DERVISH

DERVISH
THE RISE AND FALL OF AN AFRICAN EMPIRE

❖

Philip Warner

WORDSWORTH EDITIONS

First published in Great Britain in 1973
by Purnell Book Services Ltd.

Copyright © Philip Warner, 1973

This edition published 2000
by Wordsworth Editions Limited
Cumberland House, Crib Street, Ware,
Hertfordshire SG12 9ET

ISBN 1 84022 246 8

© Wordsworth Editions Limited 2000

Wordsworth® is a registered trade mark of
Wordsworth Editions Limited

Printed and bound in Great Britain
by Mackays of Chatham plc, Chatham, Kent.

CONTENTS

ACKNOWLEDGEMENTS

The author gratefully acknowledges permission to quote from the following:

Sir Ronald Wingate, CB, CMG, CIE, OBE. 'Two African Battles',
  Journal of the Royal United Service Institution, Feb. 1964, May 1964
Sir Samuel Baker: *Papers 1875-1893*
The Siege and Fall of Khartoum (Major F.R. Wingate)
El Teraz el Mankush (Sheikh Ismail Abd-el-qadir)
Wingate of the Sudan
Not in the Limelight
Ten Years Captivity in the Mahdi's Camp (Ohrwalder)
Mahdiism and the Egyptian Soudan
A Prisoner of the Khaleefa (Neufeld)
Macmillan and Co. Ltd: *The Egyptian Soudan: Its Loss and Recovery*,
  Alford and Sword, 1898
William Blackwood Ltd: *Under Crescent and Star*, A. Haggard, 1896.
  From Korti to Khartoum, Sir C. Wilson, 1896
Associated Book Publishers: *With the Camel Corps Up the Nile*,
  Lieut. Count Gleichen, 1888. *Soudan Campaign*, T.L. Pritchard, 1899
Routledge and Kegan Paul Ltd: *Suakin 1885*, E. Gambier Parry, 1886
Mrs George Bambridge and Methuen and Co. Ltd: *Departmental Ditties*,
  Rudyard Kipling
The Hamlyn Publishing Group Ltd: *My Early Life*, Sir Winston Churchill

The illustrations taken from an album of photographs recording
Kitchener's reconquest of the Sudan, which was compiled by an officer
in the Grenadier Guards, are reproduced – together with the drawings of
the Camel Corps and of the Nile gunboat in action – by kind permission
of the National Army Museum. The picture of the Mahdi is reproduced
courtesy of the Mansell Collection.

I am deeply grateful to Sir Ronald Wingate, Mr B. Arber and Mr Richard
Hill who all read the text, corrected me on various points and gave me
the benefit of their vast knowledge and experience of the Sudan.

MAPS

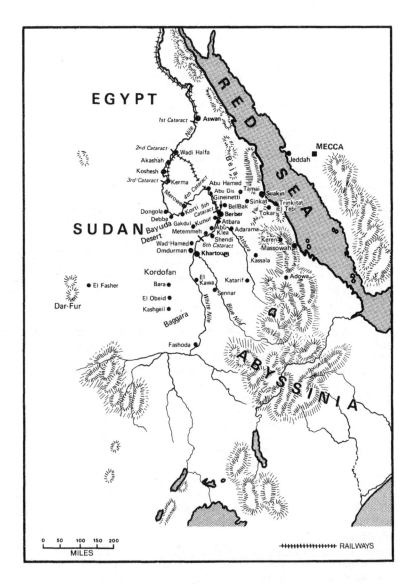

The Sudan

Preface

This is a story of great courage, great endurance and, at times, great evil. The courage of the Dervishes may have been equalled but has certainly never been surpassed in human history.

To conquer such an adversary in his own terrain, equal courage and enduring fortitude were needed. These qualities were shown by the British, the Egyptians and the Sudanese in the Egyptian army.

In this account every attempt has been made to check dates, distances and place-names, but complete accuracy is not claimed; such a claim would be absurd. Many places had several different names, and each name had several different pronunciations and spellings. Usually the best known, or the most intelligible to the English reader, is chosen. Thus Suakin rather than Suakim, and Baggara rather than Baggura, and so on. At the time of the Dervish Empire (1881 - 1898) the country was always spelt Soudan but as it is now known as the Sudan I have adopted that form. The term 'Dervish' is used to describe the Mahdi's followers, although he preferred the name 'ansar'.

'Ansar' means 'helper' or 'follower'. It is used in the Koran to describe the people of Medina who helped the Prophet Mohammed when he was in exile. It conveyed the meaning of 'disciple', and implied a reward in after-life. 'Dervish' is a much wider term and describes a variety of Moslem friars. The word literally means 'poor' (from the Persian word, 'darvesh') and all dervishes were supposed to have taken vows of poverty and austerity. Some dervish orders had adopted strange practices, hence there were howling dervishes, whirling dervishes and dancing dervishes. However, the word became widely known because of the empire which the Mahdi began and the Khalifa continued.

This empire extended over close on a million square miles and was a remarkable achievement in a era when all imperial endeavour was thought to be a prerogative of the White Man. Furthermore, the empire was established by defeating the European white man, and the particular nation concerned was Britain, the most prestigious of all military, naval and imperial countries at the time. It was not, of course, the modern maritime type of empire, such as was created by Spain, Holland, Britain, France and Portugal in the last 300 years but was the old type of land empire, which consisted of acquiring neighbouring territories and extinguishing minority dissidents in one's own domains.

This book describes the military achievement of the Dervishes as seen by their opponents and other observers. For many years it has been believed that the Dervishes were a brave, but disorganized, rabble. They were, indeed, brave, but they were also very well organized — as we see from the writings of Sheikh Ibrahim Abd-el-Kadir, a Dervish leader, who left a written account of the empire. Furthermore, they did not see the British as their main opponents. Far more important and powerful, as far as they were concerned, were the Abyssinians. Ironically, they crushed the Abyssinians but were overthrown by opponents they underrated.

1

The Setting

'The Baggara cavalry on this occasion showed remarkable and reckless daring. They evidently intended to break through our lines and divert our fire, so as to give the Dervish infantry an opening. To carry this out was hopeless, for it meant riding to certain death — but they galloped forward in loose open order, their ranks presenting one long ridge of flashing swords. Every soldier in the Sirdar's army watched breathlessly this daring feat. Nearer and nearer they came until the foremost horseman emerged almost within 200 yards of Macdonald's lines. A continuous stream of bullets from our lines was emptying the saddles, but on they came until not a single horseman was left. One Baggara succeeded in getting within thirty yards of the lines before he fell. The whole of the Dervish cavalry had been annihilated. There is no instance in history of a more superb devotion to a cause, or a greater contempt for death.

'This, however, was but a prelude to a display of almost equally reckless courage on the part of the Dervish infantry in their last despairing effort. The latter, although they had seen the fate of the cavalry, swept like a great white-crested wave towards our ranks, without the slightest pause or hesitation. Hundreds planted their banners defiantly in the ground, and gathered round them only to drop lifeless at the foot, as the price of their devotion. The carnage was fearful, as the dauntless fanatics hurled themselves to inevitable death. Most noticeable of all was the Emir Yacoub, who bore forward the great black banner of the Khalifa (his brother) surrounded by his relatives and devoted followers. Although decimated by the hail of bullets before and around them, they surged forward, until only a mere handful of men remained around the flag; and these, never faltering, rushed onwards until they dropped dead beneath it.'

So wrote an eye-witness who was not so much surprised as impressed by what he saw at the battle of Omdurman. To those in the Sudan, and to a few outside, the incredible fighting qualities of the Dervishes were already known. Nevertheless, an enemy who will fight to the death without a sign of fear or a hint of surrender – though the outcome is inevitable defeat – is an awesome sight. But even these desperate suicidal charges were by no means the whole of the story of the Dervish fighting quality. Heroism in a charge, relentless pressing home of infantry attacks even though every man had fallen before he reached the objective – these had been seen before, in other lands, for other hopeless causes. But the Dervish spirit was something different, something new. They were not brave merely when excitement and a lust for battle might make men brave, they were just as staunchly so in circumstances which could break the hardest, most disciplined, best-trained European troops. The distinction between disciplined carefully-picked troops and irregular bodies of men is that the former can stand the waiting, the shellfire, the steady losses that thin out a battalion long before it is allowed to attack, and then when it is launched forward behave with perfect discipline, meticulously keeping its formation and holding its fire until the last appalling minute; irregulars may be good some of the time, or even most of the time, but they are not absolutely dependable. It is, of course, essential that troops required for exacting tasks should be experienced, carefully-trained and superbly led. They must be intelligent. And yet after the battle of the Atbara (which took place in 1898 when the Dervishes were on the defensive):

'The scene in the Zariba after the battle was horrifying. The trenches were filled with the slain Dervishes in every position that the agony of death could assume. Many were mangled into mere fragments of humanity far beyond recognition. The artillery fire had played a fearful part in the battle and the coolness and pluck with which the enemy

12

contained themselves during the bombardment proved that the Dervish was truly brave, not merely when fired by enthusiasm in a fanatical rush, but when face to face with death, without hope of escape or hope of killing his foe.'

Three thousand Dervishes were killed in that battle. Many of them could have fled to safety. Those who did get away merely re-formed and prepared themselves for the next, equally formidable, encounter. Yet these were the disciples of the Mahdi, a man who had died thirteen years ago after a brief tenure of power. What, then, was the secret?

It is, curiously enough, a mystery which has never been entirely resolved from that day to this. The events have been chronicled, the mistakes have been rectified, history has moved on. But to anyone who looks back to that incredible sequence of events between 1881 and 1898, with its extraordinary story of heroism on both sides, of personalities of a type unlikely to appear again, set in a climate which if not the worst in the world is certainly one of the worst, that story is one of the most baffling yet fascinating of all. Possibly too it has lessons for the future. This book will not attempt to dissolve all the mystery but it will set out the facts and endeavour to assess them. It may be that the success of the Mahdist Empire stemmed from many different causes, but few, after looking at its special character, would fail to agree that it is unique in history. The striking difference with the empires of other great leaders of uneducated, ill-armed troops was that they had lesser opposition, and their empires crumbled after their deaths. This was not so in the case of the Mahdi.

The events and the people of those times are difficult to understand even as little as one hundred years later. As examples, one may wonder at Englishmen who chose to leave their comfortable country estates and endure hardship, sometimes ending in death, in a terrain of unimaginable grimness; one may wonder too at the endurance of men who survived ten years of imprisonment in a climate where any restriction of movement is discomfort; one may wonder also at the stoic pride of those Sudanese who resisted the Dervish

Empire and met a predictable fate.

First, the scene. Even today the Sudan is virtually unknown to the outside world. This is not surprising since it is difficult to explore for political reasons. The recent civil war and political disturbances between the predominantly Arab north and African south have lasted over fourteen years and cost thousands of lives; in the circumstances it is hardly surprising that foreigners of any kind have been considerably less than welcome. Fortunately, a stable regime, in which both north and south are represented, now appears to have been established. But a million square miles which contains a population speaking 115 different languages, which has 56 tribal groups among 597 tribes, is not going to be made into a modern state overnight, however brave, cooperative and loyal its people may be and indeed are.

It is a pitiless country physically. Like many other harsh and difficult lands it represents a challenge, and, as so often elsewhere, where men take up that challenge they become devoted to the cause. But to go there from choice is one thing. A very different reaction occurs when British soldiers or war correspondents find themselves sent to such a country. The feelings of the former, expressed freely in such un-English countrysides as the Western Desert, the Malayan jungle, or the Arabian peninsula, seldom find their way into print; the feelings of the latter are expressed clearly enough but tend to be excised by editors hungry for action stories but wary of long, descriptive passages. One such correspondent, G.W. Steevens of the *Daily Mail*, writing in 1898, left a description which doubtless expressed the feelings of many of his contemporaries, military and civilian alike: 'The Sudan is a man-eater — red-gorged but still insatiable. Turn your pony's head and canter out a mile; we are at the cemetery. No need to dismount, or even to read the names — see merely how full it is. Each white cross is an Englishman devoured by the Sudan.' And he goes on:

'People talk of the Sudan as the East; it is not the East. The East has age and colour; the Sudan has no colour and no age — just a monotone of squalid barbarism. Nothing grows green. Only yellow halfa grass to make you stumble and sapless mimosa to tear your eyes; dom palms that mock with wooden fruit, and sodom apples that lure with flatulent poison. For beasts it has tarantulas and scorpions and serpents, devouring white ants, and every kind of loathsome bug that flies and crawls. Its people are naked and dirty, ignorant and besotted. It is a quarter of a continent of sheer squalor. Overhead the pitiless furnace of the sun, under foot the never-easing treadmill of the sand, dust in the throat, tuneless singing in the ears, searing flame in the eye – the Sudan is a God-accursed wilderness, an empty limbo of torment for ever and ever.

'Surely enough, "When Allah made the Sudan," say the Arabs, "he laughed." You can almost hear the fiendish echo of it crackling over the dry sand.'

Yet the very next statement in Steevens's violent denunciation of the Sudan and its people is: 'And yet – and yet there never was an Englishman who had been there, but was ready and eager to go again....Perhaps to Englishmen – half-savage still on the pinnacle of their civilization – the very charm of the land lies in its empty barbarism. There is space in the Sudan. There is the fine, purified desert air, and the long stretching gallops over its sand. There are the things at the very back of life, and no other to posture in front of them – hunger and thirst to assuage, distance to win through, pain to bear, life to defend and death to face .... You are unprejudiced, simple, free. You are a naked man, facing naked nature.'

This was, of course, the appeal. The Sudan was a challenge but a challenge of infinite variety, and often in scenes of great, though stark, beauty. And although Steevens wrote about its people as 'naked and dirty, ignorant and besotted', he is, curiously enough, thinking of them with affection and pity. Whatever else he may have felt about the Sudan and its people, and whatever he said, he could not but have had an enormous respect for their achievements in the previous seventeen years. (Steevens had joined the *Daily Mail* after a brilliant career at Oxford. The paper was only two years old in 1898 but both he and it were already famous from his vivid writing. Two years later he died of an obscure fever while besieged in Ladysmith, where he was covering the Boer War.)

The Sudan was, in many respects, bigger than Steevens knew. For it is a vast country, nearly a million square miles in area. Such a figure, even when explained as being 1300 miles north to south and 950 miles east to west, means little by itself. The size of the Sudan is best expressed as being nearly one-third that of the United States or, alternatively, equal to that of Britain, France, Belgium, Holland, Luxembourg, Spain, Portugal, Italy, Austria, Czechoslovakia and Germany combined. Large countries usually have large problems, and in the Sudan they included in those days one of the most difficult of all — bad communications. This was made considerably worse by the fact that the country in effect falls into two different natural divisions. The northern half, or rather two-thirds, is desert country; the remainder is swamp, scrub and jungle. The north is Arab; the south is African. It might be said that the only thing they possess in common is the Nile. It is, of course, the lifeline to each.

Desert and jungle are not, it will be remembered, simple terms. Desert is not merely sand; it may be rock, hard sand, soft sand, or even light scrubland; jungle is not only tangled trees and creepers through which man slowly hacks his way; it may be bamboo forest, scrub, tall trees, short trees or even — sometimes — something not unlike English woodland. There is little heavy jungle in the Sudan, but there is a vast area of thorny scrub. Equally, tropical climate is not always hot. It may be freezingly cold — literally — and not only at night. It can produce unceasing rain or unbroken drought. When it is too dry it can wither up the country and its inhabitants; when it is too wet for too long it can make the country and the people seem to rot away. Tropical conditions would be considerably more bearable were it not for the insects, which seem to thrive whatever the weather or area. Flies appear in the middle of desolate wastes where there can have been nothing to support them before humans

16

arrived, and the variety of insects which can sting, infect and carry disease in the most unpromising areas for insects, is truly incredible. There is nothing benign or to be taken on trust in the tropics. A piece of dry wood, ideal for putting on a fire, will as likely as not have a scorpion in it, and a pleasantly inviting pool can hold lethal germs that will get at you through eyes, nose, ears or a mere graze on the skin. Nevertheless, men learn to live in the tropics and love them.

Fortunately for those called upon to fight the Dervishes, the campaigning area was north of Khartoum and therefore well removed from the worst conditions. Fighting wars in jungles is a pleasure which has, with the exception of a few minor campaigns, been reserved for a later generation. However, with or without a jungle campaign, life in the Sudan had enough hazards to suit even the most adventurous. All the normal tropical diseases were there, for both man and beast. So too were the animals, including lions, rhinoceroses and crocodiles.

The conquest of the Dervish Empire was brought about by using the Nile and a desert railway for transport. The Nile is, of course, more than a river: it is a form of miracle. With no Nile, or with the Nile on a different course, world history would be quite different and would probably not include the Sudan or Egypt at all. There are, indeed, other rivers in the Sudan, but the Nile is Sudan and Egypt and, north of Khartoum, what goes on apart from that great river is purely incidental. The official account of the First Sudan Campaign, prepared by the Intelligence Division of the War Office and issued in 1889, described the Sudan and the Nile with commendable brevity:

'A country in itself fertile and, especially in its southern parts, well-watered, it is cut off from the world by arid and extensive deserts, the only practicable road through which, from a military point of view, lies in the narrow valley of the Nile, often a mere rocky gorge destitute of all but water. It is true that certain caravan routes connect it with the outer world, notably the Arbain, or forty days road, leading from Assiut to Darfur; the Suakin-Berber road; and the road leading from Abu Hamed across the Nubian desert; but these, although practicable for small bodies of men in time of peace, can hardly be regarded as military routes.'

However, practicable or not, the Nile has its problems, as the War Office and its servants were to find later.

The Nile is generally held to be (despite the claims of the Amazon) the longest river in the world. From its source to the sea its length is 4160 miles. It is a vital river but it is by no means an easy or safe one. In parts it is made dangerous by crocodiles, cataracts, and some of the people who live on its banks. By the time it reaches the Sudan it has already flowed for over 1000 miles. It is joined by other rivers in the southern Sudan, then later at Khartoum by the Blue Nile (never fully explored till 1969), which rises in Lake Tana, Ethiopia, and then by the river Atbara at the town of Atbara. It flows into Egypt at Wadi Halfa and five of its six cataracts occur between Wadi Halfa and Khartoum (the sixth is in Egypt).

In 1889 the population of the Sudan was estimated at fourteen million. It is given at the same figure today, which suggests that the earlier version was considerably over-estimated. The difficulty in trying to conduct any form of census in a country like the Sudan is self-evident. But countable or not, illiterate or not, backward or not, the people of the Sudan have remarkable depths to their character, as will be seen later. They are, inevitably, a mixture. In the north they are predominantly of Arab stock, and are Moslems; in the south they are Africans, of Negro stock, and have a multiplicity of pagan religions. 'Sudan' means 'land of the blacks' but it should not be thought from this that there is a close resemblance between the Sudanese and other African Negro people. The Beja in the Red Sea hinterland are tall, thin people whose facial structure looks almost European.

The scene in the Sudan in the 1870s was little different from what it had been for centuries. The earlier history of the Sudan may be summarized briefly. In pre-Christian times, in conditions which it is hardly possible to guess at, the Sudanese had possessed an empire and had subdued Egypt. Their rule lasted 100 years and ended in 660 B.C.; nevertheless the Sudan Kingdom continued to thrive and lasted until the Romans overthrew it in 23 B.C. From then the Kingdom survived precariously but in its last stages, in the sixth century A.D., it was made Christian by missionaries from Constantinople.

Christianity did not last, for from the seventh to the fourteenth century Arabs were pressing forward to the Sudan. On the way they intermarried and settled; eventually by the sixteenth century the last remnants of Christianity were destroyed and the official religion of the Sudan became Mohammedanism (the Moslem faith).

During the period of Arab supremacy, and probably long before, the Sudan had been a rich hunting ground for slavers. The Sudanese were highly prized as slaves and this infamous trade flourished when nothing else did, for there was little in the Sudan which other countries could not provide more easily. Slaves were usually bought from local chieftains who grew rich from selling them; they made handsome money for those who traded in them. Apart from the slave-traders merchants tended to leave the Sudan alone, but in 1885 the traders were estimated to number 1500 and the captured slaves 50,000. Some of the slaves were sold in the Sudan itself but most in Egypt; the average Arab coveted a slave as modern man needs a car.

In the early nineteenth century the Egyptian situation had changed dramatically. A vigorous young officer, Mehemet Ali, seized power in Egypt with an impressive combination of speed and ruthlessness. He was born in Macedonia of Turkish parents and had risen from poverty by sheer merit. (At one stage he had been a tax-collector!) Once in power he displayed energy, ability and statesmanship such as Egypt had never seen before, and had never perhaps dreamed of. He hammered the army and navy into shape, reformed justice, established industry, and introduced an efficient system of education. (He himself could neither read nor write till he was forty.) Unfortunately, for all that, he was never quite able to shake off the moribund hand of Turkish overlordship.

The Sudan appeared at the top of his list of countries to be conquered. In the Sudan he knew he could find a reservoir of first-class fighting soldiers and control a variety of trading from ivory to slaves. In 1821 two expeditions conquered a substantial part of the northern Sudan without much more loss than those caused by tropical diseases. Subsequently the Egyptians had setbacks but not serious ones. Mehemet Ali's views of the importance of the Sudan to the Egyptian economy proved justified but the major benefits came from the slave-trade. The effects on the Sudan may be imagined. As one part of the Sudan was drained of slaves so the traders moved to another. Neither Mehemet Ali, who died in 1848, nor his successors, Ibrahim and Abbas, paid very close attention to the source of their revenue, but there were others who did, and what we know of slave-trading and conditions in the Sudan in the mid-nineteenth century does not make edifying reading.

Considerable confusion has been caused by changes in the nomenclature of territories during the nineteenth century. Apart from the spelling 'Soudan', which is now rarely used, the meaning of both 'Soudan' and 'Nubia' was quite different from today. In mid-nineteenth-century geography the Soudan was defined as 'all that portion of Africa which lies between the 10th and 20th degrees of latitude'. As Archer put it (in 1885):

'It meant in its larger extent the great zone of land more or less cultivated or fertile from the Atlantic to the Red Sea and the Highlands of Abyssinia, and from the Sahara and Egypt in the north to the Gulf of Guinea, the equatorial regions, and the Albert and Victoria Nyanzas. The Soudan thus delineated has three principal divisions: the Western Soudan, which includes the basins of the Senegal, the Niger, the Benuwe and other rivers draining to the Atlantic; Central Soudan, comprising the basins of the Shasi and other rivers running into Lake Tschad, and the Eastern Soudan, west of Wadai, which is chiefly included in the basin of the Middle and Upper Nile. Up till 1882 the Egyptian Soudan was "one ill-organized province"., with Khartoum as its capital.'

This area was of course about 2½ times the size of the present Sudan. The area of what is now Egypt (or rather the United Arab Republic) is 386,000 square miles. The area from Aswan to Sennar was known as Nubia, deriving its name from the Egyptian and Coptic word 'Noub' meaning gold. It was, however, remarkably short of that product. Its inhabitants made fine fighting troops in their own climate but died rapidly when used in colder countries.

This then was the Sudan immediately before the establishment of the Dervish Empire. At that time its neighbours were Egypt, Libya, Equatorial Africa, the Congo, Uganda, Kenya and Ethiopia. Today there are more countries and some of the original names have been changed. Out of Equatorial Africa have come Chad and the Central African Republic; the Congo is now the Republic of Zaire; Uganda, Kenya, Libya and Ethiopia are the same.

Since 1956 the Sudan has been an independent republic but for seventeen years of that time has seen bitter internal strife. Now perhaps a more stable and peaceful era may be beginning. However, this book is not an attempt to forecast the future but only to record and interpret the past. Nevertheless, anyone familiar with the period of Mahdism and the Dervish Empire would never expect the Sudanese to have an uneventful future.

2

The Mahdi

In 1844 at Lebab, an island in the Nile near Dongola, a son
was born to a carpenter who built boats. He was given the
name of Mohammed Ahmed Ibn Al-Sayid Abdullah. His
father claimed to be descended from the Prophet — a claim
that may not have been so fanciful as it sounds. An inherited
name can quite easily mean kinship. There would of course
have been many other strains, and not all of them Arabic, in
Mohammed Ahmed's line. Mohammed Ahmed was the third
son; his father died soon after he was born but it was
recorded that he too was deeply religious, and meticulous in
his devotions, so doubtless the son grew up in a strongly
religious atmosphere. The care of the family was taken on by
an uncle, also a boat-builder, but Mohammed Ahmed soon
showed that he was destined for higher things than his
family's craft. As his work as a boat-builder was not strictly
necessary for family prosperity he was allowed to give most
of his time and energies to religious devotion. This meant
studying with the *fikihs*, the holy men who taught in small
religious schools called *Khalwas*. Young Mohammed was
found to have exceptional powers of concentration and
devotion. Students applied themselves to learning the Koran
by heart and in this Mohammed's special qualities soon
asserted themselves. Other religious qualities were also noted
in him from an early age; he ate little, drove himself hard and
was a striking example of self-discipline. Soon he had more
than a local reputation. He was an exemplary pupil and was
quickly given responsibilities normally reserved for those of
many more years and much more experience.

This reputation, and this advancement, did not suit the

young Mohammed. He felt a deeper need, a need perhaps to preserve his integrity and to consolidate his thoughts. He found the opportunity in the solitude of another Nile island, Aba, where he lived a life of extreme austerity, all the while driving himself to more prayer, less sleep, more concentration.

It is, of course, easy to explain the course of events at this time. Here was a young man, highly intelligent, living in a country which was oppressed and badly administered, who had been subjected to severe religious training from an early age. He was, perhaps, more intelligent than his teachers, and, probably, more naturally devout. Possibly he understood his religion better than they did. Feeling somewhat circumscribed by his growing fame he retired to think it out. His training led him to believe that the more austere his life the clearer his thoughts would be. It is a reasonable view for anyone to take. Perhaps the isolation and austerity were a little overdone: who knows? He was said to have had revelations, and to have heard voices. So, of course, had Joan of Arc, and many like her. Such phenomena are easily dismissed by the rationalist as the fantasies of a disordered, and perhaps sick mind, but the rationalist is less confident when he comes to explain the military successes of Joan of Arc's army, or even those of Hitler, who was psychopathic indeed but able to convince saner men and drive them to deeds of which they did not know they were capable.

Inevitably, in a story such as this, there will be comparisons with the life of Christ. Superficially there may seem to be parallels. Both spent their early years in a carpenter's shop, both were highly self-disciplined, both retreated from the world while they resolved their own attitudes. No one could doubt that had Christ chosen he could have raised and led armies. The Romans were certainly aware of this. It will be remembered that the three great religions of the world all began within eighty miles of each other and they do not seriously conflict. And, of course, even the most sceptical are amazed to see the power that mind can retain over body in many religions. Yoga is but one example. There is, perhaps, a closer parallel between the Dervishes dying in the trenches at Atbara and the Christians being burnt at the stake than might be realized.

The Moslem religion, of which the Dervishes represent one facet, is the creed of one-seventh of the population of the world. It stems from Mohammed — or more correctly Muhammad — who was born in Mecca in 570 and died in 632. His precepts and sayings are incorporated in the Koran, of which the final version was produced in the year 650. Although of good parentage Mohammed had soon become a poor orphan. He had risen then from being a shepherd boy to a successful tradesman but his later life had seen much dissension and difficulty. Moslems do not care for the term 'Mohammedanism' but prefer the expression 'Islam' which means 'submission to God'. The Islamic faith expects that the Mahdi — the Guided One — will return and with the help of Jesus will control all mankind and put all wrong right.

This brief and imperfect account of Mohammed and the Islamic faith unfortunately gives no hint of its power, influence or even meaning, but does perhaps indicate why the advent of a Mahdi would have such effect. And there were, of course, many claimants to the title. Even in the time of El Mahdi in the Sudan the head of the Senussi, a confederation of North African tribes, was acknowledged by them as the Mahdi.

As a young man Mohammed Ahmed was not invariably popular. He had a way of rebuking people who were his elders and thought themselves his betters, which did not endear him to them. He criticized the idleness and corruption of the Sheikhs and religious leaders, and the fact that his criticisms were just disturbed them less than the fact that he was stirring up feelings against the established order. In 1861 he became a Summaniya dervish, that is a member of a strict Moslem religious group which derived much of its guidance from mystical devotion. He took the obligations of austerity and devotion very seriously. He was therefore absolutely horrified when the leader of his sect held a circumcision feast for his son in which all the delights of the flesh were lavishly catered for. (The religion does not require sexual abstinence but as Mohammed Ahmed well knew the presence of numbers of dancing girls at a feast was scarcely conducive to restrained behaviour.) He therefore protested and denounced the whole proceedings — much to the fury of the leader. The consequence was not the cancellation of the feast and the repentance of all concerned but the dismissal of the young Dervish from the *tariqua* (branch). It was a setback for Mohammed Ahmed but one which merely steeled the resolution of a man who was convinced of the rightness of his beliefs. He soon found another protector in the Sheikh who ruled the *tariqua* at Mesellamiya on the Blue Nile. The Sheikh died shortly afterwards but by now Mohammed Ahmed's reputation as a religious leader and teacher had increased so much that he had no need of protectors. Events were now moving fast for the young Dervish, for at Mesellamiya he met Abd Allahi. The latter was also a devotee but his approach to problems was more practical than spiritual. He was a man of action of very great ability and this meeting, with its consequence of immediate friendship, was one of the most important events in Mohammed Ahmed's career. Abd Allahi was a Baggara, a member of the cattle-owning nomadic tribes whose attitudes and way of life were as different from Mohammed Ahmed's people as Bedouins are from city dwellers. (The charge of the Baggara at Omdurman was described in the first paragraph of this book.)

As time went on Mohammed Ahmed's influence grew and his followers increased. His message was simple and unanswerable: 'Trust in God. Scorn the so-called pleasures of this world and by devotion prepare yourselves for the life to come. Trust in God, and — whatever happens — all will be well in the end.' It was, indeed, an appealing message much the same as 'Fear God and keep his commandments' or 'Blessed are the meek for they shall inherit the earth' or 'Lay not up for yourselves treasure on earth . . . .' For people who have nothing and who can expect nothing on this earth except poverty, misery and oppression the message given by the wandering *fikih* was practical and comforting. They were

encouraged to avoid pleasures they were unlikely to be able
to enjoy and they were told to practise virtues, such as
humility, which they possessed anyway. Regular prayer was
essential. The Mahdi's rules were given a slight rebellious
overtone by the fact that his followers were encouraged to
despise all those who said otherwise, and all those who
oppressed them. The process by which the policy of despising
those in authority, i.e. the Turks and their Egyptian
instruments, gave way to hatred, opposition and eventually
fighting, was a slow one, but once the initial feelings were
instilled armed clashes were inevitable. Perhaps Mohammed
Ahmed was unaware of this aspect of his teaching, in the
early stages at least, but it seems unlikely that the possibility
was ignored by Abd Allahi.

The spread of Mohammed Ahmed's message was largely
achieved by his own efforts. He became a wanderer. The wandering priest is a well-known figure in history. He brings
news; he may even bring hope. In primitive, isolated
communities his rudimentary knowledge, which often includes a little simple medicine, a little faith healing and the
ability to read and write, carried the authority which from
time immemorial went with literacy. 'Glamorous' derives
from 'grammarous'; only in the twentieth century has the
teacher lost status.

At what point Mohammed Ahmed released his great secret
is not exactly known. He was, by 1880, a well-known figure;
this was no unknown who was proclaiming his divine origin;
it was a man whom most people in the northern Sudan had
seen, a man whose holiness was beyond question, a man
whom men did not forget. Nowadays we should describe his
personality as magnetic and compelling. He was said to have
been tall, well-made, and possessing a searching look; at all
times he wore a quizzical smile. He was a familiar yet aloof
figure. Remembering him, when the people heard the great
news of his secret, they would not be surprised; there had
indeed been something unusual and mysterious about him.

The great secret flashed through the country like lightning.
Mohammed Ahmed was in truth 'the Mahdi' — the man who

is guided and who guides. He was a true descendant of the Prophet. The news was heard with intense excitement and joy by the ruled; the reaction of the rulers was less favourable.

The coming of the Messiah, the Expected Guide, was not a miracle; it was something which had to happen, the only question being when. There have, of course, been false prophets, people who have claimed to be the prophet, and indeed many of them have been highly credible. There has been at least one in every century and undoubtedly there are more to come. In order to understand this phenomenon an extensive survey of Eastern religions is required and this is not the place for it. Here we are concerned with the Mahdi and his immediate appeal to the Sudanese.

The details of the immediate successors to the Prophet Mohammed are the subject of some range of opinion. The Prophet's daughter married Ali, who thus became his son-in-law and the 'Caliph' or 'Khalifa', the 'Commander of the Faithful'. During his reign a schism developed between his supporters and those who believed that the Khalifa should be elected. After Ali's line had died out it was believed that there would be a twelfth member who would come again as the 'Mahdi'.

The Persians and the inhabitants of Southern Iraq hold to the Shia tenets of Islam and thus believe that one day there will appear a twelfth Imam (leader) who will be the 'expected one'. Other sects also hold this view. Inevitably there were wide divergences in belief and the interpretation of events. It was however widely agreed that one of the descendants of the prophet would one day emerge as the Mahdi and guide his followers to freedom and pure religion. (He might also be the immediate precursor of the end of the world; views on this point differed.) There should be no difficulty in identifying the true Mahdi when he arrived for he would bear certain signs: these were a V-shaped aperture between his teeth and a birthmark on his right cheek. One sign alone would not be sufficient. The birthmark might not show itself distinctly till later years, perhaps when an austere life and exposure to the wind and sun made it stand out more clearly, as scars often do. But once Mohammed Ahmed declared himself there was no doubting; he had both marks. This was the Madhi, this was the deliverer; the whole area quivered at the news. And all the most important Sheikhs in the Sudan came to Aba to hear the public announcement on 29 June 1881.

But not only the Sudanese took note; the Egyptians and the Turks did also. This was not surprising. They were as well aware as anyone of the explosive qualities of the Sudan, created by years, in fact centuries, of exploitation and misrule. Not surprisingly the Egyptian government was seriously alarmed: it suspected coming disaster, and it was right.

In 1856 the reigning Egyptian pasha (Turkish governor), Said, had decided to look at the Sudan for himself and was horrified at what he saw. Being humanitarian he decreed various reforms: he announced that slavery was now abolished, that slaves could no longer be used as payment of wages or taxes, and that taxation itself would be decreased; but after his departure everything went on exactly as before. In 1863 Ismail came to power in Egypt. He was Mehemet Ali's grandson, and had some, though not all, the qualities of his ancestor. The Turks thought well of him and in 1867 granted him the title of Khedive or viceroy. Ismail concentrated much of his attention on the Sudan but the task of reforming a country so vast, so difficult and so vulnerable, was beyond his powers. Nevertheless he tried. His first appointment was Sir Samuel Baker, who was given a contract 'to pacify and reform the southern Sudan'. Baker had gained a considerable reputation by tracing the Nile to the Albert Nyanza lake in 1861 and was the best, indeed perhaps the only man for the task. Ismail knew that to appoint an Englishman to suppress the trade which was so valued and natural to the average Egyptian was a direct affront to his own subjects; but he was equally aware that if he appointed one of his own subjects the man would have been coerced and bribed into joining in the traffic himself. Baker set out from Khartoum in 1870, annexed Gondoroko the following year and returned to Cairo in 1873, but for practical purposes his mission had been a failure. The slave-traders were now established in the southern Sudan more strongly than ever. This may perhaps give the impression that Baker's achievement was small. On the contrary it was near-heroic. He pressed up river under conditions which would have made many lesser men turn back: 'For the narrow and shallow parts of the stream were choked with successive masses of vegetation, through which a passage had to be cleared by cutting through the high grass with swords sharpened for the purpose. The grass resembled sugar canes, growing from twenty to thirty feet in length and throwing out roots at every joint so that they became matted in a tangled and almost impenetrable jumble; and in the wet season quantities of the mass broke away and floated on to accumulate wherever there was any impediment to the stream and formed fresh barricades. The labour of cutting away great bundles of this grass, and towing them out by thirty or forty men hauling on a rope was so extreme that numbers of the people became sick and almost exhausted after days of such work. In one day a force of 700 men cut about a mile and a half of the grass and vegetable refuse, which they piled on each side like banks upon the floating surface of the vegetation. The water flowed beneath the marsh, which swarmed with snakes and a venomous kind of ant. Crocodiles were also plentiful but these and hippopotami were shot and furnished the favourite food of the Soudanese troops.' This went on for fifty miles. The aim of the expedition was to open up the river to Gondoroko and free slaves who were held in various camps. The plan succeeded.

Ismail now looked for a successor to Baker, who had completed his mission and retired,* and found him in Colonel C.G. Gordon. Gordon was appointed in 1874, and in 1877 his powers were extended over the entire Sudan.

*Retirement for Baker meant buying a house in Devon but visiting Cyprus, India, the Rockies and other imperial outposts. He died in 1893, aged seventy-two, when planning to go lion-hunting.

Gordon was no ordinary man. He was aged forty-one on appointment and had already had a varied career. Commissioned into the Royal Engineers he had taken part in the siege of Sebastopol during the Crimean War. As the engineers spent their time making and repairing trenches within easy range of the Russian guns it is not surprising that he described the experience as 'indescribably exciting'. He spent four years in China. At the end of his time there he commanded the 'Ever Victorious Army', a mixed force of remarkably poor quality which had never had a victory until he took it over. He was a major at the time of his appointment. The whole situation was bizarre in the extreme. The enemy consisted of a wild Chinese force raised by a warlord who had begun his career distributing Bibles for an American Baptist missionary. The members of this army were known as the Taipings and soon they were in control of a considerable area of China. Back in America the leader, Hsui Chuan, was thought to be a successful missionary and a great upholder of the Christian cause. In Shanghai views were less clouded, and he was recognized for just another warlord. The word Taiping means 'Great Peace' but the local merchants knew very well what sort of peace they would have if the Taipings arrived at the walls of Shanghai, and in consequence hired an American to raise what was mistakenly called the 'Ever Victorious Army'. When the first American mercenary was killed, another was appointed, but the latter, after being reprimanded for amassing an illegal private fortune, deserted to the other side. When Gordon took over, therefore, the morale of his army was far from high.

It was the sort of challenge which eminently suited Gordon. Although religious to the point of fanaticism Gordon was no dreamer: in contrast he was a man of action and adventure, one of a long line of soldiers, and as brave as a lion. Such leaders can bring out the best in the basest of men and weld them into a tight disciplined force. A combination of courage, dedication and complete absence of self-interest has always had an irresistible appeal to rogues, who would never otherwise have believed themselves susceptible. It is the secret of many a guerrilla leader.

Few leaders can have had such a challenge. Before the advent of Mao Tse Tung soldiers in China were regarded as by far and away the lowest social animal. Gordon's army, which consisted of people whom even the Chinese army would have rejected, was partly what somebody graphically described as 'the sweepings of the jails'. If this is not absolutely true of many of Gordon's soldiers it is only because prison sentences had never quite caught up with them. Gordon was something out of their world — but an irresistible force. It is said that he led attacks with a cigar in his mouth, nonchalantly twirling a cane. There have been many men as brave as Gordon but few as coolly competent.

If Gordon had a principal fault it was that he was too trusting, too naive. Doubtless his kindness was exploited. When he was stationed at home between 1865 and 1871 he spent much time visiting hospitals and workhouses. It was said 'none appealed to him in vain'. He rescued young boys from lives in the gutter, fed them, clothed them and got them jobs. Needless to say this caused him to be branded as a homosexual by people who persist in taking a sour view of all philanthropy, but there is no foundation for the allegation. And he was no prig. He could lose his temper — as he did with the slave-owning chiefs; he could understand, without condoning, other men's thoughts. He had a powerful sense of humour, which some described as sardonic.

Gordon's personal energy was remarkable. He wrote from Katarif, south-east of Khartoum, midway between the Blue Nile and the Atbara: 'I got here today after a very hot journey. We did it in a very short time — sixty hours 150 miles. With terrific exertions in two or three years time I may, with God's administrations, make a good province, with a good army and a fair revenue and peace and an increased trade, and also have suppressed slave raids; and then I will come home and go to bed, and never get up again till noon every day, and never walk more than a mile.'

It was an understandable resolution. Fifty miles a day on the back of a camel in a temperature close on 100° Fahrenheit might make anyone think longingly of bed. And it was one of many such journeys.

On that particular occasion Gordon came across a tribe dressed in full medieval armour. They had chain mail shirts, gorgets, iron helmets with a nasal or nose-piece, bucklers, and they carried two-handed swords. Their horses were also protected by armour. It was, of course, a ceremonial occasion; they did not wear them every day. But, as Gordon rightly conjectured, this armour had once belonged to the Crusaders and probably dated back to the twelfth century. Its wearers were not so different from their forebears in the days of the Crusades, when the armour had been captured and brought south as trophies.

Gordon was addicted to sudden journeys. It was said of him 'that he sped from place to place with alacrity and without caring much whether he arrived without his escort. . . . He went single-handed and unarmed amidst not only doubtful friends but avowed enemies. His utter fearlessness, which looked like audacity, but was simple indifference to danger or even to death, astonished the enemy so much that they often submitted at once. His sudden appearance frequently dismayed the cowardly and procrastinating garrisons at the stations.' A description of a visit to Dara, south-west of Khartoum, gives an indication:

'I got to Dara alone, about 4 p.m. long before my escort, having ridden 85 miles in a day and a half. About seven miles from Dara I got into a swarm of flies and they annoyed me and my camel so much that we jolted along as fast as we could. Upwards of 300 were on my camel's head, and I was covered with them. I suppose the queen fly was among them. If I had no escort of men I had a large escort of these flies. I came on my people like a thunderbolt. As soon as they had recovered a salute was fired. My poor escort! Where is it? Imagine to yourself a dirty, red-faced man on a camel ornamented with flies arriving in a divan all of a sudden. The people were paralysed and could not believe their eyes.'

Gordon was, however, a realist. Having seen the extent of the slave-trade and the cynical incompetence of the Egyptian government in outlying stations he wrote:

'If the liberation of slaves is to take place in 1884 (in Egypt proper) and the present system of government goes on there cannot fail to be a revolt of the whole country. But our government will go on sleeping till it comes and then have to act à l'improviste. If you had read the accounts of the tremendous debates which took place in 1833 on the liberation of the West Indian slaves, even on payment of $20,000,000 you would have some idea of how owners of slaves (even Christians) hold to their property. It is quite amusing to think that the people of Cairo are quite oblivious that in 1884 their revenue will fall to one-half, and that the country will need many more troops to keep it quiet. Seven-eighths of the population of the Soudan are slaves; and the loss of revenue in 1889 (the date fixed for the liberation of slaves in Egypt's outlying territories) will be more than two-thirds, if it is ever carried out.'

Within a year of his making the statement the Mahdi had brought out the whole of the Sudan in revolt.

3

The Hicks Expedition

Gordon's idealism, energy and foresight, remarkable though they were, were not enough to conquer the problem of the Sudan single-handed. His task was to stamp out the slave-trade and replace it with some other equally profitable export; to be firm and yet conciliatory; and to win the respect and co-operation of the Sheikhs in all areas. These were difficult enough tasks but the reason he resigned after two years, firmly resolved never to return, was that he felt that every reform he instituted in the south was countered by the condonation of similar and equal abuse in the north. Nevertheless he returned after a year's absence between 1876-7, having been persuaded by Ismail that he was irreplaceable. The decision sealed his own fate.

But in 1874 he was full of hope and, probably, confidence. He established a chain of military posts with small detachments of soldiers but as he himself knew only too well isolated military posts in dangerous areas tend to reach a *modus vivendi* with those surrounding them and business goes on much as before. While he was there to keep them up to scratch all was well; without his presence and personality they would be useless.

There were, however, other problems besides the slave-traders, large and small. One of them was to arise from the activities of Zubair, a remarkable personality who had risen to wealth and fame by successful slave-trading and who had become a minor king by consent. Fortunately for Egypt he agreed to help in the conquest of Darfur, a large sultanate to the south. He and his men did most of the fighting and as a result, in 1874, Egypt acquired a vast new territory twice

as large as the British Isles. The humanitarian Ismail may not
have been making much progress in suppressing the slave-
trade but he was rapidly extending Egypt's power and
influence with very little personal effort. For he was not
successful in the south alone; the efforts on the eastern
seaboard were equally rewarding and in 1875 an Egyptian
expedition captured Harar. A halt was only reached when he
turned his attention to Abyssinia. The Abyssinians, under
King John, were made of stronger material than the
Egyptians' previous opponents and when the latter tried to
capture Adowa they met their nemesis. Two expeditions
were cut to ribbons; the Egyptians thereupon decided that
their policy of expansion to the east had gone far enough. To
Gordon, who returned as Governor-General in 1879, it may
have seemed that it had gone too far. This was now the time
when most of his journeys took place.

In this second sojourn in the Sudan Gordon assembled
around him a collection of people who could help him.
(One is reminded of Milner and his 'kindergarten' in South
Africa at the close of the nineteenth century.) They were a
remarkable group and as they figure later in the story a brief
account is appropriate now.

Rudolf Slatin was an officer serving in the 19th Hungarian
Infantry when he received an invitation from Gordon to
work with him in the Sudan. He was twenty-one years old at
the time. His father was a rich Austrian trader. The family
were Jewish but had become Catholic. Rudolf, who was of an
adventurous turn of mind, had visited the Sudan two years
before; he knew he would soon be called up for military service
and as he had not shown much talent for business or academic studies he decided to see a little of the world. While in
Khartoum he had met another unusual personality, Eduard
Schnitzer, otherwise Dr Mohammed Emin, otherwise known
and more famous as Emin Bey. Schnitzer was a Prussian doctor and a keen botanist. Both these men were so fascinated
by the Sudan that they wrote to Gordon, volunteering to
help him in any way they could. Emin was accepted at once
but Slatin had to return to complete his obligatory military

service, detach himself from the army, and to make a few arrangements before he left Vienna. If he had known what was in store for him he might have drawn back; perhaps not. He did not see his family and home again till sixteen years later. Gordon appointed him Inspector of Taxes. He might as well have made him supervisor of interplanetary travel for all Siatin could do about it. One of his duties was assessing prostitutes for taxation purposes. He requested a less onerous appointment and was appointed governor of a district in the newly conquered province of Darfur.

Another of Gordon's appointees was Romolo Gessi. Gordon had first met Gessi in the Crimea, where the latter was an interpreter (the Italians contributed a useful force to the Crimean War and this did well enough to win the substantial goodwill in subsequent international councils). Yet another was Frank Lupton, and another was Geigler who was appointed Inspector-General of Sudan Telegraphs.

Gessi's name appears as Romulus in Gordon's letters but is given by other writers as Romolo or Romola. Gessi was a brilliant and indefatigable soldier. Gordon described him thus: 'Italian subject, aged forty-nine. Short compact figure; cool, most determined man. Born genius for practical ingenuity in mechanics. Ought to have been born 1560 not 1832. Same disposition as Francis Drake.'

In 1879 Gessi conducted an arduous campaign against Suleiman, a notorious slave dealer. Gessi had just over a thousand troops of dubious quality to pit against Suleiman's 6,000 warriors. Floods delayed the enterprise and men began to desert and mutiny. He shot one of the ringleaders in front of the troops and flogged seven others. He had to cross four rivers, one of which was eighty feet wide, four feet deep and swarming with crocodiles. Eventually Gessi caught up with Suleiman and shot him and nine other chiefs 'while trying to escape'.

Lupton was a captain in the merchant navy who had come to the Sudan for adventure. He succeeded Gessi as Governor of Bahr El Ghazal province when the latter retired frustrated by the political rather than the military problems of his appointment. Lupton was still governor when the Mahdi's armies defeated Hicks Pasha and were sweeping the whole country. He tried to organize resistance but no one would support him. Bahr El Ghazal surrendered without bloodshed. Lupton became a Moslem and died of typhus in 1888 in Omdurman.

Geigler, although recruited for his technical skills, was soon involved in politics. When Gordon went to Darfur in 1879 he appointed Geigler as acting Governor-General during his temporary absence from Khartoum. Later when the 1882 fighting began he showed himself to be brave and competent, but, of course, was eventually overwhelmed.

But, successful and promising though Gordon's second tour in the Sudan was, it was not to last. His resignation was brought about by events well outside his control. The Khedive, Ismail, had been deposed by the Sultan of Turkey at the instance of the Great Powers, for he had, by his extravagance and mismanagement, brought his country to the verge of bankruptcy, and France and England, whose banks had lent Ismail large sums of money, insisted on a new manager and a regular scheme of payment. Gordon felt that the dismissal was unjust, and had no wish to serve a successor. Furthermore, he needed a rest after the tremendous strain of his long journeys, and so he left the Sudan. But enough had been done in the way of reform to show the Sudanese that the hardships of their lot were not divinely ordained. Slavery had been reduced and in places eradicated. The country had been opened up and new crops, such as cotton, introduced. Above all it had been shown that some men were unbribable and would administer fearlessly and honestly. They could see that a different way of life might be achieved. Slow reforms or, worse still, reforms followed by a return to the old system are like lighting the touch-paper to the powder-keg. On this occasion the advent of the Mahdi, with all that the second coming promised, was the flame to light the paper. Unwittingly, the reformers had contributed to making the explosion worse than it would have been. When governments are brutally repressive, there is seldom revolt. But when there is hope, and men can glimpse the way to freedom, or think they can, real trouble starts.

The appeal of the Mahdi, of course, went much deeper than the creation of a few economic and social reforms. His message aimed at fundamentals. 'The Way', as he called it, was to trust in God, despise the vanities of this world and look forward to the glories of the next. Poverty, which was the lot of most of his followers, now became a virtue; it was a symbol of one's scorn of earthly pleasures. His followers would wear nothing ornate, only the long shirt known as the *jibbah* which would be patched when it became worn. Soon the patch was worn as a symbolic badge by Sheikhs and his other richer followers. With this attitude they must fervently hate the Turks — that is, the Turkish rulers from Egypt. The Turks, he told them, were betrayers of the true Moslem religion, they drank, they ate greedily, they adorned themselves richly, and they enslaved their weaker brethren. They did this not merely because they were Turks but because they had lapsed from the true religion. The issues were therefore much more clear-cut if the oppressor was not only brutal but also evil as well. The fact that he was a foreigner, self-indulgent and corrupt, made it easier to hate him, but these were only ancillary benefits. There was in all this a beautiful simplicity. Mahdism ignored all the current views of the Islamic faith, with its interpretations made by centuries of priests. The Mahdi preached the message of the Koran. It was simple, it was straightforward, and it was understood by people eager and grateful to hear it. He burnt most of the books on theology in public, saying they were ridiculous and irrelevant; in their place he put a simple book of prayers, the Ratib, and made it compulsory reading.

The Governor who had taken over the Sudan on Gordon's resignation in 1880 was Raouf Pasha. He was thoroughly incompetent and corrupt but amazingly resilient. In the past he had been dismissed twice by Gordon, first as a Governor of Gondoroko and secondly as Governor of Khartoum.

When the Mahdi had proclaimed himself, and also made a tour to see matters for himself in areas he had not previously visited, Raouf decided that some action should be taken. As his previous career showed, he was prepared to believe that 'an arrangement' might be made in almost any circumstances — except when confronted with people like Gordon. However Raouf was no fool. He did not believe in precipitate action but he believed still less in no action at all. He decided that Mohammed Ahmed might only be an impracticable dreamer, and ill-educated at that. A show of intellectual force could well bring him to his senses. Accordingly he sent a weighty delegation of learned men to see the Mahdi. They would explain to him in simple terms that his claims were absurd but that if he came to Khartoum the Governor-General would look upon the whole affair with understanding and lenience.

In the event it worked out differently. Not for the first time had Raouf miscalculated. His gesture, so far from intimidating and bringing the Mahdi to heel, had merely sufficed to warn him that the time for action was at hand. The learned men had not merely argued; they had also hinted rather unpleasantly that failure to accompany them to Khartoum in suitable penitence would lead to unfortunate consequences for the Mahdi.

The Mahdi's reaction was unexpected. Not only did he ignore their advice, he also seemed indifferent to their threats. In fact, as Raouf soon learnt from his informers, he went to a terrifying extreme. He declared a Holy War. The great difficulty with Holy Wars is that those waging them believe that death for the cause is the prelude to eternal joy in heaven. For an oppressed near-slave this is an inspiring message. Life on earth is virtually intolerable anyway; in eternity it will be perpetual bliss. It creates very difficult opponents, for they make no effort to preserve themselves and in failing to do so often win victories. However Raouf was not at first alert to the full possibilities of the situation. He decided that a small — but not too small — punitive force would take care of matters. It consisted of two companies of Egyptians — probably a total of about 200 ill-armed and half-trained men. The expedition travelled up the Nile on the steamer *Ismailia*. It did not arrive at Aba until after dark on 12 August 1881. The commander of the expedition, Abu Saud, stayed on the steamer but told the two company commanders that the one who captured the Mahdi would be promoted. Both were anxious for this rich and easy prize so they disembarked their men in the dark and stumbled ashore. The fact that they could not see their targets and did not know the terrain did not seem important until they found themselves floundering helplessly in mud and reeds. As soon as the Egyptians were well in trouble the Madhi's followers, themselves not more than a few hundred, hurled themselves on the wretched soldiers. At this stage the Dervishes were armed only with spears but they did fearful execution at close quarters in the dark and the confusion. Very few of the Egyptians escaped, and those only by swimming out to the steamer. The joy of the ansars was unbounded. They had defeated the army of the oppressor. The *Ismailia* steamed back to Khartoum and reported the disaster. Subsequently it was assumed that in the general confusion the two companies had fired on each other by mistake in the dark, at close quarters, leaving a remmant to be finished off by the ansars.

However the Mahdi was too prudent to stay and let revenge take its course — he set off for better headquarters in Kordofan. There, in the Nuba mountains, he was secure. As the rainy season followed soon after, Raouf could do nothing for a while. The Mahdi, with the die cast, lost no time. He assembled and trained the nucleus of an army. Fortunately for recruitment there was a legend that the Holy War would be launched by the Mahdi from a mountain fastness. It was therefore no surprise to anyone — except perhaps Raouf — that the second expedition to crush the Mahdi was wiped out as adroitly as the first. On 9 December 1881, a force of 1400 men under Rashid Bey, Governor of Fashoda, was ambushed and slaughtered. Nothing succeeds like success. Recruits to the Mahdi's army poured in faster than ever.

Back in Cairo the news was received with disquiet. Raouf was removed from his post as Governor-General and transferred to other duties in Egypt. A new Governor was appointed and began to make his way slowly southwards.

Meanwhile Egypt had troubles of her own. When Ismail had abdicated under pressure his son Tewfik had taken over his post. Owing to the extraordinary complications of Egypt's bankrupt finances England and France had come together to establish the 'Dual Control'. They jointly appointed ministers to take care of Egyptian finances and this made more obvious than ever the fact that Egypt was being run by foreigners. Needless to say, the experience was not new, for ever since Turkey had conquered Egypt most of the positions of authority had been held by people from outside. Mehemet Ali himself had been a foreigner. However, the Dual Control was so blatant that it was not difficult to stir up feeling against it, and this is what was done by Arabi Pasha, a pure Egyptian and not one of the ruling Turkish-Circassian army clique. In 1882 he raised a revolt among army officers and other discontented Egyptians, and with the cry 'Egypt for the Egyptians' drove out the foreign ministers.

It might be assumed that England and France would have had no hesitation about joint action to put down the revolt, but the intense rivalry which existed between the two countries prevented this. The French* refused to take any action at all and the British merely ordered the Mediterranean Squadron to Alexandria. On 11 June 1882, a riotous mob murdered about 150 European residents in Alexandria. An ultimatum was issued to the Egyptians that they should dismantle the forts they were building; they refused and the English warships shelled them. At the end of July troops landed and took control of the town.

However, the capture of Alexandria did not mean the war was over. Strong forces still held Cairo. Consequently Sir Garnet Wolseley, hero of many a small brisk expedition, seized the Suez Canal and marched to Cairo across the desert. This move completely disconcerted the Egyptians who expected the next English attack to come from the direction of Alexandria. Wolseley had contributed to this deception by

*It seems likely that their inaction was partly caused by the possibility of another war with Germany — which would require all their resources.

41

keeping his plans secret even from his own generals. Once Arabi learned of the new turn of events he rushed to Tel-el-Kebir with 25,000 men. There he had an excellent position from which he could pick off an enemy at ease. Realizing the costliness of a daylight assault Wolseley decided on a night march, followed by a dawn attack. His 13,500 men then carried the position for a loss of only 400 men. They pressed on and within two days were in Cairo — sixty-four miles from Tel-el-Kebir.

This situation, which had developed unexpectedly, put the British government in a difficult position. 10,000 British troops now had to be garrisoned in Egypt in order to make sure there was no recurrence of trouble and also to see that reforms were carried out. The whole idea was detestable to Gladstone, who was an ardent opponent of any form of imperialism, benevolent or not. Sir Evelyn Baring, who had previously been British Commissioner on the Debt, was appointed British Agent and Consul-General in Cairo, in which capacity he was to supervise Egyptian finances and also keep an eye on Tewfik, and Sir Evelyn Wood, V.C., one of the most experienced soldiers of the age, was given the task of reorganizing the Egyptian army. One of his officers was H.H. Kitchener, a young engineer who had taken the trouble to learn Arabic. All this happened at the time when the Sudan had relapsed into the worst anarchy of its existence and the Mahdi had declared himself and won small but significant victories. Reluctantly and belatedly the British government realized that farther along the Nile was a vast territory whose inhabitants could, if they wished, make life extremely unpleasant for Egypt. Furthermore the well-being of that territory was Egypt's responsibility.

The news that then began to filter out of the Sudan was anything but comforting for a people who desired nothing more than a quiet life and a retreat from commitments. Raouf Pasha had been removed from his job in March 1882 but his successors fared no better. An expedition some 6000 strong under Yussif Pasha completely underestimated the Dervishes, was surprised and easily defeated; this annihilation was almost entirely due to incompetence but it appeared otherwise to the disciples of the Mahdi, who saw it as yet another example of divine ordination by which they had been given large quantities of stores and arms. What had been a local insurrection now seemed like the hand of destiny. The Khartoum administration raised yet another army, this time of 12,000, but the Mahdi was recruiting even faster and the morale of his soldiers was on an altogether different plane. He now needed the town of El Obeid, the second city of the Sudan, in which he could equip his army properly, establish a permanent headquarters and organize his forces on a national scale. By September he was encamped outside El Obeid with a force not far short of 30,000. On the way there he had captured some Austrian missionaries, one of whom was Father Ohrwalder, who spent the next ten years in captivity and wrote a book about his experiences.

El Obeid was a valuable prize, and the Mahdi needed it badly. But the Governor of El Obeid, one Mohammed Said, had no desire to lose it; doubtless he knew the fate he might expect if he did. Accordingly he constructed an outer and an inner ring of fortification. He received the Mahdi's request for surrender with contempt and slashed off the heads of its bearers. The Mahdi wasted no further time on words. On 8 September the attack went in.

But it is one thing to fight as a guerrilla force, to ambush and to surprise, but a very different matter to assault a prepared position without the necessary materials, tactics or training. The Mahdi's army broke through the outer perimeter and entered the town. There, in spite of low morale and desertion by the defending force, the attackers were at a complete disadvantage. The garrison were able to fire on them from parapets and rooftops and the numbers of the Mahdi's army, completely misused, proved more of a handicap than otherwise. Eventually the attackers, depleted and shattered, withdrew. Mohammed Said's forces were too exhausted — or perhaps too sensible — to try to pursue.

The Mahdi was disappointed but not perturbed. If — as it seemed — he had been defeated by superior firepower and by using the wrong tactics, he would change the tactics and wait for the firepower to fall into his hands. He settled down to besiege El Obeid and Bara, the other, though less important, town in Kordofan. In the event both fell in the following January after four memorable months.

There was of course in the meantime an attempt to relieve both towns but not surprisingly it failed. In September an expedition of 3000 men which hoped to live on the country set out into Kordofan. Thoughtfully, the Mahdi had destroyed every well on their probable route. Few armies can have been so ill-prepared or so demoralized. Eventually they were wiped out by a determined attack from the Mahdi's forces.

Unfortunately for the wretched people besieged in Bara and El Obeid the failure of this expedition convinced the Khartoum government that further attempts to relieve the beleaguered towns were doomed to failure, and they should either sit out the siege and wait for the Mahdi to tire of it or should, more hopefully still, wait for relief from Cairo. An unwilling witness of the sufferings of the inhabitants of El Obeid was Father Ohrwalder, whose capture by the Mahdi's forces was noted above. The situation of Ohrwalder and his fellow captives was anything but pleasant, for, as he put it: 'The infected atmosphere of the Mahdi's camp brought on a burning fever and constant diarrhoea . . . we had become covered with horrible vermin; it was impossible to get rid of them, they seemed to increase daily. We had no clothes to change and as we had scarcely enough water to drink, washing was out of the question.' Conditions in El Obeid were infinitely worse, as he discovered when he subsequently talked to other missionaries who were within the town:

'The poor began to starve quite at the beginning of the siege and soon were dying in considerable numbers. A little later, matters came to a terrible pass. All the camels and cattle being finished, donkeys, dogs, mice, and even crickets were consumed, as well as cockroaches, which were considered quite tit-bits; white ants too were eaten. . . . Scurvy and dysentery were rife; the air was black with scores of

carrion-kites, which feasted on the dead bodies; these ugly
birds became so distended with constant gorging that they
could not even fly away, and were killed in numbers by the
soldiers, who devoured them with avidity.

'Later on gum became the only food; there was a quantity
of this, but it brought on diarrhoea, and caused the bodies to
distend – indeed numbers died from eating it.'

Ohrwalder spares us no detail, however nauseating. Eventually, of course, El Obeid surrendered. Mohammed Said was
not killed immediately but a few weeks later was chopped to
pieces with axes.

Ohrwalder was taken to the Mahdi soon after capture and
gives an interesting description of him: 'He greeted us kindly
and asked about our nationality and our object in coming to
the Sudan, also whether we had ever heard anything about
the Mahdi; he then briefly explained to us the nature of his
divine message, and recounted his great victories over "the
enemies of God and his Prophet" by which name he
designated the Turks.*

'Seeing that we were utterly exhausted he offered us some
Kamar-ed-din (dried apricots) mixed with water but almost
before we could put it to our mouths it was full of flies. In
the meantime a certain George Stambuli, who had joined the
rebels with the other inhabitants of El Obeid, came in, and
through him the Mahdi endeavoured to place before us the
great advantage of the Islam religion. The Mahdi himself
never asked us to adopt the Moslem faith, because he feared
that we should answer in the negative. He then stretched
himself out on the mat as if he were preparing to behold a
vision.

'Mohammed Ahmed was a powerfully built man of dark
brown complexion and carefully kept skin; he had a pleasant
smile which showed to advantage the curious slit between his
front teeth. By constant training he had acquired a gentle
manner of speaking, and with these exceptions there was
nothing unusual in his appearance. He wore a dirty *jibbah*

* The Dervishes usually referred to the Egyptians as 'the Turks' because
of the Turkish overlordship.

(long shirt) on which parti-coloured strips of cotton had been sewn; on his head the white skull cap or *takia* round which a broad white turban was bound; he also wore a pair of loose drawers and sandals.

'After he had lain for some time with closed eyes he rose and offered us some more Kamar-ed-din from which he himself began to take out the flies but finding it absolutely useless to do so, he gave it up, and then went back to his tent, probably to hold a council. After a short time he again returned, wearing a clean *jibbah* patched with pieces of the vestments belonging to our mission church at El Obeid. He then began to recount to us the history of the numerous conversions which had taken place in the early days of the Prophet. Seeing that we took little interest in what he said, he got up and ordered us to be taken before the Khalifa Abdullah (the present ruler of the Sudan) while he himself retired to his own tent.'

The Khalifa was less ceremonious than the Mahdi and was soon threatening them with death if they did not change their religion. In spite of threats, and the certainty that these would be carried out, they refused to become Moslem. Eventually they were reprieved from the death sentence by the Mahdi himself.

At this point it is possible, from his sayings and his actions, to make an assessment of the Mahdi's policy and its chances of success. Clearly he himself had enormous prestige, vision and influence but the possession of these attributes did not necessarily imply continuous progress. His aim was to liberate the Sudan from its oppressors. This might appear to be a simple political/military concept but in fact was religious. The 'Turk' was an oppressor because he was irreligious and a loose-liver. He was a bad Moslem. From this evil the remainder sprang. Therefore there was no separate political aim. Eliminate the evil liver, create a new theocratic state and gradually its influence would spread. The next step must be the capture of Khartoum. After that the Sudan must be united. Later Egypt would be invaded, but that phase belonged to a later màster plan. Meanwhile religion would march hand in hand with military power.

Thus his military deputies would be four Khalifas, who would resemble the four companions of the Prophet. In the event there were only three, for the head of the Senussi, who was offered the post of third Khalifa, declined it. Each Khalifa had his own flag, and the theory was that these regional military groupings would gradually eliminate local tribal rivalries. All taxes and captured stores were to be deposited at a central repository and subsequently used to best advantage. This central treasury was known as the Bait-al-Mal; eventually it controlled trade and persuaded the Khalifa to begin trading with Egypt again. The main tax was the Zaka but the rich were also occasionally made to give forced loans to the government; these were rarely repaid. At no stage in the Mahdi Empire was there ever an' adequate financial and administrative structure for an expanding state.

In February 1883, when the news of the fall of El Obeid and Bara was learnt in Cairo, the feeling was already strong that some vigorous action should be taken to restore order in the Sudan. Unfortunately the problems of the military situation were imperfectly appreciated and the outcome was the appalling disaster of the Hicks Pasha expedition.

Colonel Hicks was a retired officer from the Indian army. In January 1883, before the news of the fall of El Obeid and Bara had reached Cairo, he was appointed Chief of Staff of the Egyptian army. The title 'Pasha' which he was then known by is a Turkish word denoting an officer of high rank. There are grades of pasha and they are distinguished by the number of horses' tails displayed on a banner. Hicks's grade was approximately equal to Lieutenant-General. He was nominally subordinate to Sulaiman Pasha, a decrepit old man said to be not far short of eighty years old. Sulaiman, however, was a Moslem and the fact that he was in command — even if only by a polite fiction — meant that this was not a war of Christians against Moslems but of the legal Egyptian government suppressing a rebellion within its territories. Subsequently Sulaiman showed great interest in the proceedings even to the extent of trying to interfere with Hicks's plans. Hicks had enough troubles without a doddering and ignorant overlord breathing down his neck, trying to frustrate him. The main weakness of Hicks's position was not, however, higher direction by an incompetent superior but the appallingly bad quality of the troops he was expected to lead. His army of 9000 was recruited from the forces defeated by Wolseley, about half of whom had surrendered without firing a shot. Their morale was not merely low: it did not exist at all.

An account of the early part of Hicks's journeyings comes from Colonel the Hon. J. Colborne, who published a book called *With Hicks Pasha in the Soudan* in 1884. Colborne had been transferred elsewhere before Hicks's column met its almost inevitable end in November 1883. Colborne was a man of personality and feeling. His book began:

> 'Then farewell home and farewell friend
> Adieu each tender tie
> Resolved we mingle in the tide
> Where charging squadrons furious ride
> To conquer or to die

'We rumbled out of Cairo railway station at half-past eleven on the morning of February 7th, 1883.

Sicubi fata vocant*

'It was a bright, crisp, sunny, Egyptian winter's day, and the date palms on the banks of the Ismalia canal showed the ashy white surface of their graceful fronds in tremulous movement, as they were carressed by a gentle breeze from the Delta.

'Our party consisted in addition to General Hicks of Major Farquhar, De Coëtlogon Pasha, Capt. Massey, Major Martin, Major Warner, Capt. Evans, Rosenberg (our surgeon) and myself.

'Capt. Forestier-Walker was left behind to bring up the Gatlings.

'We were all in high spirits and eagerly looking forward to

---

*Wheresoever the fates call.

the campaign. Three only of that cheerful company returned from the Soudan. Little did we dream, as we indulged in half-jesting speculations as to our lot in the far interior, of the dire fate in store for most of us.'

The line took them as far as Suakin, a port on the Red Sea which was famous for the export of slaves. By now they were inside the Mahdi country but thought little of it as they understood that in previous encounters the Egyptian forces had fired off all their ammunition while out of range and that the Mahdi had then attacked and cut them to pieces; with proper discipline matters would be very different.

'We left Suakin on the evening of February 11th. We were to have left at five in the morning. They told us the camels would be ready by that hour, and, not being initiated into the ways and manners of the people, we believed them. Soudanese camel drivers always say they will be ready in the morning but for some inscrutable reason they never start until the evening.

'We had sent on our Bashi-Bazouks, whose presence in Suakin was not a pleasant experience for the inhabitants. Bashi-Bazouk notions as to the distinction between meum and tuum are confused, and their exuberance of spirits is apt to take an aggressive and minatory form.'

Bashi-Bazouks had, indeed, a reputation, which extended far beyond Egypt. They were a form of mercenary cavalry employed by the Turks where intimidation was considered suitable in the collection of taxes. It was a measure of the hasty way in which Hicks's force had been scraped together that he had to employ these part-time brigands. Eventually they became too much of a problem and had to be kept well apart from anyone or anything they could damage.

Colborne viewed his surroundings with interest and was humorously pleased with what he saw. Camels fascinated him:

'He is essentially a traveller and has never been more aptly described than as a machine for travelling through deserts. A marvellous though uncouth creature he is. . . .

'The process of loading and unloading never takes place without manifest signs of disapproval on the part of the camel. His cargo is placed on the ground in two lots; he is driven in between, and at once gives vent to his indignation by angry and discordant bellowings. This is a mere formal protest.'

Colborne, although thrown off a camel and buffeted at various times, never grew to dislike them. He probably understood that it is not much fun being a camel. Nevertheless: 'With respect to the alleged ease of the camel's pace, it is probably comfortable compared with that of a giraffe: but commend me to any species of quadruped I have bestridden in preference to the camel.'

Colborne's account of his journey gives a good idea of the terrain and also explains how easy it was to lay ambushes:

'Every step our camels took westward seemed to bring us into a desert more desolate and forbidding. . . . The rocks were absolutely naked — not even a tuft of moss or lichen was to be seen. . . . A striking feature in the geology of this desert is the occurrence of homogenious isolated masses of porphyry. One of these attains a height of 1000 feet. They are coated with a black accretion about a millimetre thick. It adds to the horrid desolation of the place, this waste of inky black stone.'

And again: 'We approached it through a ravine, or, rather, a labyrinth of ravines. Indeed the road from this point to Ariab was nothing but a mountain pass, alternating with basin like valleys surrounded by amphitheatres of mountains. And such mountains. Bold, jagged, and split with deep gorges and ravines filled with dark mysterious shadows. We toiled through a succession of basins and along stony paths that would seem to offer a serious impediment to the apparently soft, velvety-gloved feet of our camels; but pointed edges or roughly covered boulders were alike passed over without inconvenience or lameness.'

He mentions — although he winces at the thought — that they shot some sand-grouse — in February. Furthermore they shot them sitting. 'Proh Pudor' [for shame], he commented but not perhaps very seriously.

Beyond the mountains they came on to a plain of shifting sand, blown up into dunes 100 feet high:

'Our camels sank deep into the fine quicksand at every step, and we were heartily glad to get on to firmer ground, however dreary. And a gloomier waste man never saw than that in which we encamped at a spot almost thirty-four miles from O'Bak. There was no water, not a vestige of vegetation, nor of organic life of any kind. The loose black boulders with which the plain was strewn gave a terrible aspect to it. They looked as if they had been blackened by fire and the whole region seemed to be the debris of a vast conflagration – the cinder of a burnt-up world. The scenery is of the type that astronomers tell us is presented by the moon – the remains of a worn-out volcano. Before reaching our camping-ground we passed the huge solitary black of granite called 'Eremit'. And further on was visible 'Aboo Odfa', the obelisk-like rock mentioned by travellers. The wind-driven sand has worn its base until it resembles in form a huge fungus or a pear. Smaller blocks of this kind are seen at intervals on the road.'

Eventually they reached Berber, where Hicks received a letter from Colonel Stewart at Khartoum, 'informing him that El Obeid and Bara had surrendered with 7000 men, 10,000 stand of arms and some mountain guns, with an immense quantity of ammunition. Colonel Stewart further stated that Darfur and Kordofan were then in the hands of the enemy.' Hicks was urged to press on with all haste to Khartoum. The news was regarded with amused incredulity; no possible danger to Khartoum was envisaged – yet.

The next stage of the journey was by steamer. Some of these had negotiated the cataract but others had come in sections on camels' backs and been assembled at Khartoum. Sailing was considerably easier than marching but progress was slow; the steamers could only manage five knots and travel was impossible at night owing to the numerous sandbanks and rocks.

On arrival at Khartoum they lost no time in having firing practice. This was by no means unsatisfactory. After three weeks Forestier-Walker arrived with the Nordenfeldt machine-guns with which he had stayed behind in Cairo so that the crews could be trained. But:

'During their passage from Cairo, men and officers had completely forgotten their drill. When the guns were attempted to be brought into action, dire confusion reigned. Men ran against each other; the ground was strewn with cartridges; hoppers were placed anywhere but where they should have been. No one appeared to have the slightest knowledge of how to feed, aim, and discharge the pieces. In the midst of all this, poor Walker — not knowing anything of the language beyond the words of command — stood aghast.'

Men of any army may smile a little sympathetically, for most of them will have known at least one vast M.F.U. — 'Military Foul-up'. It needs little effort to visualize:

'General Hicks thundered out "he had never seen such a disgraceful scene in his life" and ordered Forestier-Walker to remain for three days perpetually drilling his men in that sandy scorching camp, instead of returning with us to the comparatively "blest abode" of Khartoum. I should add that no blame can be attached to Forestier-Walker for this failure. He was shortly afterwards invalided, through sunstroke, and proceeded to England, but was destined to perish in the Soudan. He fell, fighting his guns gallantly, at El Teb.'

Colborne gave a valuable description of Khartoum as it was at this time. Apart from the Blue Nile which washed one side of the town the only other fortifications were three plain mud ramparts. The town was full of trees and there were excellent gardens and buildings established by the Austrian Roman Catholic missionaries. There was no hotel or inn. Liquor shops were plentiful and offered a variety of intoxicants. One of the local poisons was 'manufactured in Cairo and labelled "Hennessy's Three Star Cognac" (why Hennessy should be singled out as the victim of these rascally counterfeits I cannot conceive, Ekshaw and Martell are generally exempt from spurious imitations) . . .

'It is almost impossible to calculate the population of Khartoum. The mud houses and beehive huts of the narrow,

tortuous, mud-walled streets, are unnumbered, and there is
no municipal system which will permit of an exact census
being taken. Probably, the inhabitants, including slaves, may
be reckoned at something like 60,000.'

The military day at Khartoum began at 5 a.m. when the
men boarded the steamers and went down to Omdurman just
below the point at which the Blue Nile and White Nile meet.
There they drilled and practised weapon training. They were
supplied with horses on arrival. 'On one occasion,' said
Colborne, 'there was a horse deficient. Colonel Farquhar
found himself unprovided with a mount. I shall never forget
the look with which the ex-Guardsman in irreproachable
patent leather boots withered an Egyptian officer, who in
unsophisticated kindness of heart exclaimed "Malesh; Take
my mule." Poor Farquhar — than whom a smarter soldier
never donned a red coat — never abated one jot of the
minutiae of the dress parade even in the wilds. Needless to
say, the proffered mount was refused with scorn; and he
declined leaving the water's edge until a horse was procured.'

Training went on till 10 a.m. when the men fell out and
had breakfast. 'The afternoon we spent in writing, military
drawing, and sketching.' Every evening they attended the
General for a short chat. Before dinner they drank a little and
reminisced. Colborne said:

'There were moments when we truly felt

'*Coelum non animum mutant qui trans mare currunt.*
(They change the sky but not the mind who travel across the
seas.) We loved to wander back to the hunting field, the trout
stream, the lonely Irish country quarters, even Aldershot
field days, and last, but not least — the town, the club, the
ball-room, the pork and oyster suppers "after the opera is
over". Greenwich, Richmond, Hurlingham and Lord's of
pleasant memory each afforded reminiscences.'

Colborne's memories abound in literary references, quota-
tions from the classics and recollections of cultural activities.
With it all goes a pleasing tolerance. He laughs at Farquhar
for his arrogance in discomfiture but commends him for his
virtue in the same breath; he likes his fellow men (and

women) and even if he does not find the Sudan countryside pleasant he finds it interesting. The pros and cons of Britain's imperialist history have been widely and hotly discussed, but the people who made it possible, the explorers, the administrators, the officers, the soldiers, have rarely been closely considered. Colborne is, perhaps, a typical example. The leadership came from men with a similar educational and sporting background. They would ride straight. They were admirably self-contained, they could live on memories of the past and plans for the future. Long periods of isolation or tedious humdrum activity would not upset them. Like bees they ate a little of their own honey in the winter.

At Khartoum Colborne met another survival of the Crusades. It seems that these were a different contingent from the ones whom Gordon had met:

'A more interesting and less turbulent body of men were the hundred cuirassiers we found at Khartoum. They were without horses but we afterwards mounted them. Very strange was it to come across the garb of the knights of old in these mail-clad men, with helmets having the one longitudinal bar over the nose. Nothing of the kind exists in the countries which formerly rang with the exploits of Saladin and Coeur de Lion and to find the relics of the Saracens we must go to the interior of Africa.'

The next move was to Kawa 150 miles up the White Nile. On arrival Colborne wrote a letter:

'The heat here is intense, and the odours horrible. The thermometer is 120 in the tents. General Hicks, Colonel Farquhar, and Captain Massey proceed tomorrow up the river about forty-five miles in a steamer to take possession of the ford between Senaar and Kordofan, by the island of Abba. They will probably land and entrench themselves. They take with them 200 soldiers, a "Gatling", two "Nordenfeldts" and one seven pounder mountain gun. On Thursday next, the army here (leaving behind 1000 men to garrison the fort) will march under the command of Suleiman Pasha to attack the enemy entrenched forty-five miles up the river at Jebel-Ain, some distance above the ford. [Colborne and

Coëtlogon went as staff officers.]

'The Egyptian force, which is about 5000 strong, has four Nordenfeldts. The enemy are said to be in force to the number of 20,000 men. There is a fort protecting the ford, said to mount four guns, which General Hicks' steamer will engage.'

But the plan was changed. Dueim, twenty miles down river, was attacked by Baggara tribesmen before the expedition started. The attack was repulsed but it had become obvious that the initiative did not lie entirely with General Hicks. Eventually they occupied Kawa but found themselves in a state of semi-siege. The heat was almost intolerable.

Hicks pressed on. After three weeks at Kawa the journey to Jebel-Ain was continued. This time it was on foot with camels taking the load. Hicks had ordered the advance to be in column but Suleiman countered this and ordered it to be in a square. He was undoubtedly right. Had they been attacked they would never have been able to form in a square in that terrain at short notice. And the square was the proved vital formation. It was the only means of withstanding a determined enemy attack.

There were very few cases of indiscipline on this march. Colborne quoted one, then went on to say:

'I mention this case as a startling and solitary exception to the general conduct of the troops. With a steadier and more patient army I have never marched. Unlike the present Egyptian army, the officers of which are mutinous and fanatical, and whose hatred of their English officers has on one occasion at least found expression in acts of flagrant insubordination, the Soudan Field Force was permeated throughout by a loyalty and a sense of duty beyond all praise.'

Shortly afterwards a Baggara chief joined Hicks. He said his men had joined the Mahdi and subsequently left him. The story was regarded with some suspicion and he was suspected of being an enemy spy. He too was dressed in medieval armour. His arrival caused more surprise.

'The first time I met him was on the occasion of our first

night alarm. It was moonlight, though cloudy. Hearing a
bugle sound, I rushed out of my tent, and was as much
astounded as though I had seen the ghost of my great
grandfather.

'In front of me was the apparition of a knight clad in full
armour, lance in hand and sword on thigh. I rubbed my eyes
and thought I was dreaming. But the phantom vanished not,
and in truth proved to be an actual flesh and blood Knight of
the Soudan, temp 19th century.'

The man rode fully seventeen stone, being over six feet
high! So much for those stories that all medieval knights were
dwarfs compared with modern men. Possibly only smaller
armour, and children's armour, has survived and created a
legend.

On 26 June the force was attacked by Baggara cavalry,
who were driven off by well-directed rocket fire. In expect-
ation of the attack Hicks's men had strewn the ground with
caltraps, four-pointed spikes so joined that whichever way
they fell on the ground one spike would always be pointing
upwards. This, incidentally, was a traditional medieval device
for upsetting cavalry and the advance of illshod infantry.
Hicks, of course, had no cavalry with him and its absence
made reconnaissance almost impossible.

On 29 June a more serious attack took place. The enemy
was hastily estimated at several thousand but at 500 yards
the fire from Hicks's square began to take its toll.
About 500 of the enemy were killed before they rode off.
This was the battle of Marabia. Afterwards Colborne went
and examined the enemy dead. Their features were 'of a light
brown hue with well-chiselled noses and lips' — many of
them strikingly handsome. Clearly these were of Arab stock
and:

'Not only in features did we find a point of resemblance,
for in actual combat they displayed the qualities and tactics
of their warlike ancestors. They never wait to be attacked.
Their onslaught is furious. They sweep down on the foe in
one sudden rush and their plan of battle is invariably to
throw their enemy into confusion by the rapidity of their

attack, which always takes place in the open.

'We had to traverse dense woods and jungles on our march. The chances in their favour would have been immense had they attacked us while we were making our way through these obstacles but their instincts and traditions taught them that such a mode of warfare would not be chivalrous.'

This was just as well. Even though the square was formed on the march considerable adjustment was required when it halted and prepared to receive an attack. Here the enemy were chivalrous enough to attack on an open plain with no cover less than 500 yards away.

'Onwards they came, waving their banners inscribed with the Mahdi's own rendering of the Koran; but the Khedive's troops, encouraged by their English officers, had no fear. They had seen the charm-protected enemy bite the dust under their fire. Allah and the true prophet were with them, and they hurled defiance in answer to the fanatical apostrophizing of the rebellious sheikhs.

'And what gallant men they were. Right up to the cannon's mouth, right up to the rifle muzzle dauntless they rode, encouraging their followers with the promise of Paradise to break our squares. But Nordenfeldts and Remingtons are no respecters of creeds.'

After the battle, Massey and Warner went out with a small reconnoitring party to see if they could take any live prisoners. It proved impossible, as the enemy were expert at dodging and hide-and-seek.

Soon after this Massey got himself lost while out on reconnaissance accompanied by a young Egyptian officer. He was soon in a bad way and his horse was even worse. He thereupon ordered the Egyptian, whose horse was fairly fresh, to return on his own. Massey then lapsed into a coma and the Egyptian left. After some hours he came to, and tried to lead his horse; but after a few paces the horse collapsed and died. Massey went on, too weak to hold anything but his drawn sword. Then he collapsed again. A day later he was found by some Arabs who had been sent out to discover and bring in his body if it was not too decomposed; for this they were to receive £20. He survived — only to be killed later when the column was wiped out.

So the little army reached Jebel-Ain. There Hicks' concluded that the campaign was finished and the expedition should return. Colborne was now suffering from heatstroke and, much against his will, was sent back to Khartoum.

The view that the campaign was over seems, in retrospect, optimistic to the point of idiocy. But at Jebel-Ain there was no sign of the Dervishes and there was no point in going on, thought Hicks, as 'victory with as little bloodshed as possible should be the axiom of a wise General and the urgent desire of all Christian soldiers and every humane man'.

Hicks interviewed all the nearby chiefs and assured them that all would now be well in the future. They need have no fear of the Mahdi. 'They showed a little trepidation at first, but the word of an Englishman, even on the White Nile, carries with it a guarantee of good faith.'

The next stop was Dueim. Shortly before their arrival Dueim had been attacked by one of the Mahdi's armies.

'On August 23rd the rebels appeared in great force around Dueim, assaulting it with desperate energy, but they were utterly routed by the gallant little garrison, losing 4,500 men. When we were there the ground outside the Zareba was strewn with the bleaching bones of the slain. Our camp was situated on the site of the battlefield.

'At the time we were there it was very unhealthy; the heat was intense, and the stench from dead bodies was insufferable.'

Colborne was evacuated to Khartoum on one of the Nile steamers. These remarkable craft weighed about 250 tons and had engines of 32-35 horse-power. Some of them had travelled out in sections, done a spell of duty, then been taken to pieces, transported and reassembled on another part of the river. Two of them 'were converted into war-cruisers, having had thick mimosa plants nailed to the railings of the deck, and being made to carry guns and Nordenfeldts'.

While at Khartoum, Colborne was warned by the Government Medical Officer of the Sudan, 'a man of the greatest experience, who has resided here for twenty-five years', that 'milk drunk alone in this country is poison; that even the natives have to mix it with water. Eggs too are pronounced an abomination – rank poison, however fresh. Both these I was told to avoid if I wished to recover, and not to partake of when recovered.'

Food was cheap. Best mutton was (in modern equivalents) 2p a pound, beef slightly cheaper; a chicken cost 4p.

One account of the end of the ill-fated Hicks expedition came from Father Ohrwalder, who was among the people hoping to be rescued by it. When the Mahdi learnt that a column of unknown strength, but reputed to consist of 12,000 men, was on its way into the Sudan he called up all available men to his forces. Those who joined him were promised 'paradise and all its joys' if they fell fighting in this Holy War; anyone who refused would have his hand and foot cut off. There was no need to carry out the threat.

Hicks apparently left Dueim on 24 September 1883 and marched south-west through Shatl, Zeregga, Aigella, Shirkeleh and Rahad, reaching the latter on 20 October. All the villages en route were deserted and all goods had been removed. 'The ill-fated army scarcely met a living soul, but flocks of vultures followed them as if waiting for their prey.' With the army was an Austrian officer called Major Herlth, who kept a diary. After his death Ohrwalder, with great good luck, was able to obtain it from the man who had stripped his corpse.

Morale was apparently not good, particularly after several thousand troops who had been expected to join them at Shirkeleh had not appeared. Hicks was in constant disagreement with his Egyptian overlord. Camels were dying, and those who survived were in very poor condition. Nearly all the 500 horses died. And the guides were treacherous. It was an open secret that they had been sent by the Mahdi. At Rahad 500 Baggara had been due to join the expedition but these did not appear either; instead they were sniped by the enemy. A bullet came through Hicks's tent and hit the seat he was sitting on. Farquhar now did his best to raise morale.

'On one occasion some horsemen were seen a short

distance away sitting fearlessly on their horses as if challenging anyone to come out and fight them. When Farquhar saw them he mounted horse and advanced straight on them. When he approached they began to retire, but he went in pursuit and coming up with them killed two, the third he pulled off his horse, and capturing the horses brought them back to camp. In spite, however, of such a gallant example, the men were listless and out of heart; the long marches had thoroughly exhausted them.'

Farquhar may have been a 'stuffy' officer on the parade ground but like his fellow officers was superb in action.

At Rahad a German servant deserted. His name was Gustav Klootz and it is said that he deserted not so much because he feared his fate if he stayed with Hicks as because he was a socialist and therefore had leanings towards Mahdism. He appears to have been somewhat muddled in his concepts. By the time he reached the Mahdi's camp at El Obeid he was beginning to regret his decision for he was made to walk barefoot with a rope around his neck for a day and a half in the burning sun. The condition of his feet after that walk may be imagined.

When interrogated Klootz said that Hicks's army now consisted of barely 10,000, and that morale was low. According to Ohrwalder, 'The Mahdi then asked whether, if he wrote to Hicks he would be likely to surrender, to which Klootz naturally replied that he was sure nothing would induce him to do so.' The Mahdi was so pleased to hear that Hicks was now weak that he sent for a plate of fried meat which he shared with him. This was astonishing, as Moslems at that date considered it wrong to eat in the same place as Christians.

In spite of Klootz's reply the Mahdi sent a letter to Hicks inviting him to surrender. This, of course, was ignored. Hicks left Rahad on 26 October, reached Aluba three days later and on 3 November was advancing to Kashgeil, twelve miles south of El Obeid.

The force which then set out from El Obeid was enormous, numbering 20,000 in all and Ohrwalder trembled for the unfortunate Hicks whose force, through desertion, was down to 7,000. Every man, woman and child followed the Mahdi's army; all believed that 40,000 angels would appear and fight on the Mahdi's side.

Fighting began on 3 November, and Hicks's army was soon surrounded. In addition to some machine-guns, the Mahdi's army contained a good number of Remingtons: 6000 rifles, a number of field guns, and huge quantities of ammunition had been captured at El Obeid. In the initial attack the Mahdi's forces were driven back, although Hicks's force suffered heavy losses. Hicks was now desperately short of water and trying to dig wells; had he but known it there was a reservoir of rainwater a mere fifteen minutes' walk from his position.

The last entry in Herlth's diary is for 4 November: 'The general orders the band to play, hoping that the music may enliven us a little; but the bands soon stop, for the bullets are flying from all directions, and camels, mules and men keep dropping down; and we are all cramped up together so the bullets cannot fail to strike. We are faint and weary, and have no idea what to do. The general gives the order to halt and make a Zareba*. It is Sunday, and my dear brother's birthday. Would to God that I could sit down and talk to him for an hour! The bullets are falling thicker. . . .'

At that point the diary ceases.

Hicks's army could not stand and fight for they had insufficient supplies and, in any case, their mission was to press on and take El Obeid. The Mahdi's troops were now using cover and employing fieldcraft; shots poured into Hicks's army from bushes, boulders and shrubs. The doomed army made three attempts to break through the encircling lines but failed on each occasion. Finally the Dervishes rode in for the kill, with lances, on 5 November. The massacre became known as the battle of Sheikan. In Ohrwalder's words:

'According to the evidence of the Dervishes themselves the European officers fought most heroically. General Hicks was one of the last to fall; he had emptied his revolver and,

*Zareba: a fence of stakes and thorns around a camp.

holding his sword in his right hand, waited for the rush of the
enemy; he was soon surrounded and his horse wounded in
the back; he then dismounted and fought most gallantly with
his sword until he fell, pierced by several spears. The heroism
of these brave men was the admiration of all.'

Nevertheless, with their death all hope for pacifying the
Sudan was now extinguished. The prisoners of El Obeid who
had waited for a year now had no prospects of any relief at
all in the foreseeable future.

Another account of this doomed march was discovered in
1898. It was found on the body of one of the Emirs after the
battle of Omdurman, and was the diary of Colonel Abbas
Bey, the Egyptian Deputy Chief of Staff to General Hicks. It
may seem strange that a fighting Dervish should carry around
with him a diary written in pencil, and eventually die in
battle with it thirteen years later, but the Arabs have a great
reverence for written documents and rarely destroy them.
(After the battle of .Ferkeh on 7 June 1896 other documents
were found on the bodies of dead Dervishes and later proved
very useful to Wingate's Intelligence service.)

Abbas Bey's diary makes very plain the difficulties and
frustrations faced by Hicks but also shows, surprisingly
enough, that up till 1 November, when the diary ended, the
column felt that they had a reasonable chance of victory. In
the early stages there were numerous wearisome conferences
between Hicks and the Egyptians, and the irritations these
engendered made subsequent relationships distinctly edgy;
Hicks felt that the Egyptians were inexperienced and undisci-
plined: the Egyptians felt the British were overconfident and
perversely stubborn. Apparently there was a steady trickle of
losses, some through desertion, some through stragglers being
cut off, and some through skirmishes with the Dervishes
when the Egyptians left the column to obtain grazing for the
camels. Discipline was far from good and much of the hardship from thirst could have been avoided. On several occasions, when marching through bush, the square became so
disarrayed that the Dervishes could have cut them to pieces
if they had realized the position. Neglect of routine

maintenance had a seriously damaging effect on the transport. Even so, many of the Dervish Emirs doubted their ability to stop the column and would have preferred to retire and defend El Obeid (Abbas Bey of course did not know this). What the Dervishes did not realize was that Hicks's Krupp guns were in such a poor state that their range was down from 1000 metres to 100.

The remainder of the story came from yet another independent source, the Sheikh Abd-el-Kadir, of whom we shall hear more later. Abd-el-Kadir said that great damage was done to the square on the night of the 4th; Dervishes crawled right up to the zareba in the darkness and fired point blank at men, horses, mules and camels. On the morning of the 5th the column set out in three smaller squares in a desperate attempt to reach the next water-hole. But the Mahdi with thousands of Dervishes was poised waiting. When the long-awaited order came the onslaught was overwhelming and absolute. The only survivors were those buried under the great heap of dead.

As Ohrwalder wrote: 'The Mahdi was now hallowed almost as a god. He was now regarded as the true Mahdi, every Moslem believed in him, and all doubt was put aside.

'At the battle [in which Hicks's army had been wiped out] numbers of people said they saw the angels whom the Mahdi had summoned to fight against the Turks.* He now became the object of almost superhuman adoration; even the water with which he washed himself was handed by the eunuchs to the believers, who drank it with avidity as an antidote to all ills and disease.'

Khalifa Sherif, the Mahdi's right-hand man, strongly urged him to advance to the White Nile and attack Khartoum, but the Mahdi had reservations about the wisdom of doing so. However he wrote to Slatin (Governor of Darfur) suggesting he should surrender. Slatin was in Dara at the time, with only five cartridges a man, and had absolutely no

---

*It will be recalled that angels fought for the British against the Germans at Mons in 1914.

hope of holding out. He surrendered. His subsequent story, *Fire and Sword in the Soudan*, describes his near-incredible experience as a prisoner in the Mahdi's camp, sometimes as a slave, sometimes as a near-confidant, and makes extraordinary reading.

However, just when hope had all but left the wretched prisoners at El Obeid, a new message suddenly revived it. Gordon was reported to have arrived at Khartoum. The hope abated a little when it was learnt that Gordon had brought no troops with him and that he had merely offered the Mahdi terms which the Mahdi would not even consider. For a leader resolved on the conquest of the world in a Holy War the offer of the Sultanate of the Western Sudan was a poor substitute, particularly as he already dominated a much wider area. The Mahdi replied saying he was not interested in worldly possessions but wished 'to reform the people'. He suggested Gordon should join him in this crusade and sent him a complete set of Dervish garments, a *jibbah*, a *takia*, turban, girth, and pair of sandals.

It was now the turn of the Catholic sisters to suffer. In the words of Ohrwalder again:

'They had set out from Rahad with the various Emirs amongst whom they had been distributed; on the journey they suffered greatly. They were obliged to walk the whole distance barefooted over thorns and burning sand; they underwent agonies of torture and thirst, and some of them had to carry loads; one of them for a whole day had not a drop of water to drink. These brutal savages were continually beating, insulting and abusing them, and when, tired and weary, they sat down for a moment, they were driven forward under the lash of the cruel whip. On their arrival at Rahad they scarcely looked like human beings, with their faces all scorched and peeled by the burning sun; and here new tortures awaited them. One of them was suspended from a tree, and beaten on the soles of the feet until they became swollen and black, and soon afterwards the nails dropped off. In spite of all this suffering, and notwithstanding the continual threats of these barbarians that they

The Mahdi. His full name was Mohammed Ahmed Ibn Al-Sayid Abdullah

Life in the Sudan in the mid-nineteenth century: (*above*) a convoy of slaves on the march; (*below*) collecting taxes with the aid of the *kourbash* or rhinoceros-hide whip

A Dervish Emir. Although his *jibbah* is patched, as the Mahdi's had been, the material is of good quality and already a mere symbol of poverty

(*Above*) Some of the officers of the ill-fated Hicks expedition. Back row (*left to right*): Capt. Massey, Maj. Farquhar, Maj. Warner, Sgt. Bradley (Hicks's orderly), Capt. Evans, Capt. Forestier-Walker. Front row: Col. the Hon. J. Colborne, Maj. Martin, Hicks Pasha, De Coëtlogon Pasha

(*Below*) The death of Hicks Pasha

Gordon after his first visit to Africa

The attempted relief of Khartoum: disaster at the Birti Cataract, 1885

(*Above*) The Guards Camel Corps at Dongola: inspection and general salute

(*Below*) Crossing the desert

The fall of Khartoum

would be violated, these sisters clung firmly to their faith and belief '

However, one of them eventually escaped and got into the Mahdi's hut. The Mahdi said he was unaware of what had been happening but ordered the ill-treatment to cease. It did.

The Mahdi was undoubtedly sincere in his religious beliefs and made several attempts to convert Ohrwalder. These meetings produced some extremely interesting conversations, though they failed in their main purpose. The Mahdi believed God had given him forty years (he died four years later) and he planned in that time first to subjugate the whole Sudan, then to take Egypt, then to attack Mecca. At Mecca he believed there would be an intensely bloody battle. After winning, the Mahdi would proceed to Jerusalem where Christ would descend from Heaven.

Subjugating the Sudan involved a number of desperate battles with the Nubas. Although the Dervishes despised the Nubas and called them 'poor black slaves' they found them extremely dogged and brave opponents. As the Dervishes were constantly thwarted so did they become more cruel.

Ohrwalder was an unwilling witness of the treatment of some of the Nuba captives and also heard at first hand of their fighting skill. 'The Nubas fought with desperate skill. I used to hear of their bravery from the Dervishes who frequented my master's house,' he wrote. And:

'On one occasion, when the Dervishes, led by Abu Anga and followed by the Gellabas, attempted to ascend the mountain, the Nubas allowed them to advance some way and then pounced upon the Gellabas in the narrowest pass; these men were badly armed and four hundred of them were killed. . . . In another attack the Dervishes succeeded in reaching the Nuba village, burning the huts and killing a large number of them and carrying off their wives and children as captives to Rahad where they were sold as slaves.'

Eventually the Nubas agreed to submit provided they were allowed to remain free and stay in their native mountains. However, when they came down from the hills to take the oath of allegiance, they were told to follow the Mahdi to the

White Nile. The Nubas had no alternative but to agree, but during the night fled back to the hills. The fight was renewed but eventually the Dervishes broke off the attempt to eliminate the remainder in the deep recesses of the hills.

The defeat of the Nubas, although no one outside the Sudan realized it at the time, was part of the Mahdi's master plan. As Sir Ronald Wingate, son of Wingate of the Sudan, put it: 'During these years of apparent chaos there was a plan and there was an intelligence directing that plan. The plan was of great simplicity; to bring back to the true way of Islam the Egyptian empire from the Mediterranean to the Great Lakes. The Mahdi's uprising was a true religious movement directed against an alien rule by the "Turks" (and their prince the "Khedive" who had abandoned the tenets of the Prophet).'

This information derived from a source which did not become available for years after the Mahdi's death. This was a book written by the Sheikh Abd-el-Kadir, previously referred to. Abd-el-Kadir was a man of considerable learning who had taken part in nearly all the early battles. He then settled in Omdurman and wrote two books; the first was about the Mahdi and the second about the events in the Sudan after the Mahdi's death. The Khalifa was very pleased with the books but after hearing that Abd-el-Kadir in fact despised him as being vain and ignorant he ordered that all copies should be destroyed. Fortunately one survived.

From Abd-el-Kadir's writings it is clear that the Mahdi was following the principles of early Islam. The Abyssinians were not to be attacked unless they attacked first. Christians need not be converted by force but should be persuaded. After a successful battle women and children should be enslaved. Looting would be strictly controlled and a fifth of all captured property handed over to the State Treasury.

At an early stage he forbade the use of the word 'Dervish' and decreed that his followers should all be called 'ansars'. The word means 'helpers', and had been used by the Prophet Mohammed. With all this went a strict austere regime: no' drinking, swearing or luxury were permitted. (Women, whether wives or concubines, were not considered a luxury.)

Inevitably, after the Mahdi's death and some thirteen years in which corruption and apathy were bound to take effect, there was considerable slackening both in morale and impetus. But, even in 1896, Hilliard Atteridge, the *Daily Chronicle* correspondent, noted that stores were issued and checked with a method which would have won the approval of a British regimental quartermaster. Furthermore, although much of the initial religious zeal had disappeared, lessons learnt from experience made the Dervishes still a most formidable fighting force.

4

Suakir

The disaster of the Hicks column was not the only one which the Egyptian government and British prestige were going to encounter in 1883. On the very day of Hicks's defeat another ominous battle was taking place on the opposite side of the Sudan. This was the work of Osman Digna.

Osman Digna was what would later be called a great guerrilla leader. He was a forerunner of such personalities as De Wet in the Boer War, Grivas in Cyprus and Chin Peng in Malaya — all equally troublesome to the British in their different ways. Osman Digna (his full and proper name was Uthman Ben Abu Bakr Digna) came of an Arab family which had settled in the Sudan in the seventeenth century; they had subsequently intermarried and become members of the Hadendowa people. Like the rest of his family he was a slave-trader principally but also handled other goods as well. He was in partnership with his three brothers and doing nicely until his brother was captured, by a British ship, when trying to cross the Red Sea with a cargo of slaves. All four brothers were imprisoned and their property was confiscated. The family was ruined. After a half-hearted attempt to earn a living legally Osman threw in his lot with the Mahdi. It was, unfortunately for their enemies, the perfect partnership. One of the Mahdi's greatest qualitites was his ability in choosing the right subordinate commanders. He listened to Osman's story with interest, created him an Emir, which is the title of a provincial governor of considerable importance, and gave him the task of raising the eastern Sudan and capturing Suakin. In rank, Osman was now an army commander.

At first it seemed that he would be no great success. Both

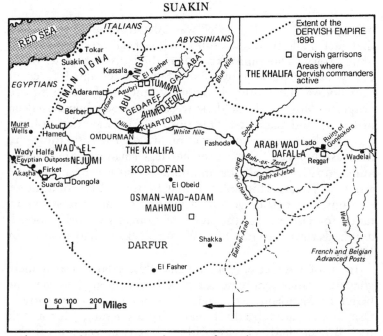

The Dervish Empire on the eve of Kitchener's reconquest

his first two attacks on government forces were repulsed bloodily; in the second he himself was wounded. The architect of his defeats was an able Egyptian soldier named Tewfik Bey. They were only minor skirmishes, but if they had been followed up Osman might have decided the task was beyond his powers and adopted a passive role. Unfortunately the government remained on the defensive. The following month a slightly smaller force — about 150 men strong — was ambushed, and all but wiped out. It was meant to be a reinforcement for a government post at Sinkat, which had repulsed the first attack, and the importance of this minor success was that Osman could now wait for Sinkat to surrender or die of starvation. Leaving behind a small besieging force he turned his attention elsewhere.

The next obvious target was Tokar, a small town about fifty miles from Suakin. Osman besieged it. As he expected, a relief force set out from Suakin and marched towards the beleaguered town. The force was 500 strong and presumably that fact made its leaders think that normal precautions were unnecessary. Their mistake, when they discovered it, was a costly one. Attacked by a small but determined force of Hadendowa the motley little army failed to form its square properly. Most of the soldiers were completely inexperienced in battle, and panicked. One-third of the Egyptian column was slaughtered; the remainder ran away. The casualties were the least important part of the battle. Osman captured several hundred rifles and all the ammuniton that was meant for the relief of Tokar. This was the first battle of El Teb, a minor encounter as battles go but a victory of the utmost importance for Osman. As the news of Osman's victories spread, hundreds rushed to join him. Within weeks he had an army of 10,000.

It is, of course, easy to assume that Osman was a mere guerrilla leader, enjoying his task but without any genuine belief in Mahdism. The view may not be entirely correct. Osman was undoubtedly a man with a grievance, for he felt the British had unreasonably ruined a very profitable occupation which did no harm to anyone of consequence. Slaves had an appalling time when they were being transported but once they were sold into ownership were usually well looked after. A man would be a fool if he destroyed his own valuable property, which is what a slave was. Osman's reaction to his punishment for being a slave-trader was probably much the same as the owner of a hen-battery today. The latter will point out that the hens are fed regularly, are housed in warm, dry, even if somewhat restricted quarters, and are safe from the hazard of foxes. Osman probably regarded anti-slavery movements as mere uncommercial nonsense. It is one thing to feel ill-used and burning for revenge, but a different matter entirely to inspire a rebel army over many years.

One final effort was made by the Egyptians in 1883. The last contingent of trained troops were now thrown into the fight. They amounted to a battalion, and they were sent to the relief of Sinkat. They never reached it. At Tamai they were overwhelmed by 3000 Dervishes, full of spirit and confidence in victory. Thirty-five Egyptians survived.

Just as the year ran out another spectacular figure arrived on the scene. This was Valentine Baker, better known as Valentine Baker Pasha. He was the younger brother of Sir Samuel Baker, and no less a personality than his redoubtable explorer brother. He had fought in campaigns in several parts of the world, including the Crimea, but at the age of forty-eight was court-martialled and dismissed from the army for allegedly trying to rape a woman in a railway carriage. With no future in Britain or British forces he went off to Turkey and fought with considerable skill against the Russians, earning the rank of Major-General. In 1882 he was offered the post of Commander-in-Chief of the Egyptian army but the offer was withdrawn before he could take it up. Supposedly Queen Victoria herself had intervened: it was said that his record with young women in railway compartments could cause his brother officers to recoil from him in disgust. However, if he was not good enough for the army he was thought to be good enough for the police and he was put in charge of the 'gendarmerie', a police force organized as a military unit.

The gendarmerie, when he took it over, was enough to daunt the bravest. It was of poor quality and untrained. When the order was given to proceed to the Sudan there was an attempt at mass desertion. But Baker did not worry. It was a command, there was fighting to do, and once he got his men organized they would, he hoped, surprise everybody.

Baker embarked his army and took it to Trinkitat, the port where the last ill-fated expedition had landed. This was sixty miles south of Suakin, and the best approach to Tokar, which he planned to relieve. He was soon at El Teb — but not before the Dervishes. The date was 4 February 1883. His army numbered 3656 and had six guns. Unfortunately for Baker it consisted mainly of Egyptian officers and men of the lowest quality, a sharp contrast to those who were with Tewfik. The ensuing massacre — it could not be called a battle — was almost incredible. The 150 Turkish cavalry panicked after starting to charge and rushed back; the effect of this was to disorganize the square which was just being formed. The Dervish numbers were given in the official report as 1200, but may have been even less. As they hacked their way into the broken square it became 'a scene of butchery which has probably never been rivalled' (Official War Office Report). Inside the square the state of affairs was almost indescribable. Cavalry, infantry, mules, camels, falling baggage and dying men were crushed into a struggling surging mass. Gradually, as the square thinned, the men escaped and fled, throwing away their arms and clothes, the rebels following and killing them as they ran.

Baker Pasha and Colonel Sartorius vainly tried to rally the cavalry for a charge, but finding matters perfectly hopeless, charged with their staffs through the rebels and gained the shore. The Egyptian loss on this occasion was 112 officers and 2250 men killed and wounded, besides the machine and Krupp guns and 3000 rifles. Among the British killed was Captain Forestier-Walker, formerly of the Hicks expedition. He was reported to have been killed 'fighting his guns with the utmost gallantry'.

Four days later Tewfik Bey, deciding that there was now no chance of relief, evacuated Sinkat having destroyed everything which might be of use to the enemy. His small force numbered only 400 effectives but also included large numbers of women and children. He was offered surrender terms, but refused. His force was then overwhelmed a mile and a half from Sinkat, after a desperate struggle. On this occasion the Dervishes were not merely slaughtering the terror-stricken; they were fighting men as brave and enduring as themselves and they paid heavily for their victory.

Andrew Haggard of the King's Own Borderers (elder brother of Rider Haggard, the novelist) had gone out to Egypt in 1882 with what was called the 1st Reserve Depot. Most of the unit were Irish, and Haggard said: 'I can honestly say that of all the unruly and insubordinate scoundrels it has ever been my lot to meet wearing the British uniform these Irish Reserve men were the worst.' Doubtless they would fight like tigers when well disciplined and led, but this would come later. As they entered the Suez Canal they met the victors of Tel-el-Kebir and were greeted with cries of 'You're too late' and 'Come for the next campaign; we've won this'. Their own men were so enraged by the taunts that it was a good thing there was water between the two ships and 'they could only reply to the taunts of the conquering heroes by shaking their fists and by howls of execration and curses'. But as Haggard put it: 'If we were too late for the fighting we very soon found we were not too late for fatigue duties, a business for which our men in their state of temper were not particularly inclined.' Nevertheless they buckled to and in spite of sickness, insubordination and occasional near mutiny, the jobs were done.

His comments on Baker's army were illuminating. 'The troops that still remained of the old army were converted from regulars into gendarmerie, at least in name and status, although they remained armed in every respect as before, and wore the same uniforms. These were placed under the command of Baker Pasha, late Colonel Valentine Baker of the 10th Hussars, who had resigned a high command in the Turkish army for entirely another purpose than to command a rubbishy lot of worthless ex-soldiers who were to be called gendarmerie.'

Baker's place as Commander-in-Chief in Egypt had been taken by Sir Evelyn Wood, who had begun service life as a midshipman and was destined to become a Field-Marshal. The title of the appointment was Sirdar and the post was paid at the rate of £5000 a year. (To obtain the present-day equivalent one has to multiply the figure by ten.)

The Egyptian army was a godsend to the British army. As Haggard wrote:

'Let any subaltern with a turn for statistics get hold of the Army list of 1883, and one of every succeeding year up to date. Let him then get hold of a list of the officers of the Egyptian army, including the medical branch, and watch their progress in rank from the day they joined it until the present day. Let him see the subalterns who have become full colonels, let him note also the colonels who have become generals. I think that before he has got half through his task he will agree that, whether they stuck to it for long or not, to have once belonged to the Egyptian army was a distinct step in most instances on the road to fortune.'

However, as Haggard soon found, pay and promotion went with an enormous amount of hard work. But there were diversions: 'We descended at that jolly old caravanserai Shepheard's Hotel — where there were plenty of pretty ladies to vary the monotony of so many military men. For the visitors from England and elsewhere had begun to regain confidence and were coming to finish the winter in Egypt. What a jolly and merry crowd they all were too! Ah indeed! Those were cheery days in Cairo, cheery enough at times almost to make the Sphinx laugh.'

The entertainments included some riotous Mess dinner nights. On one occasion the entire company took the part of a fox-hunt complete with horn, holloas and riding straight (over chairs, tables and so on) in the best hunting tradition. Most of those present fought in the Hicks expedition and the leading light and organizer of the fox-hunt, one Captain 'Sugar' Candy of the 9th Lancers, 'in the cholera season of the latter part of 1883 showed that he could do something else beside skylarking; for he did capital and very trying work in establishing quarantine cordons with his gendarmes around the centres of infection, incurring much personal risk.'

'As regards drill, we had at first two great difficulties to contend with; one was that the Egyptians seemed absolutely unable to understand the meaning of a straight line, and more especially unable to grasp the meaning of one line being at right angles to another, or of a line being parallel to another. But, in time, they improved.'

Haggard's beau idéal of a soldier was a young officer called Chamley Turner, 'very tall, very broad-shouldered, had a dark face with keen blue, almost jackdaw blue eyes. He was downright, devil-may-care, good natured, hot-tempered, and a splendid shot. He would work all day, sit up all night, get out again on parade the next morning at five or six o'clock, and work all the next day and to give his own phrase when he was perhaps a little merry, which he would quote with a stentorian laugh, "Fear! Chamley Turner doesn't know what fear is."When he first made use of this phrase to me I thought him boasting. Over and over again afterwards, until his death by drowning in the Nile I found that his words were absolutely true — Chamley Turner was the one man I have met who positively did not know what fear was.'

One example was the occasion when someone — as a practical joke — handed him a box of writing paper, but which, in fact, contained five asps. The practical joker had had all the fangs removed.

'He took the box — opened it. Up came the five snakes' heads all hissing. Did he drop that box? Not much! Exclaiming "Snakes, oh ripping!" he plunged his hand into the box, seized all five snakes at once, and with them curling round his hand and wrist in every direction, and biting him, started round to clear everyone off that verandah, which he did in about a minute and a half, or less. When he had turned every one off the place into the street or the hotel, he put the snakes back in the box and only then asked if they were poisonous.'

The Egyptians, though not talented at drill, were extremely keen. They loved drill so much they even drilled all night: 'It was useless ordering this practice to be stopped; as I have said before the Egyptians loved drilling — you could never give them too many hours of it. The habit was therefore encouraged by the native officers, and encouraged by the non-commissioned officers, who would, for that matter, gladly go without a night's rest so that they could get in an hour or two's extra drill. The result was the night was made hideous (with: left turn, right turn, about turn, present arms, order arms etc.).'

Life in Egypt had no lack of variety. There were formal dinners, and there was shooting and riding. There was also a cholera epidemic, during which the officers moved among their men, nursing and often burying them. And there was romance — 'friendships with not only Syrian and Coptic ladies but even with one or two beautiful Circassian slave-girls'.

'And when once an Eastern woman loves, or fancies she loves, she does not believe in calmly waiting until in the European way, the object of her young affections tells her that she is adored by him. On the contrary she promptly finds some means of communicating with the object of her choice. Even should he, fearful of bow strings and yataghans, seek to elude her, it is of no use; for sooner or later, whether he will or no, he finds himself somehow in the lady's presence.'

Haggard described one of his duties:

'The conscription laws in Egypt were in themselves simple enough and fair enough. All young men between the ages of nineteen and twenty-three were liable to military service for four years, and then to eight years on the reserve. The exceptions were in favour of those who were known as "Wahidani". This word – from wahid = one, means an only son; but for purposes of conscription it had a broader signification – namely to denote any son upon whom devolved the care and support of an old or infirm father or mother, or of young brothers or sisters so long as they should remain small and unmarried.

'A great deal of lying always took place upon these points. Another exception was in favour of all religious pupils, Mahommedan or Christian, of priests or persons engaged as servants in the Coptic churches or in the mosques. This was the great door of escape to the Copts, who produced false certificates. Finally of all persons engaged in the Khedive's household, and of those medically unfit. In addition, anybody could claim exemption upon payment of £100 Egyptian.'

He described the scene at the exemption commission. Whenever a mother had a pretty daughter as well as sons the daughter would be propelled forward to the judicial table. 'The girl, barely veiling the point of her chin, and with a shy but coquettish manner, would stretch out her shapely arm – and Egyptian women's arms are shapely indeed – with the petition to the nearest of us, with such a beseeching look in her lustrous eyes that it was usually accepted from the dainty fingers.' However 'one glance at the petition and one or two questions tersely put, were generally enough. The statements set out were usually found to be a tissue of lies, and the exit of that mother and daughter was more often than not so rapid that it must have seemed to them like a dream, if indeed it did not take their breath away.'

There was nothing naive about the commission. On discovering a genuine Copt they took from him the names of all the other genuine Coptic priests and servants.

'This list we found useful when presently two other Copts appeared, both claiming to be students, and both armed with certificates to that effect signed by the Patriarch. By its aid we found them not to be religious pupils at all, but first-class liars engaged in other occupations. They were ordered to be enlisted at once, and one, moreover, to be tried by court-martial on enlistment.'

But these were not the only liars the commission encountered. Some were detected; some, they feared, were not: 'The village sheikhs lied horribly on the following day, and half the conscripts whose names were called were absent, being screened by the sheikhs, whose palms had been well oiled, and who explained their absence by a hundred fictitious excuses. Among the sheikhs there was one who came to grief by thrusting himself in unnecessarily. There is an Arab proverb which runs as follows: *Al dabur zann likharb eshshu* (the hornet hums to the destruction of his own nest). This proverb applied to his case.'

When a young man had been called this sheikh had sworn he was in Cairo. The story was somewhat undermined by the fact that several people had seen him outside the court-house the previous day. The sheikh was therefore imprisoned. The next day immediately after the train from Cairo arrived the young man got off it, almost breathless, and ran to the court-house, saying he had been summoned by telegram from Cairo. Unfortunately for the story it was proved that he had merely got on the train one station down the line.

But there were diversions from the tedium of hearing a string of lies day after day. Haggard liked a ride in the early morning. One day:

'I was riding very early in the morning in Upper Egypt
when, traversing some date palms, I suddenly came by a deep
descent through a small nullah or ravine upon the Nile, which
being very low at that time of the year, was perfectly hidden
from the banks above. No sooner was I on the banks of the
river than I found myself face to face with a pretty village girl
of some eighteen summers who, denuded of even the merest
vestige of clothing, was washing herself in the river, in which,
on account of the swift current, she did not stand deeper
than her knees. The situation was embarrassing. I reined up
my horse; the maiden cast one irresolute glance at the
swiftly running stream behind her, then another at her
clothes on the bank by my horse's feet. That glance decided
her. In a second she had made up her mind. In a couple of
bounds she had sprung out of the water, and stooping, picked
up — what? Not her blue chemise; that was left on the
ground. It was her veil which she seized upon, and swiftly
covering her face therewith, she calmly waked back into the
water again.'

Perhaps the Egyptians would have been less reluctant to
take on a military career if they had not been conditioned by
the abuses of the old system of conscription. Previously once
a man had been enlisted in the army he stayed in it until he
was killed or useless. 'Then when feeble and worn out he was
no longer fit to carry arms, he was stripped even of the
uniform he stood up in, and, clad in any rags he could obtain,
allowed to find his way home as best he could to his distant
birthplace. On arrival there it was no longer a home to him;
all his relations were dead, no one knew him. Too weak to
work, he had nothing left but to die as soon as possible, to
quit the miserable existence of utter destitution to which he
was reduced.'

With the new system introduced by Baker and continued
by Sir Evelyn Wood, everything changed. They were properly
paid, given leave, medals and gratuities, and generally
well-treated. As a result it was possible to say ten years later
'the young soldiers have turned out well, and have frequently

behaved with distinguished bravery in the field.'

At the beginning of 1884 there was little to make either the Egyptians or anyone else feel confident or brave. Apart from a few isolated towns such as Khartoum, Suakin and Sennar the Mahdi controlled the Sudan. It seemed only a matter of time — and not a very long time at that — before these too would fall.

Perhaps the most depressing aspect of all was that the British government, which was nominally in charge of Egypt and the Sudan, seemed to have no idea of its responsibilities. It was a situation which would occur again later, with much the same muddled reasoning behind it. The man at the helm in the British Cabinet was Gladstone, a lifelong Liberal who believed the English had no business in anyone else's country, and who, at seventy-four, was not prepared to listen to any suggestion to the contrary.

Gladstone was a kindly man, much troubled by matters which were beyond his ability to comprehend. His policy for Egypt and the Sudan was to leave them as soon as possible, or if not able to do so, to pretend that such problems as existed there were no concern of the British government. Even Sir Evelyn Baring, the Consul-General in Egypt, a staunch Liberal, was unable to make much impact on this view. It was obvious to Baring that influence could not be exercised by half-measures. Egypt was to all intents and purposes a British colony — for the time being at least — and the Sudan, so closely linked with Egypt, was a centre of the slave trade which Britain had abolished in the British Empire in 1814 (the slave-trade had been banned by Great Power agreement in 1806) but which had never been finally stamped out. However, Gladstone, as a strong anti-imperialist, could not tamely accept the view that Britain should now increase rather than decrease her imperial influence. It probably seemed a losing battle, for further south Cecil Rhodes was openly determined to extend British influence as much as possible in Africa. But in the Sudan Gladstone decided the process of imperialism should stop. His interpretation of the Mahdist movement was 'a people rightly struggling to be free'. This view ignored the position of the slaves whose freedom was hardly likely to be assured by the Mahdi's army, judging by the Nubas' experience, and also paid no heed to the fact that Mahdism was neither a purely nationalist movement nor a purely religious one. There were plenty of Sudanese who did not wish to serve the Mahdi voluntarily, and there were numbers of Moslems who considered the Mahdist movement to be a form of heresy.

Forced to take some action, Gladstone and his Cabinet decided that as the choice was between reconquest and complete evacuation of the Sudan, the latter was preferable. In consequence in January 1884 Gordon was sent to supervise the British withdrawal, but with no special title or brief other than to report from Khartoum and carry out further instructions later.

Gordon must have seemed an excellent choice. He was an experienced and capable solider, he had served in the Sudan before, and he was a religious liberal in outlook. The surprise and annoyance of the British Cabinet was therefore understandable when he began to bombard London with a stream of telegrams which queried his instructions; equally understandable was Gordon's reluctance to evacuate the few remaining Europeans and abandon to their fate all those who had no wish to become part of the Mahdi's forces. As we have already seen, the route to and from Khartoum was difficult, and could be highly dangerous unless some agreement was reached with the Mahdi to let the evacuees proceed without molestation from his supporters. The most tiresome aspect of Gordon, as far as the British Cabinet was concerned, was his individuality. Instead of finding a simple solution to the complex problem of withdrawing from the Sudan he produced a complex one, and one, furthermore, which involved certain unacceptable compromises such as recognizing slavery in order not to alienate potential friends and allies, and fighting the Mahdi's army to prove that it would be better for the Mahdi if he gave Gordon time and the opportunity to evacuate all those who wished to leave.

Gordon can hardly be blamed for assuming that the British

government did not know its own mind, or that it had no idea of the true situation in the Sudan. For in spite of deploring the use of force it was actually authorizing it. This authorization was, however, limited to the defence of Suakin. The procedure was brisk and businesslike. The admiralty telegraphed Rear-Admiral Hewett at Suakin asking him what force he required for the protection of Suakin. Hewett asked for 500 marines, and received them. On 10 February 1884 Hewett took over supreme military and civil command in Suakin and proclaimed it to be in a state of siege. Two days later he informed the British government of the fall of Sinkat, and in consequence it was decided to·send a force to the Red Sea to relieve Tokar. Lieutenant-General Sir Frederick Stephenson, C-in-C Egypt, was then ordered by telegraph to organize a relief force, selecting his three best battalions for the purpose. He was informed that Major-General Sir Gerald Graham, V.C., would command the expedition, Colonel Herbert Stewart would command the cavalry brigade, and Colonel Sir Redvers Buller, V.C., the infantry brigade. (Buller was ideal for this purpose but less adequate fifteen years later in the South African War, for his intellect was not on a par with his courage.) The total force, which then concentrated at Trinkitat, numbered 4000. Gordon was advised of this somewhat inconsistent piece of policy by the British government, and insisted that before fighting began the rebel chiefs should be asked to confer with him at Khartoum. The gist of the message was that the rebels should disperse their soldiers before daybreak the next day, and answer the letter by the same time. No answer was received.

The bare official account sums up the ensuing events admirably:

'Sir G. Graham accordingly advanced with his entire available force.

'He found the rebels entrenched at El Teb, where they had mounted the Krupp guns captured from Baker Pasha. To turn the entrenchments he moved to the right, stormed and carried them in flank, two successive positions being taken.

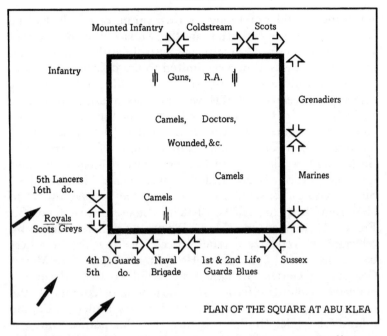

PLAN OF THE SQUARE AT ABU KLEA

Four Krupp guns, two brass howitzers, and one Gatling gun were captured, besides a quantity of arms and ammunition. The loss of the rebels was very heavy; 2100 bodies were buried in the positions captured, irrespective of those killed in the cavalry operations. The action lasted three hours and the enemy showed desperate resolution and tenacity; their strength was estimated to be about 6000. The British loss amounted to 34 killed and 155 wounded.'

Further proclamations were then issued calling on Osman and his chiefs to submit; the early ones were ignored but then there came a reply, signed by a number of chiefs, defying Graham to do his worst.

On 13 March, after a preliminary night bombardment, Graham's army advanced on Tamai in two squares. Much to its surprise it was attacked with great fury. This was the great occasion when the 'Fuzzy-Wuzzies' broke a British square. The British, who are much given to celebrating their own defeats, remembered this chiefly through Kipling's lines:

82

' 'E rushes at the smoke when we let drive
An', before we know, 'e's 'acking at our 'ead;
'E's all 'ot sand an' ginger when alive,
An' 'e's generally shamming when 'e's dead.
'E's a daisy, 'e's a ducky, 'e's a lamb!
'E's a injia-rubber idiot on the spree
'E's the on'y thing that doesn't care a damn
For the regiment o' British Infantree!
So 'ere's to you, Fuzzy-Wuzzy, at your
                    'ome in the Sowdan;
You're a pore benighted 'eathen but
                    a first-class fighting man;
An' 'ere's to you, Fuzzy-Wuzzy, with
                    your 'ayrick 'ead of 'air —
You big black bounding beggar — for
                    you bruk a British square.'

The 'Fuzzy-Wuzzies', as they came to be called by the
British soldier, had hair which frizzed out in all directions
from the head. They were the Beja, the hill tribesmen, of
whom the Hadendowa were one section. They fought
with a courage, drive and ferocity which compelled admiration as well as respect. Of their other characteristics, more
later. On this occasion they pushed in the right flank and captured some machine-guns. However, courage was not a mono-
poly of the Beja, and a battery of four guns, unprotected,
took fearful toll of the advancing enemy. Eventually, Osman
Digna's forces withdrew and the British occupied Tamai.

'The strength of the enemy was estimated at about 12,000
and their loss is put down at 2000 killed.' British losses were
less than a tenth of this figure but they were, of course,
defending, and although outnumbered three to one, had
infinitely better fire power. Nevertheless at one stage,
defensive, disciplined and well-armed or not, they could have
been swept away and killed to a man. Although the fruits of
this victory were frittered away the achievement should not
be belittled. It was a desperate battle between opponents who

were worthy of each other.

After the battle and the occupation of Tamai, Graham's force returned to Suakin. Graham telephoned for further instructions. He mentioed that 'two heavy blows had been dealt at the Mahdi and the rebels and followers of the Mahdi, who are profoundly discouraged.' He went on to say that 'They say however, that the English troops can do no more, must re-embark, and leave the country to them. To follow up these victories, and bring waverers to our side, we should not proclaim our intention of leaving, but rather make a demonstration of an advance towards Berber, and induce a belief we can march anywhere we please.' Gordon was also in favour of this march to Berber, which would have opened up the road to Khartoum and given point to the recent expensive operation; he was prepared to send a force from Khartoum to meet it.

But Her Majesty's government refused to sanction this further operation, and the force withdrew. In May the withdrawal was complete; in May also Berber was besieged by the Mahdi's troops. The policy was not merely inexcusable: it was idiotic. If the way to Khartoum had been opened, and kept open, with the forces already there, the whole history of the next thirteen years would have been different. But the government seemed determined to ignore all advice. Sir Samuel Baker, whose opinion was entitled to be respected, had suggested the appointment of a Resident and also the enlistment of the head of the Korosko Arabs, who would have fought for the British and contained Osman Digna. In Egypt a somewhat ludicrous suggestion was made that the Eastern Sudan should be handed back to Turkey. As it was held by Egypt from Turkey at an annual rent this seemed an ideal occasion to pass it back to the Sultan. The Sultan, however, declined to break the existing agreement and Egypt found herself not merely in titular possession but also having to fight a determined opponent for territory from which she could not benefit.

Gordon was in a curious position. He had been sent by a government which clearly did not know its own mind. He was subject to his own ideas and training, which were to be a soldier but also a Christian of distinctly unorthodox ideas. Lastly he was so brave that any form of caution — which would not have been inappropriate in Khartoum at that time — was anathema to him. As a contemporary said:

'Whatever Gordon's reasons, and whatever his ideas, he was one of the most gallant men who ever lived, and his fame is imperishable, not only among his own countrymen, but among all those countless hordes of the Soudan, who respected him only less than they dreaded him. He was a born leader of men, and 1 can call to mind the pride with which a native of the interior of the Soudan once showed me an Arabic letter in his possession which bore Gordon's seal.'

Haggard was one of those sent up to Suakin to reorganize the remnants of Baker's defeated force before Graham's arrival, and to see that Suakin was properly guarded. It was no mean task. He had the duty of going round the outposts at night, and as his troops had a habit of firing off their rifles for fun in any direction into the darkness, the visits were not without their moments of excitement. Apart from the possibility of running into the enemy there were such factors as pitch-dark and pouring rain to contend with on some nights. And, on one occasion: 'I then found I had run the risk of a more terrible disaster than of merely being shot, for I had ridden at least three times backwards and forwards through a regular network of wide-mouthed and deep wells, by any one of which I might have been engulfed horse and all.' Haggard sums up the situation: 'To the best of my belief, had Osman Digna sent only 100 men during the days that all British troops were absent, with instructions to win or die, they would have won, hands down, and all the dying would have been on our side.'

Morale was extremely low among the Negro troops. 'One day they actually deserted all their posts and came into Suakin to drink a strong kind of native beer called boosa — a very appropriate name since they were undoubtedly soon in a state of "booze". On this occasion I passed a pleasant afternoon in the middle of 800 or 900 mutinous wretches who were discontented with everything . . . it was jealousy which was the principal cause of the riot. The Massowahs had got all their women with them; they had also annexed all the women of the other Massowahs who had been killed. The Bezingers had no women with them, and wanted some Massowah women and could get none.' To him that hath shall be given; when fighting broke out the Massowahs got the best of it.

Throughout the 'discussion' Haggard had kept his finger on the trigger of his pistol and his eye on a target in the middle of the ringleader's forehead. He knew that if he had to fire that shot it would be the last thing he would ever do but he was equally determined that if the agitator set the crowd in motion it would also be the last thing that he would do.

At the second battle of El Teb were two survivors of the previous disaster. One was Baker Pasha, the other was Captain Harvey of the Black Watch. The van of Graham's army was led by one Lieutenant Humphrey of the Mounted Infantry, described as 'a capital fellow'. Humphrey was an excellent soldier but eventually 'died an extraordinary death on the Cairo racecourse, where, as a result of a fall while practising over a jump, he lay for eleven days with his neck broken, or at any rate dislocated. He never was moved from the spot where he fell, and was sensible the whole time till his death, and able to talk to officers who visited him in the tent erected over him, and also to make his will.'

The second battle of El Teb was no matter of machine-guns against ill-armed natives. Osman's men had the two Krupp guns and also field artillery. 'The shell-fire was very heavy and fairly accurate, the shells bursting inside the large square into which Graham had now formed his troops; but the enemy's rifle fire was high. This was fortunate, as they had any amount of Remington rifles and boundless stores of ammunition at their disposal. Baker Pasha was hit under the eye by a shrapnel bullet which lodged in the cheek-bone, but would only dismount to have his face bandaged after considerable persuasion, and remounted again at once.'

The breaking of the square was described as follows:

'As the enemy got near the square their men on the hill stopped firing; but for a change our Gardners and Gatlings got to work under the sailors (the Naval Brigade), while the infantry, who were lying down and kneeling, were firing volleys and putting a perfect stream of lead upon the advancing foe. They fell by dozens; yet not only did the remainder rush on, but even those who were shot down, if not actually dead, got up again and rushed on, brandishing their swords and spears. Some of them got right home to the square, and either stabbed a man or threw their spear before our men, now on their feet, finished them off with the bayonet. . . .

'The cavalry had as difficult a time as the infantry. They were very active in charging the enemy whenever possible; but unfortunately it seems only too probable that they suffered themselves more than the enemy, who stepped behind bushes as they approached, or, lying down behind mounds, jumped up suddenly and slashed and cut at the horses' hocks. When the rider was down, they jumped upon him and speared him. About thirty of their number who were mounted even charged back at a squadron of the 19th Hussars which was charging under Colonel Barrow, and some three of them, after actually getting through Barrow's squadron unhurt, turned and pursued them.'

The enemy carried with them a short stick curved at one end. This stick was very heavy, and they were skilled at throwing it with precision, and it was the throwing of this weapon at the horses' legs which brought them down.

'Although on subsequent occasions we again tried cavalry against these Hadendowah Arabs it must be confessed they were never a success. They had all that was required — bravery, skill and discipline. It was no use to charge with cavalry an enemy who had all the agility of acrobats — who could jump about and bound from side to side like a rubber ball. I have myself, for fun, tried to ride down members of the Amarar tribe with whom we were friendly. The man I would pursue would only be armed with a long stick instead of a spear. I have ridden right on to him, and only when actually under my horse's head would he spring to one side, striking me as I passed him with the point of his stick. And this is how our cavalry lost so many at El Teb without doing any harm to the enemy themselves.'

The victors of El Teb, little realizing how their efforts were going to be completely invalidated by premature withdrawal, were heartened by the news they heard from Khartoum. Gordon was apparently showing a happy blend of firmness and compromise. They heard with approval that he was prepared to work with his former enemy, Zubair. Although once a slave-trader Zubair now seemed to be the only man who could organize a Sudanese government to counter the Mahdi. It seemed that he was to be trusted — although, on an expedition against slave-traders, Gordon had previously had his son executed. And Gordon, in his characteristic way, did not in the least mind about Zubair's being a personal enemy of his own; he felt assured Zubair was the only man with sufficient ability and firmness for the post of governor. However, Gordon's plea was in vain and Zubair was sent off to confinement in Gibraltar.

The 'Zubair plan' had been an imaginative concept. Baring had given his whole-hearted backing to it but the British Cabinet felt that to install a former slave-trader as their representative on the assumption that he would neither establish a military tyranny nor reintroduce slave-trading was taking expediency to the point of idiocy. Most of the press opposed it, and so did the Conservatives, not only because it was immoral but also because it was a Liberal measure. Gordon, 'the man on the spot', believed he could have checked any slave-trading tendencies on the part of Zubair. When the proposal was turned down, and it was clear he would not be sent military assistance either, Gordon must have realized his fate was sealed. He knew too his efforts to save the situation had been in vain. But on the Red Sea littoral the frustrations engendered by governmental in-decision were yet to come.

Haggard was given the assignment of building a pier at Suakin, a task about which he did not know the first thing.

He obtained the assistance of an Egyptian gendarmerie sergeant-major and the subsequent result was most impressive. So great was the skill and hard work produced by the Egyptian *fellaheen* (labourers) that Haggard was no longer surprised that the pyramids had been built and had been so durable; the Egyptian was a superb builder.

Haggard had a very different opinion of Osman Digna than that held by most people; he described him as 'by origin a man of no importance. He had, according to report, been a shoemaker in Suakin, and amassing a little money, had then gone in for the slave-trade from that port to the Red Sea coast at Jeddah. Osman had, however, been pretty nearly ruined by the capture of his slave dhows by British men-of-war's boats about the time of the commencement of the disturbances, when the Mahdi, whom he personally knew, delegated to him the organization of the rebellion in the provinces of the Eastern Soudan. With the exception of the siege of Sinkat, where he was wounded, Osman Digna was never known actually to come under fire in any of the numerous engagements which took place around Suakin. He would, on the contrary, stay at a distance with a bodyguard and pray for the success of the force which he would dispatch to fight — an eminently successful proceeding as far as he himself was concerned, for although by rumour killed a hundred times, he is still alive and kicking. I have myself once or twice, while engaged with the Hadendowahs outside Suakin, seen Osman Digna's praying brigade in the distance, but he never came within rifle-shot.'

Bureaucrats, splendid, conscientious, reliable, pettifogging men, crop up in all places and at all times but are seldom so infuriating and dangerously obstructive as when they occur in armies. When Haggard arrived at the camp outside Tamai he was grateful to see a very neat arrangement of stores and water-troughs:

'The senior officer of the Commissariat whom I found there, and who was worthy of praise for all this order and arrangement, was a man called Jessop. I do not know what has become of him since, or whether he is alive or dead, but I can honestly say that, while doubtless an excellent commissariat-man, I found him a most disagreeable person to have anything to do with, so eaten up was he with red-tape and officialism. If he had had his way, he would have kept back all the water I had brought with me there at Baker's Zareba, and I should never have got to the battle, and there would have been no water for the army in front.'

Jessop was overruled by the General but that was by no means the end of the matter. Although Haggard had himself brought up almost all the water in the place Jessop refused to allow him to have any for his own two horses. He said there was only enough water for the horses of the English army officers, and that in any case Haggard had not got 'a proper "indent" made out in regular form, signed by the competent officer and other foolish excuses of the same sort. I then asked if, since water was so scarce, he would be kind enough to give me a ration of corn for my two horses. Would he? Not a bit of it! He said that all the corn was entered on the lists, that he had not proper authority. . . .'

Haggard then gave up the struggle. He merely waited till Jessop's back was turned, then took all the water he wanted. For corn he simply told his servant to go and 'find' some.

Haggard and his servant, Alfred Thacker, pressed on as soon as possible so as not to miss the forthcoming battle. They slept the night before the battle in the open, without any cover at all. There was a fair chance that they might be killed by hostile Arabs but that was not their main fear. 'The only fear we had was, as a matter of fact, lest in the brilliant moonlight we should be attacked not by Arabs but by moonstroke. Alfred Thacker kept a diary which I saw later. In it he had made the following note: The Major and me covered our faces with our handkerchiefs for fear of moonstroke, which is very prevalent in these parts.'

In spite of all their setbacks Haggard and Thacker reached the battle in time. Their efforts were well-rewarded:

'The two squares marched off, the left square being under Major-General Davis, and the right under Sir Redvers Buller. It was the left which got nearly all the fighting. As far as pluck goes the enemy were just as brave as at El Teb. They smashed up the left square for a time, and got inside it, and took, moreover, two of our Gatling guns from our blue-jackets. I never in all my life heard such a hellish din as that which prevailed for an hour or two at the battle of Tamai, and I was never under such a hellish fire as that which I was then under. For Parr, Chamley Turner, and myself, being on the transport, were left with some details in the so-called zareba; and as the enemy attacked from several sides at once, we not only got the enemy's fire, but also much of the fire from the rear face of the left, General Davis' square, and from the right, Buller's square as well.'

As if that were not enough they were also attacked by a party of the enemy.Henry Hallam Parr noted that their own troops were thoroughly rattled and managed to rally them by instilling an ever greater fear of himself. The attackers were beaten off. 'Chamley Turner and I were with him, and we three had a jolly good fight.'

All in all, it was a narrow victory. One correspondent was so sure that the battle was lost that he galloped off to Suakin before it was over, and telegraphed news of the disaster to his paper. Some people were merely amused but the senior officers were furious. The unfortunate correspondent was killed later in the battle of Abu Klea.

Immediately before the battle Osman Digna had sent a letter to the British, which containted the following words:

'Know that the gracious God has sent his Mahdi suddenly, who was expected, the looked-for messenger for the religious and against the infidels, so as to show the religion of God through him, and by him kill those that hate Him — which has happened.

'You, who never know religion till after death, hate God from the beginning. Then we are sure that God and only God sent the Mahdi, so as to take away your property. And you know this since the time of our Lord Mahomed's coming. Pray to God and be converted.

'There is nothing between us but the sword, especially as the Mahdi has come to kill you and destroy you unless God wishes you to come to Islam. The Mahdi's sword be on your necks wherever you may go, and God's iron round your necks.

'Do not think you are enough for us, and the Turks are only a little better than you. We will not leave your heads unless you become Mussulmans and listen to the Prophet and laws of God.'

After the battle a price of £5000 was set on Osman Digna's head but this was soon withdrawn on instructions from the home government as it was thought to be undignified and uncivilized to put a price on a man's head.

The courage of the enemy was admired: 'After the Arabs had captured the Gatlings, a couple of them quietly and calmly, under a tremendous fire directed on them, opened the box of a limber, found a bottle of oil in it, poured the oil over the limber, and set fire to it. After this they walked quietly away, untouched by bullets and thoroughly well pleased with themselves.' Less admired was the habit of the wounded who would stab and kill those soldiers who went to give them a drink of water or some other help.

After these successful battles Haggard was made Governor of Massowah, a small unimpressive town, and given the task of making alliances with neighbouring tribes. He travelled through wild and difficult country, 'where the smell of lions and other wild animals was as plain at times as in the Zoo at Regent's Park.

'I am getting too old now ever to be surprised at anything or I must confess I should have been surprised when, shortly after leaving Mr Baramberas [an Abyssinian chief], I suddenly came, in the middle of the jungle, upon a French bishop in full canonicals, wearing a gigantic cross round his neck, and riding a mule. I found he was Monseigneur Tovier of the French Mission at Senheit. We had a short chat in the middle of the dried-up watercourse!'

It is interesting to see that in the nineteenth century the remedy for human ills was religion. With the right religion the lion would lie down with the lamb, and good fellowship would prevail. The problem however was: what was the true religion? Everybody, of course, knew that it was his own. Yet there was often amazing tolerance. Keren, in Abyssinia, was a Moslem city, yet it housed a Christian mission, which had a school, a nunnery and a flourishing printing press.

The ability not to be surprised, and to adjust rapidly, was vital. Back in Suakin, Haggard and a Colonel were having coffee. They were told that some natives wanted to see them. Thinking they might have useful information they had them shown in. But the visitors wished to sell not information but trophies: one had a human head, the other a hand! 'As it was important to have these people on our side the bearers of these grisly spoils were treated quite courteously but at the same time asked to take them somewhere else.' Then the two continued with their interrupted coffee.

Of his brother officers he wrote: 'We fought together, drank together, had together good times in Cairo, and rough yet cheery times in the Soudan. There was not one of them much above thirty when he died and most of them were between twenty-five and thirty.'

The Arabs besieging Suakin were remarkably adaptable. When they caught suspected spies they cut their hands off and sent the spies home with their hands tied round their necks. The area round the town had been mined by the defenders. These mines were of various sorts; some were made to explode automatically, others were connected with an electric battery by a long insulated wire enclosed in gutta percha covering. It was for a long time all of no use. 'The Arabs had eyes like cats, and they had the courage which can only be inspired by the most implicit faith in religion. They used to cut and carry away hundreds of yards of insulated wire, then dig up the mines, which they always found, no matter how well concealed, and in some extraordinary way move them without themselves sustaining any injury whatever.

'It was a most extraordinary thing, for so gingerly were some of these mines set that dogs occasionally exploded them!'

Occasionally the Arabs were not so lucky. Once a large

mine went up in the middle of a group. Some of the human fragments were blown as far as sixty yards: 'some human souls had been released from the earthly trammels with awful rapidity.' Weapons were torn and twisted, 'not one of the rifles having left on it one atom of the woodwork of the stock.' (This ability of high explosive to strip the stock from a rifle was also noticeable in the Second World War.)

Then as now, the bomb disposal experts of the Royal Engineers displayed coolness and indifference to danger. 'To do in cold blood a thing of that sort is far braver that to do a plucky thing in action' thought at least one of their comrades, and many will agree.

They thought mortars 'antediluvian' weapons but having a use for them sent to the citadel at Cairo for supplies. They proved useful though erratic. They would have been surprised to know of the widespread use mortars would have in two world wars, but in the nineteenth century trench warfare was scarcely envisaged.

Haggard frequently spoke highly of the Egyptians, who were now trained and disciplined. One of these was Sergeant Redwan, who was shot in the neck. 'When I went to speak to him as he lay there holding his gaping wound together with his hand he exclaimed simply, "Oh, Maalesh, it is nothing, and now that the Bey has come to speak to me I shall be all right." And there were others like him, and as brave.'

In 1885 the British government handed over the administration of Massowah and the surrounding territories to the Italians, who, wishing to stake a claim in Africa, had asked the British government to approve this annexation. They gave the reason that some Italian travellers had recently been assassinated in the area. Everybody knew the real motives, but Britain was in a friendly mood and, as the territory was claimed though not occupied by the Sultan of Turkey, she assented to what might prove to be a reasonable future for the local inhabitants. But 'such was the extraordinary nature of the compact which had been made between the British government and the Italians, that it had not even been thought necessary to inform the Governor-General of the Red

Sea littoral of the proposed handing over of one of his towns to a foreign power.' In the event, the Italian landing party was lucky not to have been greeted by a burst of gunfire.

When Haggard was sent away to other duties another eloquent officer was on his way to Suakin. This was Major E. Gambier Parry. Parry did not enjoy his voyage out. 'A life on the ocean wave seemed a horrible fate' but it had its diversions, such as the concert given on board. Like all army concerts it unearthed much unexpected talent. As usual the most popular items were the most sentimental such as 'a song sung by a trumpeter boy, not more than fifteen years of age. He stood up a little nervously before the audience and sang a song the name of which I never heard but the verses finished with:

"It's only a leaf in my Bible
I picked from my poor mother's grave."
It brought tears to the eyes of strong men.'

On arrival at Suakin he gave a brief description of the conditions: 'The inhabitants depend for their water supply on two or three wells about a mile from the town. The supply is at all times limited. Towards the close of the dry season, when the water becomes very scarce, it turns thick and is dark· brown in colour.' He collected some interesting statistics from the sick returns, which, in that unhealthy town, were considerable. 'I found that at least 65% of the total number of cases occurred among the men of under 25 years of age while the men between 35 and 45 escaped with comparative immunity.'

Parry gave an account of Osman Digna which is in complete contrast to that given by Haggard: 'Most people now know Osman Digna's history but for those who do not it may be as well to give a short sketch of his antecedents. This person, then, was born at Rouen, and is the son of French parents, his family name being Vinet. He was called after his father, George, and began his education at Rouen, but after a while was moved to Paris. A few years after that his parents went out to Alexandria in connection with some matter of business, and shortly afterwards his father died there. His mother then married a merchant of Alexandria, Osman Digna by name. This man took a great fancy to his stepson, young George Vinet, and brought him up as a Mohammedan, sending him to complete his education to the military school at Cairo, where he had for his companion Arabi. Here he studied tactics and the operations of war under French officers. It was at this period that his father migrated to Suakin where he set up as a general merchant and slave-dealer, and very shortly was doing a very lucrative business. At his father-in-law's death George Vinet continued to carry on the business under the same name. A few·years passed, and when the war broke out in Egypt, in 1882, Osman Digna espoused the cause of his old friend and companion, Arabi, and became one of England's bitterest foes as the Mahdi's lieutenant. In appearance Osman Digna is a fine looking man, tall and well-propotioned though rather fat. He wears a long black beard, and has lost his left arm. He never gets on a horse, and in the few engagements in which he has thought fit to risk his valuable life he has always been present on foot.' (This criticism of Osman's courage proved premature.)

Before long Parry was engaged in the defence of Suakin. It was not easy, for the outposts were badly sited and the enemy were extremely ingenious. 'None of us knew when we lay down at night whether we should be alive in the morning.' He went on:

'I was lying on my camp bed with my sword on and my revolver ready to my hand . . . suddenly the stillness was interrupted by the most awful scream it has ever been my lot to hear — a loud, long wail of agony, as of a man mortally wounded, crying out with his last breath. It was a sound that absolutely seemed to curdle the very blood in one's veins. Then came a rush through the camp as those men who had been in their tents turned out. A few random shots were fired without effect and the enemy, if ever seen at all, disappeared.

'With the stealth of a wild beast, and with the wriggle of an eel, a party of Arabs must have entered the camp unnoticed by the sentries, and then rushing in through one door of a tent have stabbed and hacked with their long spears as they rushed through and out of the tent the other side. One poor fellow had been stuck with a spear right through the stomach, and with a last frightful and pitiful yell had expired at once.

'How the Arabs managed to enter the camp we never discovered; but this sort of thing was repeated by them over and over again in the face of double sentries and guards and pickets all over the place.'

Parry had some doubt about the 'friendly Amarar'. He suspected that after dark they went out of the camp and joined with the opposition in making attacks.* 'In the face of the acknowledged treachery of these people it was curious that no attempt was made to put a stop to this sort of thing; but we English are a confiding people.'

The British soldier grumbled, but made light of it all. In this country where Parry said 'the sun was a curse, where pestilence and fever were hatched by it, and where men fled from it to escape, if it were possible, its pitiless power', the British soldier showed astounding adaptability. 'You would see him carrying on an energetic conversation with a native, and making up for his deficient knowledge of the language by talking at the top of his voice. Then you would see him trying to make a pet of a camel, or riding one as if he had never ridden anything else.'

The government, though wildly out in its idea that the troops could recuperate in the hills during the hot season, at least had the wit to decide to build a railway to Berber. The practical details were — as usual — misunderstood, and the toughest work fell to the army. 'The navvies received the princely remuneration of twelve shillings a day and time work, a free ration and free kit; while our soldiers received only as many pennies extra working pay as the navvies did shillings.' The troops also had to guard the head of the line, which meant standing and keeping alert in the full glare of the sun. 'There were one or two instances where men came in

*Compare South Vietnam, where some of the cleaners in military camps were night-time guerrillas.

with a line across their faces as though cut with a knife, where the sun had caught them below the shade cast by the front of the helmet and opened the flesh.'

Rations improved as they settled in, and a quantity of tinned food arrived. 'We get a variety of these provisions and I think tried pretty well everything prepared either by Messrs Moir, or Messrs Crosse and Blackwell. Our favourite things were the Oxford sausages and the herrings a la Sardini, both of which were excellent. Stewed beef steak, haricot mutton, mutton ragout, and grouse aux truffles were also among the most appreciated. The tinned vegetables were not at all bad, but we fought rather shy of these for fear of colouring matter.'

Parry goes on to say:

'We heard one morning that a shipload of oranges had arrived in harbour for the use of the troops, and "when practicable"said the orders on the subject, "an orange a day will be issued to each officer and man. This indulgence," added the order, "is not to be looked upon as a right." '

(During the Second World War it was laid down with great emphasis, 'Leave is a privilege, not a right.' In the event, it was doled out, like the oranges, with every attempt at fairness and liberality but that did not prevent the curt menacing note occurring in all references to it.)

However, the War Office did not spoil the troops in Suakin with too much tenderness. At first soldiers used to write on top of the envelope 'On Active Service' and not stamp it, but this practice soon ceased when the recipients were charged *double* postage at home. Subsequently the generous concession of charging single postage was instituted.

'Few people can understand the enormous pleasure letters afford to soldiers on active service. When there is so much work and so many hardships to be undergone, a letter, giving a glimpse of home, is an untold joy.'

Parry thought very highly of newspaper correspondents 'always in the front when fighting was going on, and always to be found where the bullets fell thickest, and where danger was to be met with. Then after the fighting was over, or perhaps after a long march, they would ride miles in the hot sun, and sit up half the night to write home the doings of the day.'

When the railway building and the move up-country were set in motion the troops were joined by the 9th Bengal Cavalry. They were a magnificent regiment but they were trained to fight with sword and carbine. Nevertheless they were told to use lances in action and if they did not know how to do so then to learn quickly. (Normally it took two years to train a lancer.) The result of this was that when they went into action they threw away their lances and drew their swords.

At night, work went on by the electric light generated on HMS *Dolphin*, 'which gave a curious, weird appearance to the mass of men'.

The first objective of the advance was Hasheen, a village on a hill. The square, which was fully 800 yards across, was made up as follows:

'The front face was composed of three battalions of the 2nd Brigade, viz. the 49th, the 70th and the Royal Marines; the other regiment in this brigade, the 53rd, having been left behind to look after the camp. On the right face were the Brigade of Guards, and the left face was formed by the Indian Brigade, viz. the 15th Sikh, and the 17th and 28th Bombay Native Infantry. The troops inside the square, besides the Commissariat and Transport Corps, were the 17th and 24th Companies of the Royal Engineers, some Madras Sappers and Miners, two rocket troops of the Royal Artillery, and a battery of Gardner guns. The cavalry force in front was composed of two squadrons of the 5th Lancers, two squadrons of the 20th Hussars, and four squadrons of the 9th Bengal Cavalry. There was also in front a battery of Royal Horse Artillery, and the greater part of the Mounted Infantry.'

And so they went on. At Hasheen, 'After a long march in burning sun and under heavy fire, the men moved as if on parade, taking advantage of every bit of cover the ground afforded.'

But the bush was very thick and soon the cavalry were in trouble. They were ambushed. Wheeling about to re-form, they were soon in even greater trouble for 'they were simply overrun by the Arabs. With surprising agility these fellows sped over the ground after the retreating horsemen, seeming almost to fly through the bush as they sprang from place to place. Rushing up behind the horses, they would hamstring the poor animals, and thus bring the riders to the ground.' Anyone who fell was soon despatched, however hard he fought. Some of these Arabs were caught in the next charge 'when they produced their usual tactics, and lay themselves flat on the ground when they saw the cavalry approaching, doing their best to hamstring the horses as they passed but the lance put an end to many of these thus sacrificed to their temerity'.

'The roar of the musketry was now general over the whole field, the enemy were firing away in the valley and along the lower ridges of the mountains where the mounted infantry were driving them back, the 49th and the Marines were showering bullets down from their point of vantage, while the rattle of the musket in the bush told of the Guards being hotly engaged. Volley succeeded volley, and amidst the crack, crack, of the rifles, the booming of the guns re-echoed through the mountains, as the Horse Artillery pitched their shells with unerring precision into the enemy wherever he showed thickest and in the greatest numbers.'

It was truly a battle between equals. Both sides were equally brave, equally resourceful, equally good marksmen. Neither could take anything for granted. 'There was no hurry and the men moved with the utmost steadiness under the galling fire poured in upon them. Every now and then the square would halt and reply with a volley or two; but they were unable to see the crafty enemy, who took good care to hide himself behind the thickest of the bush, and the rocky ground of the hills.'

Among the casualties were doctors 'present in the very forefront of the action all through the day', at risk but bringing 'kindness and gentleness to the suffering'.

The battle, so hard fought, was not put to any practical use. The enemy merely withdrew from Hasheen to stronger positions in the hills behind. Both sides celebrated it as a victory. One of the trophies of the British force was 'a youth who had led the charges on the Guards' square riding on a white camel. His great grief was that his white camel had been killed, and he seemed to find it a hard matter to get over this. I do not think he ever showed any particular signs of gratitude for the kindness he received; but this was hardly to be expected from a representative of the race who hated and detested us most bitterly.'

This feeling of intense hostility was mentioned again in their next encounter. The fruits of the last victory having been thrown away the force set off – this time in the direction of Tamai – to build a zareba as a staging post. As soon as this had been done they were attacked; the Arabs stampeded the transport camels first and while these were crashing panic-stricken through the British lines the Arabs followed 'hacking, hewing right and left, ham-stringing and ripping up the wretched camels. Mules, horses and camels were huddled into one hopeless mass of inextricable confusion, while the air was filled with the screams of men and animals and the roar of the musketry.'

This battle was even more intense than the last.

'The enemy dashed onwards, with almost irresistible impulse, falling in terrible numbers before their well-directed volleys, and not being stopped until they were actually touching our bayonets. Led by sheikhs carrying white banners inscribed with the Mahdi's name they charged again and again, rushing up to the face of the square and engaging our men hand to hand. Many of these Arabs would fall before the rain of bullets, but, picking themselves up instantly, they would dash forward with the rest, till, pierced through and through, they reached the square at last, positively riddled by the fire. So Arab and Englishman hacked and hewed and shot and thrust, till blood flowed out on the ground like water, and black and white men alike bit the dust or writhed in death agony on the hot sands of that parched-up desert.'

It was as well that the British soldier was steady, for he was outnumbered, and often out-manoeuvred. Sometimes, when the Arabs worked round or infiltrated, he had to stop firing for fear of hitting his own men. Then it was bayonet against spear.

'I ought to mention an incident of the fight, showing how the enemy are animated by a bitter hatred for us, and how this hatred is not confined to the Arab men alone, but fills the hearts of their women and children also. For one single instant the smoke cleared off and showed the swarming hordes of Arabs leaping and dancing in the bush, while they rushed forward in endless numbers to demolish us if possible; and as we thus gained a momentary view, there stood out between the two opposing forces a boy, aged not more than twelve years, without signs of fear, actually throwing stones at us. But the Arab fire was growing hot, ours opened again, and the fate of that boy was sealed, not because there was the slightest wish on the part of our men to slay the little fellow, but because one and all were hopelessly doomed before that terrific and deadly hail. There were women, too, fighting like the men, and dressed in the Mahdi's uniform. It was horrible to think of their being there, and worse still to think that they had to fall. But there was no help for it; and in the short half-hour that the fight lasted there was no time to pick and choose, and though we never knew till afterwards that there were women in the enemy's ranks, the dead bodies of several lying in the field told more surely that anything else of the bitter enmity there was between us.'

The courage and discipline of the Mahdi's troops made them worthy, though difficult, foes. 'The enemy's tactics were well-planned . . . they carried out an attack on both sides simultaneously without any shouting or word of command, and without showing in force for a moment . . . a strong reserve, numbering some thousands, was always in readiness.' These were the comments of an experienced soldier, respecting but not always liking what he saw. He also had something to say about the British weapons, and was strong in his criticism of the Martini-Henry rifles. These jammed (he called it 'clogged') easily. They had suffered from this fault from the beginning. The trouble lay in the clumsy bottle-shaped cartridge-case, which had originally been described as 'experimental' but which had never been replaced. Instead the old cases were sent back and refilled. Sometimes the base of the cartridge came right off, leaving the rifle permanently jammed.

The bayonet too was far from satisfactory. 'We hear a lot about the wonderful quality of British steel; but why are our soldiers armed with a weapon which, when put to the test, simply doubles up like so much soft metal. Every soldier's life is valuable, and our soldiers are not so numerous that we can afford to sacrifice them to the love of economy of some, and the short-sighted policy and indifference of some few more.'

There were two kinds of ammunition in use, one for the Martini, the other for the Snider. Revolver ammunition also came in two different calibres (.450 and .455) and was poor quality at that. 'An Arab shield made of crocodile skin or rhinoceros hide would, we found, turn a revolver bullet at forty yards.'

Parry mentioned how difficult it was to help the wounded Arabs, who often tried to kill those trying to give them first-aid. However he did not consider that a reason for ceasing to try. 'The Arabs knew no better but we did. Kindness they did not understand, and gratitude was foreign to them; the first they looked upon as weakness, the second as an impossibility from a Mohammedan to a Christian. Many of the Arabs wounded entreated our people to kill them in order that they might be despatched to a happy land by the hand of the infidel.

'It was on this occasion that our balloon was first used [for observation over the scrub], and it was also memorable as being the first occasion on which we had ever made use of a balloon on active service. The balloon, which was made of goldbeater's skin, covered with a netting, was taken up to the Right Water Fort the night before and unpacked in a ditch, when filling it was at once commenced, so that it should be ready to ascend by daybreak next morning. When I reached the Water Fort just before daylight, after a hard night's work loading up water, I found the balloon inflated and quite ready for the ascent. I was rather disappointed at its size and fully expected to see a larger one. The basket or carriage beneath the balloon did not seem capable of holding more than one person. The actual measurement of the balloon was twenty-three feet in diameter, and its weight altogether ninety pounds. When filled it contained seven thousand cubic feet of gas, brought all the way from Chatham, a distance of nearly four thousand miles.

'Very soon after our convoy was formed up ready to start, the balloon began to rise slowly to a height of about two hundred feet, being fastened to the ground by two lines attached to the car. An admiring crowd of natives witnessed its ascent in silence, and did not seem in the least surprised, much to my disappointment, as I had expected to see them struck with amazement at the sight of a man floating in the air. However, these natives seem astonished at nothing, and I do not believe they would have been surprised if they had seen a regiment provided with wings and suddenly begin to fly.'

'When the convoy was ready to move, the balloon, still two hundred feet up, was made fast to a cart in the centre of the square. It was rather difficult to avoid jerking the cords which held it, and thus running the chance of breaking them; but extreme care was taken when crossing any rough piece of ground, as it would not have been pleasant for the occupier of the car if he had suddenly found himself floating quietly toward the mountains miles beyond the reach of any friends.'

On the march food and water were a problem.

'The condensed water was good enough when it was fresh but after being kept a day or so in the tins it began to smell and became filled with a white slime. I never heard how this slime was accounted for.

'The bouilli beef was rather salt and why the army was

ever supplied with such uneatable and unsuitable stuff is wonderful indeed.'

The bouilli beef was the precursor of the 'bully' beef which has stayed with the army ever since. It would have been quite easy to have driven a few animals out with the convoys and slaughtered them when required. However 'eminent medical men' had decided that the salt beef was the cause of dysentery, and doubtless delivered their views with an impressive display of authority. Ice was available on the ships but was never used for any form of refrigeration. 'Instead of this the men were fed on an eternal supply of tinned meats, till everyone was simply nauseated with the stuff and turned from it with loathing and disgust.'

The Hasheen zareba was eventually abandoned, partly because the supply convoys were too heavily attacked and suffered too many losses. The withdrawal was not easy:

'About four thousand of the enemy then attacked us furiously on all sides with their usual astounding bravery. Many of them jogged in their peculiar manner right up the square before they fell, while others walked quietly back into the bush after endeavouring to penetrate our ranks. Their coolness under fire was simply astonishing; and it was marvellous indeed that day after day men could be found to charge three or four battalions of infantry in the face of the awful slaughter that invariably took place.'

On one move, Parry said that he and his friends took a change of clothes and a deal box. On the side was painted 'Military Documents'. This rendered it absolutely safe from thieves: it contained no military documents at all but 'a bottle or two of whiskey, several tins of Brand's essence of meat, cocoa and milk, potted meats and sardines'. (That was intended for at least four people.)

Apart from stores all convoys carried a plentiful supply of rumours, among which were: the Mahdi was a prisoner of the Abyssinians and Osman was going to give himself up the next day; the government had decided to stop the war and railway-building would cease; they were now going to fight Russia, advancing in a two-prong attack through Asia Minor and India. (Two- or three-prong attacks seem essential to any military rumour: it is a pity they are never true because war fought in accordance with them would be a much more rapid and exciting affair.)

The arrival of Australian reinforcements on 29 March 1885 was greeted with great enthusiasm. 'They all wore the familiar red serge coat, albeit rather strange out here, but they very soon changed into Kharkee like the rest of us.' Parry commented on their arrival as follows:

'Let us hope the readiness with which our Australian and Canadian colonies came forward voluntarily, and extended to the mother country the hand of help, when surrounded with a sea of troubles unparalleled in her history, may serve as a warning to our foes of the latent strength of the British Empire, and at the same time be the beginning of that great Imperial Federation which is to bind the whole together in one indissoluble union for the protection of our commerce, the defence of our possessions, and the supremacy of our country's flag.'

Mounted infantry played an important part in this campaign, though usually misused. They were armed with rifles and their function was to engage the enemy at distances over 400 yards. However, they were often thrown in as cavalry, being supplied with swords but without proper training for that role. Their function should never have been to charge but, as it was succinctly put, 'to fire and scuttle away'. Too often, however, they were used purely as cavalry.

After considerable experience of marching and counter-marching — for what reason he could scarcely imagine, and suspected a similar ignorance on the part of the Higher Command — Parry was evacuated with some unspecified fever. The campaign was over, Osman Digna clearly had no intention of engaging in anything but minor harassing activities for the time being, and the railway line to Berber was to be discontinued. Had it been built a year before it might have saved Khartoum. There was no need for Parry to stay but doubtless he would have preferred to leave on his feet. It was not to be so. He was clearly very ill, though not too ill to admire the nurses. 'Women teach us many things, but above all they teach us unselfishness.' He went on:

'One of the greatest drawbacks to our hospital was the enormous number of rats. I awoke one night to find upwards of a dozen in my cabin. They were the most confident rats I ever saw, and they seemd to know perfectly well that, being a cripple, I was unable to get at them. They would take a jump right across from the bunk at one side of the cabin on top of me, but I got accustomed to them at last, and quite content they should enjoy themselves so long as they did not crawl over my face. Besides the rats, there were thousands and thousands of cockroaches of all sizes, the largest measuring an inch and a half long. Some people would have objected to these more than the rats but I preferred anything to the cold paws of a rat on my face. That was really objectionable, and what was worse, it generally woke one up with a start.'

Not long ago, during the so-called 'Emergency', a soldier lying naked on his bed in an attap hut in Malaya had an interesting experience. Two rats, which had begun fighting in the rafters, fell onto his chest and continued their combat there. But at least, unlike Parry, he was a fit man and could take action.

5

The Fall of Khartoum

Long before the events described in the last chapter had reached their abortive conclusion, Khartoum had been lost, Gordon killed, and the Sudan abandoned. The decision to leave the Sudan to its own devices had, of course, been taken when Gordon was sent to organize the evacuation of the remaining troops; it was therefore not to be expected that the British government would react to the loss of Khartoum by a vast punitive expedition. Government policy was one of withdrawal in order to save money and effort. Although warned by Gordon that abandoning the Sudan would eventually save neither, but rather would increase the threat to Egypt, the government chose to ignore the facts of the situation and the experience of history. Gordon was not, of course, advocating direct rule by the British. He was, in fact, a pioneer of one of the most skilful of British compromises — indirect rule, which was subsequently associated with the name of Lugard. The principle of indirect rule was to back the most responsible of the local chiefs, provided they were also acceptable to the local people. It was no use at all picking a bright young man of obvious ability. He would be ignored — and perhaps murdered. The nominee must be someone known to be of royal blood — even if he did devote most of his energies to drunkenness and fornication, and very little to justice, administration and education. Gordon, who was a realist, felt that his former enemy Zubair would provide an effective challenge to the Mahdi's power, and that the rivalry of these two would occupy them to such an extent that neither could give much trouble to others. The government were not unaware of the advantages of this course but they took a highly critical view of Zubair. They felt that Gordon's trust in him was too great, and that he might well turn on his backer, conquer the Mahdi, and go on to establish a tyranny in the Sudan which would be infinitely more dangerous than anything the Dervishes seemed likely to produce.

As we have seen, after a bad start in the Eastern Sudan, the situation had been put under control by General Graham's brisk expedition. Had this army — or a part of it — been sent to Berber, Khartoum could probably have been evacuated without loss of life. It would not have been an easy task, for Suakin was 250 miles from Berber, but it could have succeeded. In the event it was not allowed to try, and all that happened was that the same battles were fought again around Suakin the following year.

From 12 March 1884 Khartoum was in a state of siege. The hottest months of the year were approaching, when sandstorms, flies and crippling heat would make life seem less than tolerable. Gordon was sustained by two factors: religion and a natural belief that any government could not really be as stupid as the Gladstone government appeared to be. Soon, he felt, reason would intervene. He suspected that his suggestion to use Zubair would fall on deaf ears but he felt sure that a Turkish military expedition — paid for in cash but not too expensive — would put an end to the Mahdi's aspirations. He even suggested that it might be paid for by public subscription. If the government was unwilling to act over the Sudan he suggested they should hand the country over to Turkey; the Sultan would know how to combat the Mahdi's movement. The government was, of course, unwilling to do anything of the sort — to do anything at all, in fact. The garrisons at Khartoum, Kassala, Dongola and Berber should fend for themselves as best they could.

Berber fell in 1884; the news was received by the government a month later. There was no news of Khartoum; nothing had been heard since April. The government had to wait another month before receiving a message saying that Gordon was holding on but that he would like to hear news of the relief expedition. There was of course no expedition at the time, and a message was sent to that effect, but as the reply took three months to reach Gordon it made no difference.

Back at home, however, public feeling was more humane than the government appeared to be. A public outcry, supported and fanned by press activity, drove the Cabinet reluctantly to take action. In August, a relief expedition was authorized.

But it is one thing to decide to take action and another to know what action is best to take. Had the decision been made earlier, procedure would have been relatively simple. An expedition like General Graham's could have forced its way to Berber, and then gone up the Nile to Khartoum. But Berber was now in the hands of the Dervishes and it was unlikely that they would leave any convenient wells on the route from Suakin. It would not have been easy before but now that line of approach looked suicidal. The Nile, with all its difficulties, was the only possibility. For this Lord Wolseley — 'our only General' — was appointed. Wolseley, although not universally popular, was a first-class fighting soldier to whom the unorthodox was an acceptable challenge. He had already shown by the success of his 'Red River Expedition' in Canada that he understood the problems of rivers and cataracts. The expression 'all Sir Garnet', derived from when he was the meticulously efficient General Sir Garnet Wolseley, passed into the language as a catchphrase for perfect organization. Wolseley reached Cairo in early September, and soon made very clear that this was going to be no repetition of the disastrous Hicks expedition. The basis of his army was 7000 British troops from first-class fighting regiments, and he planned to transport them in 800 boats, with flat bottoms, oars and sails. Drawing on his Canadian experience he brought in 300 Canadian boatmen alleged to be expert. The expedition was excellently and swiftly organized, and on 5 October sent out to relieve Khartoum. In hindsight Wolseley's preparations were perhaps a little too full and too deliberate. A 'flying column' sent as an advance party might have reached Khartoum and tipped the scales far enough to have saved Gordon's life. With the news, which the Mahdi could not but know, that a massive expedition was following up, it seems likely that the siege of Khartoum would have been lifted.

The tragedy of the fall of Khartoum on 26 January 1885 was that it was nearly prevented by Gordon's own efforts. When he arrived on 18 February 1884 he found the town defended by rudimentary fortifications of a medieval pattern (although they had in fact been constructed within the last three years). These comprised a ditch and a rampart with forts and bastions in between. The defensive line required more manning than he had troops for, and his 7000 badly-armed and even more badly-officered garrison forces were by no means unshakably loyal. Furthermore, it seemed likely that the Mahdi would have his own supporters – a dangerous 'fifth column' – in the town. Like all sieges, this one was to involve a large force of civilians who needed to be fed and organized but who were probably more of a liability than an asset in an emergency. It was to have a curious feature in that the besieged were able to move up and down the Nile in paddle steamers, going outside the besieging ring but unable, for all that, to bring in help or evacuate the garrison to safety. Gordon put down a screen of barbed wire and buried mines (he was not a sapper for nothing), and even provided a local currency. He was optimistic always and speculated at times on the possibility of recapturing Berber. In the best tradition of besieged forces he was as active as his attackers, and, by sallies and adroit use of the Nile, sometimes made them wonder who had the initiative. These sallies progressed from local attacks to deep raids, one probing as far as a hundred miles behind the Mahdi's lines. Unfortunately one of these expeditions was a little too venturesome and was ambushed; nearly a thousand men and a resourceful leader were lost. This was in September 1884, when Wolseley was just beginning his preparations in Cairo. Even more foreboding for Wolseley was the fact that the Mahdi, who had been relatively inactive during the Moslem fasting month of Ramadan, was now determined to wipe out the opposition at

Khartoum. His army was said to number 60,000. The news of this threat came to Gordon. In the now desperate situation he took a desperate decision. The help which must surely be on the way must be hurried up. He decided to get a message through by means of the Nile steamers which had so far managed to run the Dervish blockade with impunity. For this mission he chose Colonel Stewart, with the French Consul and another officer, to travel as far as possible down the Nile with information about the desperate plight of Khartoum. But luck was not with them. Although pursued, they were making good headway when the steamer stuck on a rock in the last cataract. Fortunately — as it seemed — they were signalled to the shore by a friendly sheikh. He promised them camels and a safe escort for the short remaining journey. With relief at their good fortune they went into his house to eat and to wait for the camels to arrive. They were then murdered. It was still September. Gordon, of course, did not know.

Had Gordon realized the ponderous nature of the expedition that was due to relieve him even his optimism might have sagged. Fortunately, perhaps, he did not. In October he uncovered a Mahdist plot to betray the town. At intervals the Mahdi invited him to surrender but he left most of these letters unanswered. Even in late October, when the Mahdi was able to prove by quoting from the papers of the dead Colonel Stewart that the expedition had perished, Gordon did not lose hope. He had enough food for six weeks, and relief *must* arrive by that time.

In November the Mahdi launched a brisk attack on the fort at Omdurman. After desperate fighting his forces cut it off from the rest of Khartoum and waited for it to surrender. Gordon became thoughtful. He had not previously had a high opinion of the fighting qualitites of the Dervishes, thinking they had been flattered by weak opposition. Now he began to believe that they were capable of carrying the Khartoum defences.

In December food was running short. The little steamer *Bardeen* had been running up and down the river, often through a hail of bullets and shells, taking messages out and bringing them in. The incoming messages came via Kitchener, who had been sent up as a small advance party to reconnoitre the situation and make any contact with friendly tribes which seemed feasible. On 13 December the boat took out a last plea:

'If some effort is not made before ten days time the town will fall. It is inexplicable, this delay. If the Expeditionary Forces have reached the river and met my steamers one hundred men are all that we require, just to show themselves.'

On the 14th he wrote another paragraph:

'Arabs fired two shells at the Palace this morning. . . . I am on tenterhooks. 1030 am. The steamers are down at Omdurman, engaging the Arabs, consequently I am on tenterhooks. 1130 am. Steamers returned; the Bardeen was struck by a shell in her battery; we had only one man wounded. We are going to send down the Bardeen to-morrow with this journal.

'If I was in command of the two hundred men of the Expeditionary Force, which are all that are necessary for the movement, I should stop just below Halfeyeh and attack the Arabs at that place before I came on here to Khartoum. I should then communicate with the North Fort, and act according to circumstances. Now MARK THIS, if the Expeditionary Force, and I ask for no more than two hundred men, does not come in ten days, the *town may fall*; and I have done my best for the honour of our country. Good bye.

C.G. Gordon'

He held out for six more weeks. In December the town's inmates began to harvest unripe grain; in January he sent out of the town all who wished to join the Mahdi. By mid-January Khartoum was in much the same state as El Obeid had been earlier. On 13 January the garrison commander at Omdurman, which had held out with the utmost fortitude, was told by Gordon to surrender. During the next week Gordon spent most of his days on the palace roof, eagerly scanning the horizon with his telescope for the help which never came. A ray of hope appeared a week later, when information came from the Dervish camp that their forces had been defeated down river by the relief force. This superficially cheering news for Gordon in fact sealed his fate, for the Mahdi realized that if he did not now take the city the opportunity might be lost for ever. On 26 January the final attack went in just before dawn. Exhausted and thinly spaced though they were, the garrison gave what they could, but the Mahdi had wisely directed that the ramparts should be heavily bombarded while the infantry probed for gaps. The battle could not, and did not, last long.

Most of the Dervishes ran riot in the city, slaughtering and plundering, but one small party had other intentions. In spite of the Mahdi's instructions that Gordon must not be killed they made their way straight to the palace. According to one version of his death, they chopped down the few guards who tried to resist them and forced their way to the staircase that led to his quarters. At the head of the stairs, fully dressed in white uniform, with sword and revolver which he made no attempt to use, he faced them. As the first spear went into his body he made a gesture as if of disdain. Other spears completed the work, and his head was hacked off and taken triumphantly to the Mahdi. The latter was genuinely angry. (Since the martyrdom of Thomas Beckett in Canterbury Cathedral, and probably long before, there have always been stupid men who have tried to curry favour with their masters by anticipating their wishes — usually wrongly.)

Meanwhile the relief expedition was still pursuing its relentless but pointless course. Wolseley had left nothing to chance. His Canadian 'voyageurs' had got the boats up over the cataracts and made steady progress with a combination of sail and oars, but it had taken too long. It was already December by the time they reached the Third Cataract. The problems they had already overcome were immense. Much of the Nile was uncharted or, worse still, badly charted, and the expedition was not only carrying food for itself but also for the thousands it planned to evacuate from Khartoum.

There was, however, an emergency plan. At Debba the Nile route turns sharply east, moves south again at Abu Hamed, goes on to Atbara and then swings south-west again towards Khartoum. This stretch includes three more cataracts, and it was clear that if a swifter dash was necessary it could be made from 'Debba or Korti a little further along, thereby cutting out that great bow in the Nile. With luck this force could work with Gordon's steamers at Metemmeh. It was risky because there were only enough camels for a small force and the countryside was doubtless swarming with the Mahdi's troops. Nevertheless, the risk must be accepted, and on 30 December Sir Herbert Stewart set off with a carefully selected force numbering 1100 men. The distance was 170 miles. Two thousand men and twice that number of camels were thought to be the minimum sufficient force but the expedition, desperately short of manpower, still struggled on.

One of those in the Camel Corps was Count Gleichen, a lieutenant in the Grenadier Guards. As a Guards officer he found the uniform of the Camel Corps somewhat incongruous — red serge jumpers, yellow-ochre cord breeches, dark blue puttees, and white pith helmets; he thought they looked as if they had been left over from the last civil war. The Canadians, some of whom only spoke French, and some of whom — incredibly — had never been in a boat before, arrived in thick grey tweed and shiny hats. Like many a traveller before or since, Gleichen and his companions were quick to discover the local conditions and customs — and adapt to them. They formulated rules for shopping:

'1. Always get the article into your possession before you start to haggle.
2. Bargain in the dark so as to pass off your bad piastres.
3. Offer never more than half what they ask and go away if you do not get it at your price; they will then follow you and conform to your wishes!'

'Mounting a frisky camel is exciting work for the beginner, and nearly always results in a cropper. The mode of procedure should be thus; having made your camel to kneel by clearing your throat loudly at him and tugging at his rope, shorten your rein till you bring his head round to your shoulder, put your foot in the stirrup, and throw your leg over. With his head jammed like that, he cannot rise, and must wait till you give him his head. Unless you do as directed, he will get up before your leg is over; if this happens, stand in the stirrup till he is up, and then throw your leg over, otherwise you will infallibly meet with a hideous catastrophe.'

They travelled up the Nile at 2¾ miles an hour, managing twenty miles a day. It was very dull. 'I tried reading, I tried writing — no good; the only thing in which I met with any success was in going to sleep.'

They got to know their camels well. 'A camel's hind-legs will reach anywhere — over his head, round his chest, and on to his hump; even when lying down, an evil-disposed animal will shoot out his legs, and bring you to a sitting posture. His neck is of the same pliancy. He will chew the root of his tail, nip you in the calf, or lay the top of his head on his hump. He also bellows and roars at you whatever you are doing saddling him, feeding him, mounting him, unsaddling him. To the uninitiated a camel going to you with his mouth open and gurgling horribly is a terrifying spectacle; but do not mind him, it is only his way. He hardly ever bites, but when he does you feel it for some time!

'They used to get colds in their noses, too, at night, especially the flank ones; sometimes they caught cold if the saddles were removed too soon; sometimes also they fought in the lines, and got their ropes into fearful confusion. They used to break away at times, and wander all over the lines, causing great sorrow to their riders, who came to seek them and they were not.' Eventually Gleichen got so used to camels they even appeared in his nightmares.

He found it 'unwise to trust to the names of villages marked on most official maps, for the natives knew not the names'. Eventually he discovered that the names varied from one generation to another, 'the head man of the district calls it after himself, wherefore a name only lasts till he dies and the next man gets it'. Dongola was a case in point. On all the maps two Dongolas were marked — Old and New, but Old

Dongola was not a town at all but merely a collection of ruins on the opposite bank and some seventy miles upstream from the proper Dongola. 'The Sheikh of Old Dongola did not know his ruins by that name at all.'

They crossed the river at Akhir, being transported in 'nuggers' (solid one-masted boats which could hold five camels). They pressed on. At one point 'not having my eyeglasses at the time I saw what looked like gazelles in the distance and proceeded to stalk them. They turned out to be camels' skeletons.'

Women en route were a disappointment. They were 'appallingly hideous, ranging from the coal-black negress to the yellow nondescript, a mixture of every race in Africa and Asia, and sometimes with a dash of Southern Europe! Their charms were arrayed in the native dress of grease and dirty sheets.'

When they arrived, Korti was a delightful spot, 'with a grove of palms along the steep banks of the river; immediately behind them fields of grass dotted with slender mimosa trees, broad pitches of tall green dhurra. . . . By the time we left it for good it was a deal worse than the Long Valley at Aldershot.'

At Korti they did a little training. 'The ground we passed over mostly was covered with large pebbles of all sorts, sizes and colours; agates, crystals, garnets, and blood-stones were there in hundreds. One of the men (Woods) used to walk out every afternoon and come back with a large assortment of what he called diamonds and rubies; but long afterwards he definitely got the laugh of us.'

'Stable' duty caused them to take unnecessary trouble with camel hygiene but 'you might as well groom an Irish pig. With infinite pains you beat the dust out of his skin, remove as many as you can of the ticks and maggots which infest him, wipe his nose (if he has a cold) and finish up by washing off any mud. What is the result? The moment your back is turned over he goes, and enjoys a delicious roll in the dust and dirt again, making himself filthier than before.' The natives, more sensibly, preferred to plaster the camel with mud, keeping off heat by day and cold by night.

News was frequent but consistently unreliable as much of it was sent by the Dervishes to deceive and lure them into dangerous positions.

On Christmas Eve a private died of enteric.

'Sir Herbert Stewart gave up the flooring of his tent to make a coffin, though there was not the slightest chance of getting any more planks. Not many Generals would have done that.'

The advance was to be in two stages: to proceed to the Gakdul wells (about a hundred miles away), seize them, and leave a holding force, and then to collect up the full force and with it proceed to Korti, Gakdul, Metemmeh.

With the GCR (Guards Camel Regiment) was 'a little dog of unknown breed, something between a King Charles Spaniel and a Dandie Dinmont The only thing certain about his parentage was that he was English, for he strongly resented any attempts at familiarity on the part of pariahs or other foreign dogs, and had attached himself at once to one of our companies at Assouan. He had tramped the whole day from Assouan to Korti, and now he was coming with us to Khartoum if possible. Though his body was small, Jacky's heart was big for, besides being an affectionate little dog, he refused to be carried on a camel, however tired, and trotted along with his nose in the air, disdaining all offers of help. He went through most of the fighting afterwards and came back with us to Korti, where I eventually lost sight of him. Let us hope he returned to his native shores in safety.'

Gleichen expressed the feelings of many desert explorers before and since:

'How flies and insects manage to exist in the Desert was always a puzzle ˙to me. I always imagined that insects required a certain amount of dampness, but no — the common or garden fly was as much at home on the driest slopes of the Bayuda Desert as in a lodging-house kitchen in England.'

As they pressed on, wear and tear began to take effect.

'If a camel dropped in his tracks, his load and saddle were

taken off him and loaded on another (already loaded) camel. The few spare camels had been used up long ago so the stores had to be packed at any cost on animals already weakened by fatigue and short rations. The way the poor brutes toiled on was something marvellous; you would see one go slower and slower till the tail of the animal in front he was tied to seemed nearly coming off; then he would stop for a second, give a mighty shiver, and drop stone-dead.'

Progress though difficult was uneventful. They were heading for the wells at Abu Klea, firmly convinced that they would not encounter much resistance on the way: 'Little did I think, when scrambling my rounds that night in pitch darkness, that some nine or ten thousand of the enemy were within half a day's march of us.' The next day, they knew.

The battle began gradually. 'A redoubled fire from the Arabs showed that they saw our movements, and soon the hills were alive with them, running parallel to our square and keeping up a hot fire all the time. Men fell right and left, and the whistling of bullets overhead was incessant. Skirmishers were accordingly told off to the front and flanks and they succeeded in greatly reducing the enemy's fire.'

But the square pressed on, as it had to. The main Dervish attack was expected from the right; on the left 'the Wady became alive and black with vast masses of Arabs, who had apparently sprung out of the ground'. Gleichen was on the right, so he missed the full initial effects of this, but 'suddenly a terrific shock was felt, accompanied by re-doubled yells and firing. I found myself lifted off my legs amongst a surging mass of Heavies [Heavy Camel Regiment] and Sussex [Royal Sussex Regiment] who had been carried back against the camels by the impetuous rush of the enemy. Telling the men to stand fast I forced my way through the jam to see what had happened. Heavies, Sussex, and camels of all sorts were pressing with terrific force on our thin double rank, and it seemed every moment as if it must give; but it didn't. A rain of bullets whizzed dangerously close past my head from the rifles behind into the fighting mass in front. Everything depended on the front and right faces standing fast. And well did they stick to it. With the rear rank faced about, the men suddenly withstood the pressure, and, do what they would, the Arabs could not break into that solid mass of men and camels.'

They won the battle — but at a cost:

'It was an awful slaughter. On the knoll immediately outside the square lay the bodies of eighty-six Englishmen, waxlike in death and covered with dust and blood. Hardly a square foot but was hidden by the stiffening carcasses of men and camels; here B-'s corpse, the head nearly severed from the body; there C-'s a bullet hole through the face and a gaping spear wound in the neck — it was horrible. I did not care to look any more, lest I should come across the mutilated bodies of more friends. Dead Arabs in hundreds strewed the ground, mostly with a fiendish expression on their still faces. Here and there the Mahdi's uniform and straw cap proclaimed one of superior rank, but the greater part by far were clad in (originally) white garments, wound round the waist, and fastened over the left shoulder — the shaven head covered with a white cotton skull cap. In some cases their clothes had caught fire from the nearness of the discharge of the rifles, and several of the heaps of bodies were smouldering. Arms of all sorts and broken banner-staves were scattered over the field; spears in hundreds, some of enormous length, javelins, knobkerries, hatchets, swords and knives. I even found a Birmingham bill-hook, with the trade-mark on it, in an Arab's hand, sharp as a razor and covered with blood and hair; how it got there I know not, so I confiscated it for the use of our mess.'

They marched on. After a drink at the wells and as much rest as they could manage on a bitterly cold night, for which they had no suitable covering, they were called to an early parade and set out at 4.30 a.m. When the sun went down they were still marching, and at 10 p.m. they were resigned to the fact that they would march till dawn, or longer if they had not previously reached the river. They got lost, once in a dense wood of thorny mimosa trees; so lost were they that subsequently they never discovered where the wood had been, let alone how they had reached it. 'Men in dozens went to sleep on their camels, and strayed from the column, one or two never being seen again.' But dawn came, and still no sign of the river. At last, when it was known that the Nile was only four miles farther on, it became apparent that there would soon be other troubles to contend with. 'Numbers of sharpshooters were seen in the grass round about. Bullets kept spattering in on us from invisible marksmen in the long grass all the time.' And then real disaster. Sir Herbert Stewart was hit, and was obviously fatally wounded. Gleichen himself was hit but by great good fortune it was only a ricochet, and it was turned again by a brass button! It was now apparent how wise Stewart had been to halt the column and take up a defensive position. 'The enemy had largely increased in numbers, and a continuous rain of bullets went into and over the camel zareba. Every other minute a dead or wounded man was carried past on a stretcher. Cameron, the special correspondent of *The Standard* was killed just about this time; poor St Leger Herbert was found stiff and cold amongst the camels shortly afterwards − another valuable man gone.'

By 3.30 in the afternoon, Colonel Sir Charles Wilson, who now commanded the column, decided there was no possibility of reinforcements arriving (they were expected to be following close behind) and therefore gave the order to march. But, as the wounded and the baggage would slow down the pace, the force was split in two halves, the first being left to defend itself; the second to press on. The plan worked. The forward detachment took the brunt of the next attack. On this occasion the Dervishes displayed no fieldcraft but rushed recklessly on. 'Aiming low, and firing steadily as on parade, our men mowed the Arabs down like grass, not one got within eight yards of the square.' The attack wilted and faded. The column pressed on and reached the river. 'Still, perfect discipline was observed. Not a man left his place in the ranks until his company marched up to take its fill. The front face having drunk itself full was marched to relieve the rear face, and so on, in order that, in case of attack, no flank should be left undefended.

'But, of course, it was one thing to reach Metemmeh and another to occupy it. The Dervishes were in possession. It was a well-built, well-defended little town . . . . Suddenly there was a heavy report from the walls, and a round stone shot, as we afterwards discovered it to be, whizzed over our heads and buried itself in the ground close by. This was entirely unexpected, and most unfair we thought it at the time. However, not much time was given us to think; for a second and third followed the first, each nearer than the one before.' It was a Krupp; these weapons were said to be war surplus from the Franco-Prussian War.

At that moment four of Gordon's little steamers came down the river. It was not a large reinforcement but it was useful. However, they brought news that Gordon was desperately hard pressed though still holding out, and that 3000 Dervishes were less than two days' march away, fully determined to avenge the defeat at Abu Klea.

But in spite of the intimidating noise of tom-toms the enemy did not attack. 'Those tom-toms got on one's nerves, especially when on outpost duty at night. You would hear them growing louder and louder in the darkness till they seemed to come quite near – till you expected a momentary attack – and then they would die away in the distance, only to advance again ten minutes afterwards with their infernal tap! tap! tap! tap! tap! – how we did curse them.

'On the 31st January, the convoy arrrived from Gakdul, with stores, three guns, and a couple of mails, but, alas, no instructions whatever from headquarters, and no fresh camels. Neither did they bring any news; they had not heard or seen any of the enemy; the wounded at Abu Klea were doing well and had not been attacked. St Vincent and Guthrie had died of their wounds but that was all. Sir Redvers Buller, whom we so eagerly expected to take command, had not turned up, and our only reinforcements were some more Naval Brigade and the three guns aforesaid. We were somewhat disappointed at these small results of the convoy's journey; but still there was the fresh supply of food, and so far we were all safe; so really there was not much to grumble at. We little knew what news the morrow would bring forth.

. . . .

'Next day, 1st February, was a Sunday, and we paraded as usual for church in our Sunday-go-to-meeting red jumpers and trousers. It struck me at the time that all the staff wore a very serious look, but none of us were prepared for the awful news they had to impart. Gradually it trickled out amongst the officers that the worst possible catastrophe had happened. *Khartoum had fallen* and Gordon was probably killed.'

6

After Khartoum

Although the death of Gordon and the fall of Khartoum
marked the end of British government interest in the Sudan,
faint and ineffective though that interest had been, it did not,
of course, mean that the army could now quickly depart and
forget all about it. There remained a sizeable expeditionary
force in a vulnerable position, and after taking Khartoum the
Mahdi might feel urged to try to avenge some of his former
defeats — notably Abu Klea. Wilson had gone up river with
two of the steamers till they were within sight of Khartoum;
their first intimation of what had happened was a tremendous fire from the banks and the town, whereupon they
reversed quickly and set off down stream. Doubtless they
were using more more speed than was wise, for in the
Shabluka cataract both steamers were wrecked. The troops
managed to get ashore and constructed a makeshift fortification while a message was sent down river for another
steamer to evacuate them. It was a delicate moment but, as
Gleichen reported, 'hard work soon took our minds off
brooding on the subject.' Gravel buttresses were thrown up
against the walls of the fort outside to stop any shells that
might otherwise have knocked down the rubble masonry, and
a hedge of thorn bushes was started as an outer circle of
defence. Pending relief, a detachment was sent back to
Gakdul for more stores. Gleichen was in charge of the rearguard of this party. By 3 a.m. on the first night twenty-three
dead camels had been left behind.

The party were not happy about the men left behind in
Gubat. 'It seemed on the cards we might find them in small
pieces when we got back.' Their route took them through

Abu Klea, which was a far from pleasant experience so soon after the battle. Potiphar, Gleichen's camel, obtained his discharge from army service here; 'he collapsed into a hole and sat there roaring; when I had hauled him out by main force he fell into another and refused to budge; so I left him there and made my way on foot!' Doubtless Potiphar had the wisdom to change his residence before anyone came back to look for him on the return trip, but he was, in fact, apprehended again.

But there was no return trip. A steamer had gone up the river independently and rescued the shipwrecked party just in time. They then learnt that the expedition to relieve Khartoum had failed by two days.

From Christmas Day 1884 to 26 January 1885 the garrison of Khartoum had lived on coarse bread made from the pith of the palm-tree, on gum, and on a little tobacco. Their situation was well known to the Mahdi, who would not have attacked had he not thought the relief expedition would soon get through. Wilson considered the Mahdi would have taken Khartoum earlier if he had wished to do so. He also obtained two more accounts of Gordon's death, both from eye-witnesses. One said Gordon was taking a party to the house of the Austrian consul when he ran into a group of rebels. He fell in the first volley. The second account said Gordon met the group at the gate of the palace and fired his revolver at them. He was killed in the return volley.

Both versions were considered to be reliable and to be substantially similar, but the version given earlier had been accepted as a more correct one.

Khartoum had been besieged for 317 days, which was only nine days less than the siege of Sebastopol in 1855-6.

On the way back Gleichen encountered Sudanese troops:

'Most of them had arrayed themselves in blue jerseys, and stocking caps whilst a good many wore regulation British trousers with red or yellow stripes. On my asking where they had got them from, they told me simply they had walked out amongst the Ingleez, and taken whatever they could pick up. This propensity evidently accounted for many deficiencies in our weekly kit-inspections. They had not the slightest notions of meum and tuum; everything was public property even among themselves. If you saw some quaint article lying about, and wished to possess it, the nearest person, whether he was the proprietor or not, would sell it to you and pocket the proceeds. They were very keen soldiers, and if you made friends with them, nearly every one had a pet spear-head or sword, covered with dried blood and hair, which he produced out of some inner recess of his shanty and showed you with great pride.'

Travelling back one night, 'Just before the turn in to Gakdul, I was riding in front, when I heard some extra-ordinary noises in the distance. At first I thought it was jackals, but soon the noises turned into a wild sort of moaning I could not understand. At length it dawned on me it was Arabs singing; if they happened to be the enemy, I thought, how on earth am I to keep forty straying camels out of sight of them in the moonlight?' Fortunately they were friendly, but Gleichen did not stop for a course in musical appreciation.

One of the least pleasing aspects of the return journey was the number of stores which had to be left behind. They had been sent up as a basis for a further push ahead, and now the returning troops were tantalized by seeing large quantities of food which they could neither consume nor transport. 'After stowing away as much as we could in our kits, we stowed away the remainder in our stomachs.'

'The Heavies had been in much the same fix, having had several magnums of champagne sent to them the very night after they left Gakdul. The fellow in charge of the liquor, finding his camels requisitioned and the Heavies flown, thought it was a pity to waste good wine in the desert, so he packed what he could to take back on his own camel, and drank the remainder — two magnums — himself at a sitting; good performance, I call it. The poor chap, Costello, of the 5th Lancers, died soon afterwards, though not from the champagne.'

On the way back they met a long promised consignment of

boots 'but that which we had looked forward to as a real godsend turned out to be of such small sizes that the men could hardly get their feet into them. They were as hard as bricks, there was no grease to soften them, and the only way of using them was to slit them open at the end, and shove your toes through. As for the officers, no two had the same foot-covering: field boots, lawn-tennis shoes, garters, puttees, and boots in all stages of decay and attempted repair were worn.'

In Korti Gleichen tried to renew contact with Potiphar. Unfortunately after recovery the camel had been sent away on another errand. 'Though I made every inquiry afterwards about a big white camel, with a blue and white noseband, a vile temper, and hole in his side big enough to put your helmet in, I never heard any more of him. Peace be to his bones!'

Soon they were on the Nile, travelling in fair comfort by day and camping by night. The latter had its occasional incident:

'That evening as we lay comfortably in the sand after dinner, smoking our pipes before we turned in two gigantic spiders made their appearance in our midst. Up we all jumped, over went lanterns and plates, and it was not till C— had valiantly slain the beasts with his slipper that we ventured to return to our places. It's all very well to laugh and to treat spiders with contempt, but a bite from one of these brutes is no joke. Imagine a yellow brute with two pairs of beaks, a body rather longer than your thumb, and eight long red legs covered with stiff and spiky red hairs, the whole beast barely to be contained in a soup plate, and you have an idea of the apparitions which made for us that night. They devour little birds, their bite is by way of being poisonous and they are horrible to look at. No wonder we bolted.'

It might be thought that in those days travellers would be able to buy interesting local goods in the bazaars. It was not so: 'in it [the bazaar] you could get every variety of fifth-rate French and Manchester cottons, cutlery, gimcrack stationery and gaudy trash, but hardly any native work whatever.' The chief things noticeable about Dongola, Gleichen claimed, were a very fine old fig-tree, and a greater tendency to lying and cheating than anywhere else in Egypt.

Nearly everything came from Europe, the only native articles being those of consumption and a few pieces of jewellery, 'generally rather ugly than otherwise'.

Gleichen and the Camel Corps were not the only people to have trouble in returning from the unsuccessful attempt to relieve Khartoum. What was known as 'The River Column' also had some hazardous adventures. Its commander was General Earle, who was later killed by a Dervish sniper; its second in command was Colonel, later Major-General, Henry Brackenbury. Brackenbury recorded his experiences because he felt that 'the advance and return of four regiments of infantry through a hundred miles of cataracts and rapids in an enemy's country deserves, as a military operation, some permanent record, and because death has removed the only other officers possessing sufficient knowledge of all details to write that record with accuracy'.

The River Column had set off upriver at the same time as the Camel Corps was making its drive overland. Its mission was 'to punish the murderers of Colonel Stewart and of the Consuls and to advance by Berber to co-operate with Stewart's* force in an attack on the Mahdi before Khartoum, under Lord Wolseley's personal command'. Wolseley, by this time, might have seemed too rigid a thinker to handle this particular expedition; his insistence on whale boats had had to be altered in favour of local boats only after it had been conclusively proved that the latter were far more suitable for negotiating the Nile cataracts. The River Column was led by the first battalion of the South Staffordshire Regiment, totalling 545 men of all ranks. They performed with great efficiency and distinguished courage. In these days, when regional affiliations — admittedly not of long standing — have been obliterated in 'large regiments' it is worth remembering what their value could be. The South Staffordshire Regiment

---

*This was, of course, General Sir Herbert Stewart, of the Camel Corps.

proved themselves the equal, if not the superior, of many better known regiments, which included on this occasion the Black Watch, Gordon Highlanders, Duke of Cornwall's Light Infantry and Essex Regiment.

The River Column had an experience which is not unfamiliar to others who have hoped for local co-operation. They were told to make contact with local sheikhs who might be useful. One was Said Hassan, Sheikh of Amri Island and King of Zowarah. He was alleged to have behaved with gallantry against the Mahdi's troops. 'His first act was to beg for money for himself and his ragged retinue, and to try to drive as hard a bargain with me as he could. I promised him finally a pound a day for himself and his followers, provided he would help us with labour and supplies when we reached his country — payment to be contingent on results. He never was of the slightest use to us; and as, when we returned to Abu Dom, he did not hesitate to return among the rebels, I have little doubt that he had only followed the traditional policy of the Soudanese sheikhs, to have some family on each side in a war, so that, whichever side wins there may be some in power to intercede for those on the beaten side. In fact, so well is this policy recognized among them that the members of the family who have been on the wrong side are thought none the worse for their apparent treason.'

Their heaviest clash with the Dervishes was at Kirbekan, where General Earle was killed. Here the Dervishes displayed their usual astonishing courage but were cut down by 'withering fire' mainly from the Black Watch. The Dervishes were not the only local troops to show courage on that day. 'The Egyptian camel corps had at the commencement of the day taken up a position in front of the high ridge and protected the flank of infantry in its advance. In that position they remained throughout the day, assisting by their fire to keep down the fire from the heights, and shooting, or in some · cases pursuing and capturing, the rebels who attempted to escape towards the east, along the southern slope of the hill. Their conduct was witnessed by the Staffords, who remained so long upon the shoulder of the hill, and was the theme of much praise. When the Staffords stormed the hill one Egyptian soldier charged up the hill, all alone, on their extreme right — a most gallant feat.'

The significance of this victory was in its effect on the morale of both sides. So great had been the impetus of all Dervish attacks that it had given rise to 'the idea that unless in square formation they [the British] could not stand against Arabs; today the troops had learnt they could beat their enemy in hand-to-hand combat in the rocks, fighting in loose order.'

The way down river, after the news of the death of Gordon, was extremely hazardous. The expedition had the warning evidence of Colonel Stewart's wrecked steamer to show how the slightest steering error in that swift current could take them on to jagged rocks. Boat drill was therefore meticulously exacting. On the way up the column had suffered from exhaustion, scorching heat and frustration; now, on the way down, they had the possibility of a rapid death instead of a slow one. At one point:

'Two great rocks stood out in mid-stream. It was necessary to pass between them. The least error in steering would be fatal. To make the turn too soon would bring the boat on to the right-hand rock; to wait too long would sweep her on to the left-hand rock. Sitting under the shadow of a great rock I watched this triumph of skill over a difficulty that to anyone unaccustomed to such work would have seemed insuperable. Boat after boat came down with lightning speed, the men giving way with might and main to give steering-power; the bowmen standing cool and collected watching the water, and only using the oar should the steersmen seem to need help; the steersmen with marvellous judgement bringing round the boat at the right moment. Now and then an error of half a second brought a boat on to the edge of the left-hand rock, and she rose and fell like a horse jumping a fence. But in the day's work only one boat of the Gordons and one of the Staffords were wrecked.'

A little later they were not so lucky:

'As my boat shot down we passed the adjutant of the Gordons, with his boat stuck fast in the very centre of the boiling rapid — a useful beacon to the following boats. Four others of the same battalion were on the rocks. The adjutant had a narrow escape for his life. Thrown into the water as his boat sank, his head struck a sharp rock, and he was severely cut.'

Of the 'voyageurs' Brackenbury had this to say:

'Out of the contingent of 377 men that left Canada, ten had died, six of whom had been drowned in the Nile. Their six months engagement expiring on 9th March, eighty-nine of them had re-engaged, and sixty-seven of those had ascended the Nile with the River Column. Without them, the ascent of the river, if not impossible, would have been far slower and attended with far greater loss of life. Without them, the descent of the river would have been impossible. Officers and men had worked with unceasing energy and a complete disregard of danger.'

Wolseley said:

'The life of the men has been of incessant toil from the first to the last day of the expedition. In ragged clothing, scarred and blistered by the sun and rough work, they have worked with constant cheerfulness and unceasing energy. Their discipline has been beyond reproach; and I do not hesitate to say that no finer, more gallant, or more trustworthy body of men ever served the Queen than those I have had the honour to command in the River Column.'

The last word on the withdrawal from the Sudan might well go to Lord Cromer, the Consul-General in Egypt from 1883, though hindsight might not agree:

'As a mere academic question I think that the policy of withdrawing from Khartoum was undesirable, but I decline to consider that, in view of the circumstances which then existed the question of desirability or undesirability of withdrawal was at the time of any practical importance. A long course of misgovernment had culminated in a rebellion in the Sudan, which the Egyptian government were powerless to repress. They therefore had to submit to the time-honoured law expressed in the words Vae Victis. The abandonment of the Soudan, however undesirable, was imposed upon the Egyptian government as an unpleasant but imperious necessity for the simple reason that after the destruction of General Hicks' army, they were unable to keep it. This, as it appears to me, is the residuum of truth which may be extracted from all the very lengthy and stormy discussions which have taken place on this subject.'

But later he added:

'The Ministers who objected to the employment of Zubair Pasha were perhaps in some degree wanting in imagination and elasticity of mind. They could not transport themselves in spirit from Westminster to Khartoum and Cairo. The arguments which they applied against General Gordon and myself appear to me to be rather those of debaters trained in the art of dialectics than of statesmen whose reason and imagination enable them to grasp in an instant the true situation of affairs in a distant country widely differing from their own.'

The last word on many another country than the Sudan: but, foolish or not, the Sudan had been abandoned. Egypt however had been too long connected with the Sudan to be able to sever the connection easily; and the Dervishes, on the crest of overwhelming victories against allegedly superior opponents, were to continue on a path of military conquest until decisively defeated.

The Mahdi died in June 1885 and was succeeded by the Khalifa Abdulla. (Khalifa means successor.) Though the situation was not greatly changed, two new factors had entered the scene. The Mahdi was no longer there to make mistakes or to be proved fallible. He was enshrined as a superhuman saint. Whatever went right in the future would be the result of the Mahdi's teaching; whatever went wrong was in no way a weakness of the divine message of Mahdism but only of its followers. The second factor was that the Khalifa was a dynamic, barbarous Baggara, devout in his way, but essentially a military despot.

The Khalifa, whose name was Abdullahi Ibn Muhammad, was however a more significant figure in the Dervish Empire than the Mahdi himself. Slatin – as we see later – gave an unflattering picture of him, and this is not difficult to understand as Slatin was deeply conscious of the humiliation of his own position, particularly when the Khalifa was being kind to him. The Khalifa, whether in personal or political relations, was always operating from a position of strength. He was a strong barbarian, able to be kind because he always had his own way; not surprisingly few people would risk incurring his cruelty. Tyrants such as the Khalifa are easier to live with than well-meaning but weaker men. Thus in Norman Britain, life was undoubtedly better under William the Conqueror than it was under Stephen, even though the former's idea of a joke was to chop off captives' feet and toss them over the walls of a besieged castle; under the well-meaning, genial Stephen, it was 'nineteen long winters when God and his saints slept', simply because he was so weak that all his subordinates became petty tyrants.

During the Khalifa's rule in the Sudan, a few tribes risked defying him but their example was not followed; their fate was too impressive. And for fourteen years he held together as motley a collection of subject people as any ruler has ever had the misfortune to administer. With it all he tried to carry out the Mahdi's wishes — to extend the Dervish Empire. Empire is, of course, a word which almost defies definition but it is not unfair to call the polyglot heterogeneous tribes and areas ruled from Khartoum as an empire; for within the boundaries of what was known as the Sudan it was neither a state nor a nation. The Khalifa established the internal Sudanese empire by military despotism but kept it in being by appointing Emirs as local governors, by raising taxes, and by administering justice through a hierarchical system of courts. Admittedly the Emirs were often brutal, the taxes harsh and unfair, and the justice unequal,but it was infinitely better than anything that had preceded it. It was a remarkable achievement in view of the Khalifa's complete ignorance of the outside world. But he failed to push the boundaries of his empire beyond the Sudan, and the Abyssinian war ended in a stalemate in March 1889, and he was defeated on the frontiers of Egypt the following August.

After these two frustrations, it was clear that the limits of expansion had been reached.

Out of all this emerges the picture of a shrewd, practical, devout man, shrewd in his choice and handling of subordinates, practical in that he condoned the slave-trade as being necessary to the economy, and devout in that he clearly believed in the Mahdist creed. In the last phase of the war his belief that his forces would gain final victory in sight of the Mahdi's tomb caused him to miss earlier and better military opportunities. But all that was far in the future. In 1885 he was merely 'the successor' — a mere disciple of his dead leader.

In the years which followed the Mahdi's death Sir Evelyn Baring, later Lord Cromer, was carefully rebuilding Egypt. The task was Herculean but he had astonishing success. Reform was needed everywhere, in the labour system, in justice, in irrigation, and in taxation. The whole financial system of Egypt was in a corrupt chaotic mess. But with cool-headedness and a sane policy concisely explained in his book *Modern Egypt*, published in 1908, Cromer set up the basis of a stable, prosperous, and modern state. As soon as the financial situation permitted the foundations of the new Egyptian army were laid. At first it consisted of only eight battalions, but even at the point when the Sudan situation looked at its blackest, in 1885, it was increasing its strength and efficiency. In March 1885 Sir Evelyn Wood was succeeded as Commander-in-Chief by Sir Francis Grenfell.

Grenfell held the post till April 1892 when he was succeeded by Kitchener. It is often thought that the reconquest of the Sudan was not begun till 1896; in fact the first step was taken as early as December 1885 when Grenfell's army attacked a Dervish force on the frontier at Ginnis. (Ginnis would, perhaps, have been forgotten, quite unjustly, were it not for the fact that the British with the Egyptian army fought in red coats for the last time in their history. They would still fight in conspicuous uniform before camouflage took its full effect nearly a hundred years later but at Ginnis it was farewell for ever to the thin red line.)

Important though Ginnis was, its significance was later overshadowed by two considerable victories by the new Egyptian army over the Dervishes in 1889. The first was at Argin, near Wadi Halfa, in July; the second at Toski in August. These were not great battles but like many small critical engagements had far-reaching effects. In this situation they were enough to show the Dervishes that the path to the conquest of Egypt was far from open.

At this point the influence of another personality, no less than that of Cromer, Gordon, Kitchener or Grenfell, was making itself felt on the Egyptian scene. This was Reginald Wingate, who in 1891 published a book entitled *Mahdiism and the Egyptian Sudan*. The title-page described it as being by Major F.R. Wingate, D.S.O., R.A., Assistant Adjutant-General for Intelligence, Egyptian Army. Wingate came of a family which had considerable ability both military and commercial. When they traded they made money; when they fought they won victories. Orde Wingate, the Chindit leader in 1943, was a member of this family; Reginald Wingate was his great-uncle. A considerable insight into their qualitites may be gained from reading *Not in the Limelight*, the auto-biography of Sir Ronald Wingate, Reginald Wingate's son. All through his career as a regular officer Reginald Wingate had been intelligent, hard-working and religious. Two character-istics marked him especially; he always had a great number of friends, and he never ceased perfecting his ability in languages. In 1883 he was appointed to Sir Evelyn Wood's staff in the Egyptian army. His career to date had not been particularly lucky and this was one of his first pieces of good fortune. In the event it was even luckier for others than for Wingate. But life was not easy. He survived a cholera epidemic, but caught typhoid. He was with the River Column. From the beginning he showed considerable ability at gathering Intelligence. On Wingate's skill in appointing agents, on his knowledge of Arabic in questioning them, future tactics and strategy would depend. He had other duties too, for his principal post was Staff Officer to Sir Evelyn Wood. After a spell of leave to enable him to shake

off the effects of typhoid he was made A.D.C. to the General,
who by now had been appointed G.O.C. Eastern Command in
England. Wingate, however, had no money of his own and
wished to get married, so he managed to obtain a transfer
back to the Egyptian army, with its better pay and prospects.
In 1886 he became Assistant Military Secretary to the
Commander-in-Chief, Sir Francis Grenfell. Much of his time
was given to Intelligence work and three years later he was
appointed Director of Military Intelligence.

'Intelligence' sounds an absorbingly interesting and rewarding activity. In fact, it is more likely to be the opposite. This
has probably been true from the earliest days of warfare.
Even for the agent who is at risk in gathering his information,
boredom may be a constant companion. He must be infinitely
patient, painstaking, self-effacing. Many of his contacts may
be people he despises: he will certainly distrust them. Being
at risk may be boring; once the excitement has worn off the
very fact of being constantly vulnerable may be tedious in
the extreme.

If this is so for the man in the field it is infinitely more so
for the person who processes the scraps of information. He
has to assess their reliability, sift through a mass of utterly
useless information, try to calculate the age and reliability of
the gleanings he believes to be genuine news, and to try to
produce something reasonable on which plans can be based.
He has always too little or too much.

Wingate, of course, was up against the problem that has
bedevilled all intelligence officers through history. He could
never really be sure how far some of his agents were playing a
double game. Counter-intelligence may mean that false and
real information are being mixed; Wingate was shrewd
enough to know that some of his agents would be working
for the Dervishes as well, and he might suspect that the
Dervishes had a better and wider network of spies than his
own. And, of course, no intelligence officer can fail to be
moved by the disappearance of one of his agents, knowing
only too well what the unfortunate man's fate is likely to be
— and certainly was, at the hands of the Dervishes.

Wingate achieved a considerable reputation for his activities in the Sudan, and it was fully deserved. He had poor and unreliable maps, dubious sources of information, no resources of photography, and very little useful assistance. Long afterwards, in all countries, there developed highly sophisticated Intelligence systems with methods of cross-reference, checking information, and so on. Wingate had no one but himself.

7

In the Dervish Camp

Long after wars are over it is usually possible to piece together a picture of what life was like among the enemy. The picture which finally emerges is not always a true one and has usually lost some of its freshness. By contrast the picture that came from the Dervish camp in 1896, before the final phase of the war had properly begun, was both new and vivid. That it was so was due to the misfortunes of three unfortunate European prisoners: Rudolf Slatin, Joseph Ohrwalder and Charles Neufeld. The first two men have already figured in these pages. Curiously enough, all three were German-speaking although of very different experience and temperament; their variation in outlook and the fact that they spent their captivity separated from one another makes their testimony all the more interesting and valuable.* Slatin was a Catholic of Jewish origins who, having been appointed by Gordon, had discharged his duties with vigour and courage. When the Mahdist movement got under way Darfur was one of the first provinces to feel its effects. Slatin fought a series of vigorous engagements but then, as much for the sake of his supporters as for himself, when all hope was at an end, he surrendered on the promise that all the people with him, including women and children, would be spared. This was just before the fall of El Obeid in January 1883.

Slatin was a man of exceptional talent but has, inevitably, been criticized. In the last stages of his battle with the Dervishes, before he was taken prisoner, he had become a Moslem. This change of faith seems to have been due less to

*Slatin and Ohrwalder were Austrian; Neufeld was a German.

religious conviction than to the belief that his Sudanese troops might fight better at this stage if they were led by a Mohammedan rather than by a Christian. However, the form of Mohammedanism he adopted was unorthodox, and he therefore incurred the distrust of Christians and Moslems alike. Although he was respected, and probably liked, by both the Mahdi and the Khalifa he went through some difficult periods in captivity when a rash move would have cost him his life. Some of his captivity was harsh; other parts were tolerable. The suspicion with which many regarded him was not shared by Wingate, who became his firm friend. Slatin's knowledge of the Dervishes was of great value in the reconquest of the Sudan, in which he worked closely with Wingate. Subsequently he became Inspector-General of the Sudan for fourteen years.

Slatin escaped from the Dervishes in 1895. He wrote a lengthy account of his experiences before and after captivity under the title *Fire and Sword in the Soudan*. This was translated by Wingate from the German and published in England in 1895. Wingate provided a similar service for Father Ohrwalder, whose writings were much less coherent and complete, and published them as *Ten Years Captivity in the Mahdi's Camp*. The astonishing fact about both originals and translations is that they were completed so quickly.

Slatin throws much light on what happened during times which would otherwise have remained obscure. He gives interesting as well as gruesome details on the end of the Hicks expedition. He describes the period after the fall of Khartoum. One of his own experiences at that time was of suddenly being confronted with Gordon's severed head. On that and other occasions he realized that to show emotion would be considered a sign of weakness and probable treachery, but he found the ordeal hard. He also describes how, when Khartoum was sacked, its inhabitants were tortured to make them disclose where their valuables were hidden. 'There was no sparing of the lash; the unfortunate people were flogged until their flesh hung down in shreds from their bodies.'

He describes other more sophisticated forms of torture,

many of which were applied to older women. Young women were reserved unscarred for the harems of the Mahdi, the Khalifa and the Emirs, in that order. A general amnesty was proclaimed the day after the fall, but it made no difference; rape, murder and torture went on without halt.

In spite of the excesses of the Mahdi's followers Slatin had a considerable respect for the man himself. He made a brief summary of the Mahdi's achievements:

'Now what has the Mahdi done, and wherein lay his power to revive a religion which had become so debased? What was the nature of his teachings? He had preached renunciation; he had inveighed against earthly vanities and pleasures; he had broken down both social and official ranks; he had selected as clothing a jibba, which became the universal dress of his adherents. As a regenerator of religion, he had united the four distinct Moslem sects . . . he had made a collection of specially selected verses from the Koran, which he called the Rateb, and which he enjoined should be recited by the entire congregation after morning and afternoon prayers – a ceremony which lasted at least forty minutes, and had strictly forbidden the drinking bouts which were an invariable accompaniment of marriage ceremonies in the Sudan. A simple meal of dates and milk took the place of the costly marriage feast.

'At the same time he had forbidden dancing and playing, which he classified as "earthly pleasures", and those found disobeying this order were punished by flogging and confiscation of all property. The use of bad language was punished with eighty lashes for every insulting word used, and seven days imprisonment. The use of intoxicating drinks, such as marissa or date wine, and smoking, were most strictly prohibited. Offences of this description were punishable by flogging, eight days imprisonment, and confiscation of goods. A thief suffered the severance of his right hand, and should he be convicted of a second offence he lost his left foot also. As it was the general custom among the male population of the Sudan, and especially of the nomad Arabs, to let their hair grow, the Mahdi had directed that henceforth all heads should be shaved. Wailing for the dead and feasts for the dead were punishable by deprivation of property.

'In order that the strength of his army should not be decreased and endangered by desertion, owing to the severe mode of life he had prescribed, and fearful that his doctrines which were considered unorthodox should be made known in the various foreign countries he had already conquered, he absolutely prohibited passage of persons through these districts for the purpose of performing a pilgrimage to Mecca. Should any one cast doubt on the Divine nature of his mission, or should there be the slightest hesitation to comply with his orders, on the evidence of two witnesses, the delinquent was invariably punished by the loss of the right hand and left foot. [And sometimes without the witnesses' testimony.]

'As, however, most of these dispositions and ordinances were entirely at variance with the Moslem law he therefore issued most strict injunctions that the study of theology and all public commentaries thereon should cease, and ordered that any books or manuscripts dealing with these subjects should be instantly burnt or thrown into the river.

'Such were the teachings of the expected Mahdi, and he had left no stone unturned to carry into the fullest effect the ordinances he had made. Openly, he showed himself a most strict observer of his own teachings; but within their houses, he, the Khalifa, and their relatives, entered into the wildest excesses, drunkenness, riotous living and debauchery of every sort, and they satisfied to their fullest extent the vicious passions which are so prevalent amongst the Sudanese.'

How Slatin knew these details of the private life of the Mahdi he did not disclose.

The Khalifa, of course, made no claim to be a religious leader. He was however fully determined to maintain and strengthen the position he had inherited. In the early stages he had to contend with the Mahdi's relations, who did not feel he was a worthy successor. The 'sweetener' on these occasions seems to have been the presentation of large numbers of attractive female slaves. There were other discordant elements, in the shape of rebels and dissatisfied sheikhs; these were not to be bought with bribes but had to be reduced by armed force. Soon too he was at war with the Abyssinians.

The reasons for this war, and its bloody course, were not known until Ibrahim Abd-el-Kadir's writings came to light many years later. The campaign was of supreme military importance to the Dervishes and was prosecuted with appropriate vigour. In comparison, the siege of Khartoum and the various efforts to relieve it were of no consequence. Khartoum was certain to surrender sooner or later and it was of little concern to the Dervishes whether a relief expedition reached it or not. The Mahdi was supremely confident (and, in view of the forces launched against the Abyssinians, with some reason for being so) that the Dervishes could sweep away Gordon, the River Column and the Camel Corps with no difficulty. The defeat at Abu Klea did not shake this confidence but merely caused a minor modification of plan in that the Mahdi brought the Khartoum siege to a military conclusion. In view of what we now know of the power displayed in the Abyssinian campaign it seems that the would-be relievers of Khartoum were lucky indeed that they did not arrive any earlier. Had they done so and entered the city they would have encountered military strength far beyond their most pessimistic estimates. At least, this is the conclusion one must draw from Abd-el-Kadir's writings and the events of the Abyssinian campaign. Subsequently, when the Egyptian army had been retrained and equipped with improved weapons, when Wingate had organized a first-class Intelligence service, the railway had been built, and the Khalifa's Dervish Empire was much decayed owing to famine and maladministration, it was an altogether different situation, or Kitchener might have occupied a very different niche in history.

The war with Abyssinia was religious in origin but, once it had begun, soon became one of those desperate struggles in which one devastating battle is merely the prelude to another, and peace can only occur when both sides are too destroyed and exhausted to continue. The religious basis was that King John of Abyssinia was a Christian infidel who had siezed Islamic lands around Harat. He was also, although the Dervishes did not know it, being aided by the infidel English in return for allowing Egyptian garrisons to escape from the Sudan through his territory. Gordon did not know this either till 21 October 1884. When he did find out, he disapproved entirely, on the grounds that King John was an unreliable and cruel ally.

During 1885 there were a number of bloody contests between Abyssinians and Dervishes at frontier posts. While the attention of Britain was focused on the last days of Khartoum the Dervishes were much more interested in Gallabat, which they had been besieging since the previous September. At the end of January 1885 Gallabat was relieved by an Abyssinian expedition which succeeded in evacuating 3000 people but left the town in Dervish hands.

The Abyssinians soon made attempts to recover it. Their first expedition was defeated but the second made what seemed to them suitable amends by capturing the town, sacking it and burning it. From then on the war is a story of raids, some on a large scale, of marches through forbidding mountains, of massacres, reprisals and battles in which the dead were numbered in thousands. But on both sides, and particularly on that of the Dervishes, there was considerable sophisticated military skill.

The forces engaged were enormous. In the first large battle, in June 1887, the Dervishes marched to Gallabat with an army said to number 60,000. The Abyssinians, under King John, cannot have been many less. On this occasion the Dervishes were the better armed and destroyed the Abyssinian army with rifle fire in much the same way as they themselves had often been destroyed in previous battles. But even the fearful casualties of this encounter did not cripple the Abyssinian resolve or their war effort, although the loot from the Abyssinian camp was apparently prodigious. The Dervish victory was said to have been due to the skill of the Emir Abu Anga, but Anga was soon to disappear from the scene, for, in Slatin's words, 'he suffered from constant

illnesses and was always trying to cure himself'. He had
grown immensely stout, owing to the good living in which he
indulged, 'which contrasted greatly with that to which he had
been formerly accustomed; he suffered much from indigest-
ion and used to treat himself with a poisonous root which
came from Dar Fertit. One day, however, he took an
overdose, and in the morning was found dead in bed.'
Ohrwalder, however, says he died of typhus which was
prevalent at the time.

After Abu Anga's death his command was taken over by
Zeki Tummal. The Abyssinians took a little time to recover
from their crushing defeat but their resources were very great
and their determination equally so. The Dervishes fortified
the position at Gallabat. Unfortunately for the efficiency of
their defences the perimeter was fifteen miles long, and
Tummal, not having the numbers to man them properly,
contented himself by stationing bodies of men at regular
intervals. The dispositions were not even, and Abyssinian
spies soon learnt that they were much the weakest on the
western side. The leader of the Abyssinian Amhara tribe,
having learnt of this, broke in; subsequently the Amhara
completely wasted their efforts by pillaging and driving off
thousands of women. 'King John, who was in his tent, having
received news that the Amhara, whom he had frequently
accused of cowardice, had succeeded in entering the lines,
whilst his own tribe, the Tigré, had failed, fell into a passion,
and, ordering his followers to carry him on his seat – a small
gold angareb covered with cushions and carpets – he was
brought into the middle of the fighting line. The defenders,
noticing a crowd of followers clothed in velvet and gold,
directed their fire on them; and when King John had almost
reached the defences he was struck by a bullet which,
breaking his right arm above the elbow, entered his body. The
courageous man, declaring that his injury was of no consequence, continued urging on his men, but soon fell back
unconscious on his couch, and was carried to the rear by his
followers, who had suffered great loss. The news that he was
wounded spread among his troops like wildfire, and though

on the point of success they retired. On the evening of 9 March 1889 King John expired in his tent.'

The Amhara, as cowardly as he had expected them to be, were the first to flee on hearing the disastrous news. The others were not so quick off the mark, but once they learnt that the army was disintegrating they too turned for home, and a rear party which was taking back the partly embalmed body of King John was attacked by follow-up groups of Dervishes. The King's crown, sword and a letter from Queen Victoria were all captured. After this, although not totally destroyed, the Abyssinian army lost for the time being the will to fight. Owing to the sudden death of the King the country was disrupted by internal rivalries, and before long the Dervishes were raiding the frontier again.

However, progress was by no means even for the Dervishes. One of their setbacks was caused by a young man called Abu Gemmaiza. In the western regions of the Sudan the Dervish Emirs were looting and oppressing in a manner quite alien to the Mahdi's doctrines. According to Slatin's account, Abu Gemmaiza was a solitary youth who had been driven from his home and was sitting under a fig tree (Gemmaiza) reading the Koran at a time when the Dervishes were raiding the neighbouring village. As he appeared to be both holy and knowledgeable he was asked by the desperate villagers what they should do. The young man told them. 'Fight,' he said: 'do you not know that he who falls fighting for his women and children goes straight to Paradise?' The effect of his words was remarkable. The entire district rose in arms and slaughtered the Dervishes. Immediately the rebellion grew and all attempts at suppression failed. Unfortunately for the rebels, when one group after another of Dervishes had been defeated, Abu Gemmaiza died of small-pox. His successor lacked the same magical inspiration; after a gruelling battle his troops were scattered and he himself was killed. The Dervishes took their revenge and the whole country seemed littered with corpses.

At approximately the same time (the exact chronology of these events was not recorded) the Khalifa decided to invade

Egypt. To do this he needed to call up all his best fighting troops. However, when he tried to enlist the remainder of the Batahin, a famous fighting tribe from the area north of the Blue Nile who had already supplied many men, he encountered opposition. This may have been due to the fact that they resented the Baggara domination, but whatever the reason it brought a fearful penalty. Sixty-seven Batahin were rounded up with their wives and children. The men were then executed, watched by their families who were subsequently allowed freedom — for slavery or starvation. Slatin was taken along when the Khalifa went to witness the results of his decree:

'The unfortunate Batahin had been divided into three parties, one of which had been hanged, a second had been decapitated, and a third had lost their right hands and left feet. The Khalifa himself stopped in front of the three scaffolds, which were almost broken by the weight of the bodies, whilst close at hand lay a heap of mutilated people, their hands and feet lying on the ground: it was a shocking spectacle. They did not utter a sound, but gazed in front of them, and tried to hide from the eyes of the crowd the terrible suffering they were enduring. The Khalifa now summoned Osman Wad Ahmed, and pointing to the mutilated bodies, said "You may now take what remains of your tribe home with you." The poor man was too shocked and horrified to be able to answer.'

Slatin mentioned that every one of the sixty-seven had met his fate heroically. Whether any of the mutilated were likely to recover he did not say; it seems unlikely unless some form of cauterizing was promptly applied. However, it may have been done by their wives; doubtless the victims served their intended purpose of being a hideous warning to anyone else who felt like disobeying the Khalifa's order. (The Batahin had themselves earned a reputation for ferocious cruelty.) The outcome of the expedition to Egypt was the crushing defeat at Toski on 3 August 1889, when Grenfell annihilated the Dervish army under Nejumi. The Dervish force amounted to a mere 5000 and the whole expedition seemed suicidal to all concerned.

Omdurman had now become the Dervish capital and Khartoum was allowed to fall into ruins. But matters were bad for the Dervishes quite apart from reverses in the field. There was no rain for a year, grain was very scarce, and most of the people were starving: 'I dreaded going home,' Slatin wrote, 'for I was generally followed by several famished beggars who often forcibly attempted to enter my house.'

When eventually rain did fall and crops grew there was a plague of locusts; it seemed indeed as if a curse had fallen on the land.

Slatin's fortunes ebbed and flowed. He was expected to keep up a household, but had little money to do so. Occasionally he was sent presents of wives — one of surpassing ugliness — but he did not want them and could not feed them. Several times he fell under suspicion of treacherously communicating with the enemy — well founded suspicion, of course, for he was in touch with Wingate — and was loaded with chains. He was lucky not to have been executed. The Khalifa had troubles enough, and probably only kept Slatin alive because it flattered him to have a slave of such former prestige, although he may have genuinely liked his prisoner.

Slatin must have been a master of soothing diplomacy because he was constantly having to extricate himself from suspicion of real or imagined complicity. In a general atmosphere of unrest, when war between the Khalifa and a faction led by the Mahdi's sons seemed imminent, Father Ohrwalder escaped. The Khalifa summoned Slatin and angrily accused him of assisting Ohrwalder. Slatin was able to protest truthfully that he knew nothing of it, and fortunately was believed. The Khalifa was more preoccupied at the time by the rebellion than by the loss of one insignificant prisoner.

The rebels were persuaded to lay down their arms and given promises of safety, but neither in Omdurman nor elsewhere did these promises have the slightest value. The only variation in the pattern of executions was in the way they were carried out.

147

Slatin was soon back in favour:

'When Zeki Tummal (a Dervish general) was in Omdurman the Khalifa carried out a series of manoeuvres between his forces and those quartered in Omdurman, and personally took the command; but as he had absolutely no idea of military science, and as the thirty thousand troops of whom he disposed were entirely without discipline, the manoeuvres resulted in the most hopeless confusion and disorder; and the blame for this invariably fell on my devoted head, for the Khalifa employed me as a sort of aide-de-camp, and when he became inextricably muddled up he hurled abuse at me, and said I had purposely perverted his orders to make mischief.'

At the end of all this appalling chaos the Khalifa told Slatin he was very pleased with him and gave him two black female slaves as a token of his appreciation.

One day, because of arrangements made by Wingate, Slatin was able to attempt escape. It was a perilous, nerve-racking occasion. When the message reached him that camels would be available Slatin set off bare-foot, armed only with a sword, and accompanied by a faithful servant. The camels were expected at Khor Shambat, north-east of Omdurman.

'The night was dark. During the day the first showers announcing the beginning of the rainy season had fallen; and, as we crossed the cemetery, I put my foot into an old grave which had been washed out by the rain, and my foot got twisted in the bones of a skeleton on which I had stepped. It seemed as if the dead as well as the living were conspiring to throw difficulties in my path; but in spite of the pain, I struggled on, and reached Khor Shambat. We crossed to the other side where it was arranged the camels would await us. We searched up and down the banks . . . .'

But there were no camels. They waited for several hours, searching desperately, even taking the risk of calling out. It was no use. Eventually they retraced their steps and got home just before dawn. This was in June 1894. Wingate's bribes had not been large enough.

Six and a half months later he tried again. The code-word for his helper was 'I am the man with the needles', but when the 'helper' arrived he told him escape was now impossible unless Slatin sent a message to Wingate asking for more money. Slatin did not do so, suspecting it was a trick, but on 20 February camels did arrive and he made a start.

The journey was hazardous beyond Slatin's wildest nightmares. First Slatin and his guides were spotted by another group of travellers, who fortunately were easily bribed to secrecy. Next the camels fell sick and would not eat. Their pace slowed. They had to hide in the hills, they were short of food, they became exhausted by hunger, heat and effort, but eventually on 16 March they limped into the frontier post at Aswan.

Slatin had many observations to make on life in the Dervish Empire. He had some sympathy for the original concept of the Mahdi but was heavy in his criticism of the Khalifa. He gave an account of the latter, as follows:

'He joined the Mahdi at the age of thirty-five, and was then slim and active, though a powerfully built man, but latterly he has become very stout, and his lightness of gait has long since disappeared. He is now forty-nine years of age but looks considerably older, and the hair of his beard is almost white. At times the expression of his face is one of charming amiability, but more generally it is one of dark sternness, in which tyranny and unscrupulous resolution are unmistakeably visible. He is rash and quick-tempered, acting often without a moment's consideration, and, when in this mood, even his own brother dares not approach him. His nature is suspicious to a degree to everyone, his nearest relatives and members of his household included. He admits that loyalty and fidelity are rare qualities, and that those who have to deal with him invariably conceal their real feelings in order to gain their own ends. He is most susceptible to flattery and consequently receives an inordinate amount from everyone. No one dares speak to him without referring to his wisdom, power, justice, courage, generosity, and truthfulness.'

These attributes were not of course unique to the Khalifa, and it was felt by many that Slatin might have given more thought to the fact that the Khalifa had been remarkably

149

moderate and understanding as far as he himself was concerned. Slatin's imprisonment could have been — as we shall see when we look at the situation of Neufeld — infinitely worse. But he could say little good of the Khalifa:

'Without the smallest rhyme or reason he has caused the death of thousands of innocent people. He had the right hand and left foot of a certain Omar publicly cut off in the market-place because he had failed to make lead, which he said he could do, and for which he had received a small sum of money in advance. During the horrible execution and slaughter of the Batahin he had been present and had looked with pleasure on the slaughter of his victims.'

The last remark was contradicted earlier in the book when Slatin said that the Khalifa was not present at the actual execution of the Batahin. Still there is no reason to suppose that he did not consider the scene a useful warning for those wishing to avoid conscription.

But there was one brief glimpse of a kinder side:

'In spite of his tyrannical nature the Khalifa shows to greater advantage in his private life. He is devoted to his oldest son Osman, who is now twenty-one years of age, and has been instructed in all the commentaries of the Koran by able Mohammedan teachers. He had a large red brick house built for his son and had it furnished with all the comfort available in the Sudan. An attempt was even made to lay out a garden on the stony ground within the enclosure.'

Slatin had taken careful note of the Khalifa's military resources, which must have been of great value to Wingate. The total number of armed men at the Khalifa's disposal was 105,000, and these possessed 40,000 rifles; however, Slatin went on to say that there were only 22,000 Remingtons and, as some of those had been altered to suit the owners, not all were reliable. Although there were seventy-five field guns, only six were Krupps, and ammunition for all was short. It is interesting to note from the detailed figures Slatin gave that Osman Digna had 1800 troops only, no heavy guns, and only 450 rifles of all varieties. All these weapons had been captured in earlier battles including those of El Obeid and

Khartoum.

The Khalifa erected a tomb to the Mahdi in Omdurman. It had a square base of stone, thirty feet high and thirty-six feet across; the walls were six feet thick. Above the square was a fifteen-foot high hexagonal wall, and above that a dome forty feet high. At each corner was a smaller dome. 'Directly beneath the dome, and over the Mahdi's grave, a wooden sarcophagus was erected, covered with black cloth.' After the reconquest of the Sudan Kitchener had the tomb destroyed but this was thought to be a petty act and the tomb was subsequently rebuilt in 1947 by the Mahdi's son.

Ohrwalder's early experiences in captivity have already been mentioned. His account describes Gordon's death as taking place on the palace stairs. He was himself in El Obeid at the time but later 'visited Khartoum, and went to the palace where I was shown some black spots on the stairs which they told me were the traces of Gordon's blood'. Ohrwalder felt that Gordon 'carried his humanitarian views too far, and that this excessive forbearance on his part both injured the cause and considerably added to his difficulties. It was Gordon's first and paramount duty to rescue the Europeans, Christians, and Egyptians from the fanatical fury of the Mahdi, which was specially directed against them. This was Gordon's clear duty but unfortunately he allowed his kindness of heart to be made use of to the enemy's advantage.'

Ohrwalder was critical of Gordon for allowing the families of Dervish warriors to remain in Khartoum. Any appeal for food by women brought an immediate response from him, although it brought starvation for all that much nearer.

'He was entirely deceived if he believed that by the exercise of kindness and humanity he was likely to win over these people to his side; on the contrary they ridiculed his generosity and only thought it a sign of weakness. The Sudanese respect and regard only those whom they fear and surely those cruel and hypocritical Mahdists should have received very different treatment to civilized Europeans.'

These were strong words from a missionary priest but

Ohrwalder had more experience on which to base his opinions than most people had. Ohrwalder also criticized the Mahdi:

'Although he was continually warning his followers to despise the good things of this world he surrounded himself with every sort of comfort and luxury, appreciating to the utmost the very pleasures which he declaimed so violently. His wives attended on him in turns but no regularity was preserved. They annointed his body with all sorts of precious unguents, but his speciality was the expensive "Sandalia" (a perfume prepared from sandal-wood and oil) and so saturated was he with these perfumes that when he went forth the air was laden with sweet-smelling odours.

'The courtyard of his harem was full of women, from little Turkish girls of eight years old to the pitch-black Dinka negress or copper-coloured Abyssinian; almost every tribe in the Sudan supplied its representative so that one might say the entire Sudanese woman-world was to be seen here.'

Mahdism did not, of course, require sexual abstinence in any form, so Ohrwalder's Christian-based opinions were not entirely appropriate. Strangely enough, he had considerable sympathy for those members of the harem who were out of favour with the principal wife; deprived of expected favours 'many unfortunate girls were left weeping day and night for their miserable fate, robbed of their happiness and liberty'.

In August 1884 El Obeid had an unexpected visitor, a Frenchman named Oliver Pain. He stated, somewhat improbably, that he had come to bring the submission of the French nation to the Mahdi and, more credibly, that he detested the English. The Dervishes refused to believe he was French at all but assumed he was an English spy. Subsequently Pain confessed, though not to the Mahdi, that he was the correspondent of a French newspaper and that he had come to the Sudan to get a first-hand story on the Mahdi. However, his troubles were soon at an end for he died of dysentery while accompanying the Mahdi's army and was buried in the desert.

Ohrwalder did not reach Omdurman till April 1886. He

found the city very crowded, ill-organized, and with food problems. He mentioned that in September 1886 another Mahdi adherent died in appalling discomfort. This was Gustav Klootz, the muddle-headed German who had deserted from Hicks's expedition. Long before 1886 he had lost all faith in the Dervishes.

'He had left Omdurman in September 1886, for Gallabat, intending to escape into Abyssinia; but having no money he was forced to walk the entire distance, and the great fatigue he had undergone made him seriously ill; he lingered on for a time, but eventually died; and perhaps it was fortunate that he did die, for only a few days afterwards an order arrived from the Khalifa ordering him to be thrown into chains and brought back to Omdurman where a miserable death awaited him.'

Abu Gemmaiza* is described more fully by Ohrwalder than he was by Slatin. Slatin did not mention that Gemmaiza belonged to the Masalit tribe who 'are savage and cruel to a degree; they are in the habit of making waterskins out of the skins of their slain enemies. Slatin Bey told me that when in Darfur he had two of these skins — of a male and female, which he kept as curios.' Gemmaiza was said not only to have begun his career as a leader under a fig-tree but also to be accompanied by the shade of the tree wherever he walked. He was also said to be capable of increasing food to feed thousands, of producing milk from his finger-tips, and to be able to make a palm-tree grow out of barren ground and produce fruit all within an hour. Some believed that he was the true Mahdi. Ohrwalder stated that he died of small-pox in February 1889.

There is much in Ohrwalder's book about internal jealousies among the Dervishes. Some of the Emirs commanded his respect, but only for their fighting qualities. Among them were Nejumi, killed at Toski, and Abu Anga, but the one of whom he had the highest opinion was Osman Digna. He considered that Osman Digna's actions in 1883 and 1884 had

*Ohrwalder spells the name 'Gemaizeh'.

completely frustrated the attempts to keep the lines open, and had led directly to the fall of Khartoum. Osman Digna seems to have achieved almost as much psychologically as by arms, for the stubborn fighting qualities of his men, and their adroit handling, convinced the British government that a relief expedition through Berber was impossible. For seven years after the initial actions Osman Digna continued to harass Suakin, although his fortunes ebbed and flowed. After the first two or three years of intermittent activity he found that apathy had reduced his forces, and at the end of 1886 had hardly any men left to command. However, in January 1887 he collected another 4000 men from Omdurman, and besieged Suakin once more. He also mounted a swift and bloody punitive expedition against the Amarar tribe who had first deserted then defied him.

Kitchener, later to be Commander-in-Chief ('Sirdar') and thus liberator of the Sudan in 1898, was in 1887 appointed 'Governor General of the Eastern Sudan and the Red Sea Littoral'. Kitchener was a quiet, shy, religious, meticulously efficient Royal Engineers officer. Professionally he had shown himself to be highly competent but he was too withdrawn to be popular with his contemporaries. He had been in Egypt since 1882, and his time had been divided between the routine duties of his corps and certain special intelligence assignments. He had accompanied the unsuccessful relief expedition of 1884, and was about to return to England when the Eastern Sudan appointment came through.

His appointment to this independent command soon revealed that he had plenty of original ideas about reconquest, whatever the British government may or may not have had in mind. (At this stage it was not contemplated.) Initially his effective command did not extend beyond Suakin but he took steps to expand it, first by trying to re-establish local alliances, next by military conquest. In neither did he achieve much success. On 17 January 1888 he directed his first battle. Osman Digna was then at Handub, fifteen miles from Suakin. Kitchener's direction of the battle was little short of chaotic. He sent forward infantry with locally recruited forces, but misjudged the distance they had to cover. Although taken by surprise initially Osman Digna was quick to display his normal cool military quality. Noting the disposition of the enemy troops he hurled his men onto the rear of Kitchener's infantry and had some satisfaction in seeing the new local levies disappear over the horizon. When Kitchener arrived with his cavalry his black infantry were already fighting desperately, though still skilfully. Kitchener ordered a withdrawal but was shot through the jaw soon afterwards.

However, the force was extricated safely, and Kitchener was made a colonel. After convalescence he was returned to Cairo and given command of the cavalry at the battle of Toski. When Grenfell resigned in 1892 he was appointed Sirdar in his place. He cannot, perhaps, be said to have deserved the appointment by his handling of troops in the field; nevertheless, subsequent events proved that the appointment – said to be at the instigation of Cromer – had been sound.

While these events were going on yet another European was obtaining a close-up view of the Dervishes, but in far worse circumstances than Slatin or Ohrwalder had known. Charles (Karl) Neufeld was a trader who had come to Egypt in the early 1880s. Although German-born he had acquired such fluency in English and Arabic that he was employed by the army as an interpreter. In the spring of 1887 he set off on a little piece of private enterprise which was, for him, to have the most disastrous consequences. Since the loss of the Sudan, which provided three-quarters of the world's supply of gum-arabic, there had been a desperate shortage of the raw material. As we have seen it had been used for food in the last stages of sieges, but its standard use was on the back of stamps. Neufeld planned to trade in gum-arabic, collecting it himself. The risk of such a venture was enormous but so would be the gain. He was warned against the hazardous enterprise, but nevertheless persisted. Subsequent events followed a predictable pattern. Plans miscarried, the journey proved much more difficult than anticipated, and treachery was afoot. After a brisk engagement he was taken prisoner. Even at this stage his experiences proved worse than those of his fellow Europeans. On first being taken captive Neufeld had assumed that the fact that he came from Germany, a country which had no interest in the Sudan, would make life easier, but the Dervishes, not surprisingly, made no distinction between English and German. The result was that he got the worst of both worlds. When brought before the Khalifa he talked freely and imaginatively about fortification and troops in Egypt, and was regarded, naturally enough, with disfavour by his fellow citizens. Because, as he put it, he 'hesitated a little before replying but not long enough to allow my European blood to cool sufficiently to reply "politely" to the imperious black [the Khalifa] confronting me' he incurred the special animosity of the Dervishes:

'At dawn the following morning a Dervish came to me, and crossing my right hand over the left at the wrist, palms downward, proceeded to bind them together with a rope made of palm fibre. When the rope had, with a bit of wood used as a tourniquet, been drawn well into the flesh, water was poured over them. The agony as the ropes swelled was excruciating; they "bit" into the flesh, and even now I cannot look on the scars on my hands without a shudder, and almost experiencing again the same sensations as those of twelve years ago.

'With the perspiration rolling off me with the pain I was enduring, and no longer able to conceal that I was suffering, I was led forth to be the sport of the rabble. Made to stand in the open space, bareheaded, with thousands around me, I believed the moment for my decapitation had come, and muttering a short prayer I bent my head, but was at once pulled to my feet again; the populace wanted their sport out of me first. Dervishes rushed at me prodding with spears and swords, and while this was going on, two men, one on each side of me, with the mouths of their *ombeyehs* [war trumpets made from elephants' tusks] blew their loudest blasts. One powerful man in particular, with a large spear, gave me the idea it was he who had been told to give the final thrust; and when he had made a number of feints, I tried in successive ones to meet the thrust. One of the men guarding me, taking the chain attached to the ring round my neck, pulled me back each time, much to the delight of the assembled people.

'The ropes with which I was bound had now done their work; the swollen skin gave way, and the horrible tension was removed as the ropes sank into the flesh. If I had exhibited any feeling of pain before, I was now as indifferent to it as I was to the multitude around me. A messenger from the Khalifa asked me "Have you heard the *ombeyehs?*" a bit of the Khalifa's supposed pleasantry, when it was by his orders that the *ombeyehs* had been placed against my ears. On nodding my reply, the messenger continued "The Khalifa has sent me to tell you that he has decided to behead you," to which I replied "Go back to your Khalifa and tell him that neither he nor fifty Khalifas may so much as remove a hair from your head without God's permission. If God's will it is then my head shall be cut off, but it will not be because the Khalifa wills it." He went to the Khalifa with this message, and returned saying "The Khalifa has changed his mind; your head is not to be cut off; you are to be crucified as was your prophet Aisse en Nebbi (Jesus the Prophet); after saying which, he told my guards to take me back to the rukooba while preparations were made.

'By this time, what with fatigue and privations on the journey, my head almost splitting as the results of the *ombeyehs'* blasts, the agony caused by the ropes binding my wrists, and the torture of scores of small irritating and stinging flies attacking the raw flesh on my hands, I was about to faint.'

But he did not faint, and after being taken to the place of execution was suddenly pardoned. His bonds were taken off and he was given abundant food. He passed some food to the *ombeyeh* blowers and derived a grim satisfaction from seeing one could not enjoy it 'as his lips — great thick black ones they were too — were as raw with blowing the *ombeyeh* all night as my hands were with the ropes'.

Slatin, fortunately for Neufeld, suggested to the Khalifa that if Neufeld was taken to a prison he would probably be converted willingly to the Mohammedan religion. He was, of course, in chains:

'I was taken at once to an anvil sunk in the ground until the striking surface was about level with it; first one foot, then the other, had to be placed on the anvil, while more anklets with chains connected were fitted to me. I had now three sets of shackles, and another ring and chain was fitted to my neck. During my twelve years in: chains, and amongst the hundreds who came directly under my observation, I never saw, as has been illustrated in some papers, any prisoner with chains from the neck connected with wrists or ankles.'

However if the burden of the chains was not too insupportable the atmosphere in the prison was. Many of the other prisoners were old soldiers of the Egyptian army who had been taken prisoner at the fall of Khartoum and elsewhere 'and they waited day after day, week after week, and year after year, still hoping that the Government for whom they had fought would send troops to release them; but with the greater number their release came only with death — at the gallows, and the Khalifa's shambles, or by disease and starvation.'

Neufeld's conversion to Mohammedanism proved a slower process than his captors had expected. The sticking-point was that while Neufeld was quite prepared to accept the orthodox Mohammedan faith he was not ready to be convinced by Mahdism. This was done purposely. He knew that to refuse Mohammedanism could have fatal consequences but he also knew that if he accepted Mahdism he would soon find himself having to prove the genuineness of his conviction by leading a troop of Dervishes against the British. In spite of setbacks his condition gradually improved. His greatest danger was that his captors might suddenly become upset or excited and finish him off; the abiding risk as a prisoner of a primitive but nervous captor is that he will suddenly do something which a few minutes later he will regret. The prisoner therefore may be beaten up without reason one minute, and then presented with food he cannot swallow by a guard who is now as full of remorse as he was of irrational anger a few minutes before.

Neufeld wrote:

'My first spell in prison was one of four years. After nine months the rings and chains were removed from my neck, but the fetters I wore continuously — with the exception of thirteen days — during the whole of my captivity.'

He described a typical routine under these conditions:

'There were thirty guardians, each armed with a "courbag" (rhinoceros-hide whip) with which to keep their charges in order. There were no sanitary arrangements, not even of the most primitive description. All prisoners had to be fed by their friends and relatives; if they had neither they starved to death, as the prisoners, charitable as they were to each other in the matter of food, had barely enough to eat to keep body and soul together, for the best and greater part of the food sent in, was eaten by the guardians.

'At sunrise each morning the door of the common cell was opened, and the prisoners were allowed to shuffle down to the banks of the Nile a few yards distant, for their ablutions and for water for drinking.' [Prayers were recited at intervals throughout the day.]

'It has been found impossible, even in the most guarded and disguised language to insert here a real word-picture of a night in the prison. The scenes of bestiality and filthiness, the means employed for bringing the most powerful man to his knees with a single blow, the nameless crimes committed night after night, and year after year, may not be recorded in print. At times, and sometimes for weeks ii succession, from 250 to 280 prisoners were driven into that small room; we were packed in and there was scarcely room to move our arms; jibbehs swarmed with insects and parasites which in themselves made sleep impossible and life a misery. As the heat grew more oppressive, and the atmosphere — always vile with the ever-present stench of the place — grew closer with the perspiring bodies, and with other causes, all semblance of human beings was lost. Any prisoner who went down on such a night never got up again alive; his cries would not be heard above the pandemonium of clanking chains and bars, imprecations and cursings, and for any one to attempt to bend down to assist, if he did hear, only meant his going down also. In the morning when we were allowed to stream out, five or six bodies would be found on the ground with the life crushed and trampled out of them.

'Occasionally, when the uproar was greater than usual, the guards would open the door and, standing in the doorway, lash at the heads of the prisoners with their hide whips. Always when this occured death claimed its five or six victims, crushed and trampled to death. I wish I might say I had drawn on my imagination for what is given above; I can but assure you it gives but the very faintest idea of what really occurred.'

The hardships of prison life were greatly alleviated for Neufeld by various people, who included 'an old Greek lady, Catarina, who was a ministering angel alike to prisoners and captives' — and Father Ohrwalder: 'Surely the recording angel has placed to the right side of the account the little deceptions practised by Father Ohrwalder to gain access to the prison, when the few piastres of baksheesh he could afford were not sufficient to satisfy the rapacity of the guards, in order to bring me some little dainty when, God knows, he was bringing me the lion's share of what he was in absolute need himself. Time after time he was turned away from the gates, and this, too, after having paid the baksheesh; but his persistence secured his seeing me every one or two months during my first three years in prison, and the scraps of news he brought from the outside world — news to both of us though a year or two old — gave me something to think over and turn over in my brain until the next visit. Death, as I told Father Ohrwalder, I did not fear, but my great fear was insanity.'

Gradually Neufeld's lot improved, although he was still chained. In early life he had begun to study medicine and as a trader had become known as a practical physician. Now his reputation reached Omdurman and he found himself doctor to the gaolers' harems. His duties frequently included childbirth. The only medicine he could procure was permanganate of potash, with which he treated everything; this was applied in crystal, not liquid, form and the 'results were eminently satisfactory both to the patients and myself'.

The prison population included a very wide variety of people, and even women:

'Married women were sent to prison on all sorts of charges, ranging from suspected conjugal infidelity to the delivery of a certain lecture. A charge of infidelity "not proven" as the Scotch have it, was followed by imprisonment and the application of three hundred stripes with the courbag, and when the woman had recovered from these she would be sent into the house of one of the gaolers to be the maid of work for everyone there; she would have to grind corn, attend to the children, carry water, and be driven as a slave night and day for weeks. A Mrs Caudle or a termagant received from fifty to eighty lashes and she too on recovery would be sent into one of the gaolers' harems to work as hard as her possibly innocent and more severely punished companion in misery. A few weeks of such treatment sent the women back home completely cured of the faults for which they were sent to prison to be corrected, besides which the relation of their experiences acted as an effective deterrent on budding Mrs Caudles and others.'

However, being a part-time doctor did not prevent Neufeld from being employed unloading boats, with the rhinoceros whip to keep his efforts constant. Once, when he was recovering from typhus, a young gaoler tried to extract money from Neufeld, believing he had some. The upshot was that the gaoler knocked him out with a *safarof* (a form of boomerang used in the Sudan in precisely the same way as boomerangs are used in Australia) and had him condemned to 500 lashes. However, after about sixty Neufeld lost consciousness and the flogging stopped.

A flogging at this prison was an appalling punishment:

'The maximum number of stripes ever ordered was a

thousand, and this number was often actually given, but in every case the stripes were given over the clothing. The rules of flogging were generally as follows: the first two hundred on the back below the region of the lumbar vertebrae, the third and fourth hundred on the shoulders, and the fifth hundred on the breast. When the maximum number of one thousand lashes was ordered, they were always given on the same parts as those of the first two hundred, and this punishment was resorted to for the purpose of extorting confessions.'

Neufeld mentions that large numbers died under the castigation or as the result of it later. Hideous though these punishments were they may in fact have been less in effect than a hundred strokes of the cat-o'-nine tails, which had gone out of use in England for certain military punishments only a few years before

When Neufeld was flogged it was usually because he had defied his captors. He found the experience worse mentally than physically:

'There was I, a European, a Prussian, a man who had fought with the British troops in what transpired to be the "too late" expedition to release Gordon, a white and a Christian, chained and helpless, being flogged by a black, as much a captive and a slave as I was, and yet my superior and master. It is impossible for anyone not having undergone a similar experience to appreciate the mental agonies I endured.

'I may have been self-willed and strong-headed; I may, if you wish have acted like a fool in my constant defiance of the Khalifa and the tenets of the Mahdi, but now, looking back on those terrible times I feel convinced that had poor Gordon lived, my actions would at least have met with his approbation.

'Death, in whatever form it came, would have come as a welcome visitor to me; but while doing all in my power to exasperate my captors to kill me something – hope, courage, a clinging to life, pride in my race, or personal vanity in defying them to the end – restrained me from taking my own life, though heaven knows, if ever a man had a good excuse for doing so, I had.'

Earlier, Neufeld had mentioned what happened to married women who were suspected of adultery, but of which there was no proof. If the woman was foolish enough to confess, as she sometimes did, possibly with the aid of torture, she was buried up to her neck in the ground and then stoned to death. A man could have four wives and a harem full of female slaves and concubines, but a woman was restricted to one husband and master. Infidelity even by a concubine was punished with flogging. However, divorce was much easier than in other countries. A man merely had to say 'You are divorced' and that was that. If a woman was pregnant she' would declare the fact; if the child was male the divorce was null and void; if it was female the husband had to support the mother for two years and the child for seven.

Neufeld not only had an exacting time during his twelve years' imprisonment but after his release, also suffered from accusations of being a collaborator. Where he might have expected widespread admiration for his courage and endurance he found suspicion, disbelief and even hatred. He had been dismissed as a speculative trader who had gone on a foolhardy expedition into the Sudan, and no one subsequently troubled to find out more about him. Slatin was well-known as a competent governor, and was regarded by the Dervishes as something of a military genius on account of the resistance he had put up before being captured; however, there were doubts* about him too, and had he not been backed so wholeheartedly by Wingate his subsequent career might have been quite different. Father Ohrwalder was a priest who had managed to escape — he was generally commended. Neufeld, the most indomitable of all, got no credit for his staunchness; neither the German nor the British government raised a finger on his behalf; in fact the German government disowned him in 1890 on the basis that he had lived in Egypt so long that he had lost his German

*Wilfred Scawen Blunt attacked him and there were many who deplored his conversion to the Islamic faith.

nationality. It was said that he had neglected opportunites to escape (of which there had been none) and no credit was given to him for useful information he had managed to pass to the advancing relief force. During the final stages of his captivity he had been set to making saltpetre and casting coins; he had made sure that the former was useless for gunpowder and that the latter used up vital parts from the Khalifa's river steamers. Confronting these bizarre accusations was too much for his health, and it was only when Sir George Newnes serialized his story in *The Wide World* Magazine and Chapman and Hall published his book in 1899 that the evidence to support him came to light. After his recovery he continued to lead an adventurous life until his death in 1918; in the First World War he acted as an interpreter to German military missions in Africa.

Neufeld felt that Kitchener made a grave error and caused the death of many British soldiers when he later 'gave quarter'. He was well aware that in saying so he would be accused of vindictive bitterness but he reaffirmed:

'For let it be remembered that when a dervish sits or lies wounded, he is wounded to death, and only by force of will keeps himself alive until he dies happy at the moment he sends his spear through the heart of his would-be saviour. I repeat, the Sirdar committed a grave error in extending to the dervishes the advantages of civilized warfare. I who have lived amongst the people, who have discussed with their greatest exponents of the religious law, and made comparisons between the administration of their and our laws consider that I am well qualified to express an opinion.

'The day after the battle of Kirkeban [in 1885 — the Gordon relief expedition] an outpost was being sent forward. Moving its position it espied a wounded dervish making signs for water. One of the soldiers slipped off his camel to give him some, and his comrades moved on. As time went on and their chum did not catch them up, they came back to see what had happened. There he was, still attending to the wounded dervish, his hand resting on his shoulder, but there was no movement from either. Approaching — this was the tale plainly written. The lines of the ground showed that the "Tommy" had taken the wounded man in his arms, and half supporting and half dragging him, had placed him in a sitting posture in the shade, with his back against a rock; then, taking his water-bottle, he began to pour the life-giving drops down the throat of the dervish, for he still grasped the empty water-bottle. With returning life came, of course, returning strength — sufficient strength for the dervish to slip off his knife, poise his hand for a second of time behind "Tommy's" back while he was occupied with his mission of mercy, and then, plunging it in with sufficient force to divide the spinal column, the dervish died happy as "Tommy" fell dead across his shoulder. That dervish was glorified in the Sudan, and thousands of others were waiting the opportunity of dying as gloriously.'

The problem of course was that the wounded Dervish wanted to die, but wanted to die killing. In that way he would go straight to heaven. Life on earth, with such a golden opportunity missed, would be agony for him. Many British soldiers, kind and merciful by nature, died before they realized that a wounded Dervish was nearly as dangerous as an unwounded one, and learnt to give them a wide berth.*

In Neufeld's view the fighting qualities of the Dervish were so great that he feared they might be underestimated by the English. At night they would be unbeatable, he thought:

'At close quarters the dervish horde was more than a match for the best drilled army in Europe. Swift and silent in their movement, covering the ground at four or five times the speed of trained troops, every man, when the moment of attack came accustomed to fight independently of orders, lithe, supple, nimble as cats and as bloodthirsty as starving man-eating tigers, utterly regardless of their own lives, and capable of continuing stabbing and jabbing with spear and sword while carrying half a dozen wounds, any one of which would have put a European hors de combat — such were the

---

*The same experience was repeated in Burma in 1944 when wounded Japanese would use their last grenade on their would-be helpers.

75,000 to 80,000 warriors which the Khalifa had ready to attack the Sirdar's little army. Artillery, rifles and bayonets would have been of little avail against a horde like this rushing a camp by night.'

During the battle of Omdurman two Dervishes came to Neufeld to have bullets extracted. Neither bullet was very deep and he dug them out with a penknife.

'Maybe, with a European, chloroform might have been necessary for the extraction of the bullet in the arm but with the Sudanese — have I not already said that a dervish can continue leaping and stabbing with a dozen severe wounds in his body. A dervish can and will kill at the moment when the ventricles of the heart make their last contraction. Bodily pain, as we know it, is unknown to them. Many times have I applied, and seen applied, red-hot charcoal to sores with the patients calmly looking on. With my present patients, after dabbing a little carbolic acid on the wounds, I asked what news they brought.'

Not least of Neufeld's worries after he had been released was the account then current of his hero Gordon's death. As he put it, 'the first to relate the story of Gordon's death was a man whose tongue Gordon threatened to cut out as the only cure for his inveterate lying, and when he escaped and reached Cairo, in telling his tale he sustained his reputation'. Neufeld noted that the accounts of Ohrwalder and Slatin both bore a suspiciously close resemblance to this man's account. But as Neufeld put it:

'Those who knew Charles George Gordon will believe me when I aver that he died, as they must all believe that he died — in spite of official and semi-official accounts to the contrary — as the soldier and lion-hearted man that he was. Gordon did not rest his head on the hilt of his sword and turn his back to his enemies to receive his mortal wound. Gordon drew his sword and used it. When Gordon fell his sword was dripping with the blood of his assailants, for no less than sixteen or seventeen did he cut down with it. When Gordon fell his left hand was blackened with the unburned powder from his at least thrice-emptied revolver. When Gordon fell, his life's blood was pouring from a spear and pistol shot wound in his right breast. When Gordon fell his boots were slippery with the blood of the crowd of dervishes he shot and hacked his way through, in his heroic attempt to cut his way out and place himself at the head of his troops. Gordon died, as only Gordon could die.'

Hero worship? Wishful thinking? Perhaps. But when we look at Gordon's previous career the official version of his tame acceptance of death at the hands of a few Dervishes seems hard to believe. The detailed account given at first was subsequently contradicted, then reaffirmed. In one version Gordon was wearing an immaculate white suit, which seems a little improbable, in another a dark one. However one looks at it, it seems unlikely that Gordon did not die fighting.

8

The Reconquest of Dongola

By the year 1896 Egypt, thanks to Cromer's reforms, was in a sounder economic position than ever before, and because the financial background was secure it had been possible to improve the army beyond all recognition. As has been noted, there was nothing wrong with the Egyptian soldier if he was properly armed, trained, equipped, paid, fed and led. When the army was given a little more verve and dash by the introduction of some black Sudanese infantry it was clear that this was a force to be reckoned with. However, there was no certainty that it would be used. Although the stories which came from the Sudan, notably through Slatin and Ohrwalder, convinced the outside world that the Khalifa's regime was an appalling tyranny, this on its own would not convince Britain that she had any obligation, moral or otherwise, to go in and 'restore order'. Public conscience had been a little troubled by the failure to support Gordon but what went on in the wilder parts of Africa was thought to be none of an ordinary British citizen's business; the right people to rectify that situation were the missionaries. There was, of course, a feeling of irritation and ignominy that the British had been tumbled out of the Sudan by an ill-armed collection of fanatics, but it had all happened too long ago to matter. Rather more significant was the thought that if Britain, or her protégé Egypt, did not reoccupy the Sudan someone else soon would. There were plenty of interested parties France, Belgium and Germany in particular. Of these France looked the most dangerous contender. Anglo-French suspicion and rivalry had not diminished over the years — and there were well-founded rumours that the French were planning to claim the area of the White Nile. In the event, however, it was none of these countries which spurred the British government into taking action, but Italy; and it was not because Italy was getting too strong but because she had proved to be dangerously weak. In 1884 Britain, in agreement with other powers who were making equally advantageous arrangements for themselves, had declared a Protectorate over Somaliland. France and Italy were quick to establish themselves in the same area with French Somaliland and Italian Somaliland, but in 1896 the Italians overreached themselves and were defeated by the Abyssinians at Adowa. Furthermore, they now came under great Dervish pressure at Kassala. It was reported that they thereupon asked the British government to make a military move which would relieve this pressure. To everyone's astonishment Britain promptly authorized an expedition to reclaim Dongola.

The niceties of the reasoning behind this move do not concern us here. Cynically, the motive was thought to be less to aid the Italians than to warn off the French from making inroads into the Sudan. Cromer, who had planned to use Egyptian revenue to build an Aswan dam — a dream which many would have before the dam was built — was not informed until the orders had been given. He was taken aback; it was one thing to support an army, another entirely to finance a conquest of some half million miles of territory. Nevertheless he raised the money. It was a considerable relief no doubt to feel that the campaign would be concluded by a Sirdar who had been appointed almost as much for his economical habits as for his military prowess.

It might have been thought that as the British government had ordered the retaking of Dongola, the British government would be pleased to foot the bill. This view was soon shown to be an illusion. The entire responsibility was left to the Egyptians. Eventually the British government had to produce a loan of £800,000 (and subsequently wrote it off) but that was only because Egypt's finances were subject to the 'Mixed Tribunals'. The Mixed Tribunals, consisting of representatives from Britain, Germany, Austria, Italy, France and Russia,

had been established in 1876 when Egypt was so hopelessly
in arrears with the interest on her borrowings that she would
have needed to pay over half her entire revenue each year to
keep up with it. The Mixed Tribunals, acting in the interest of
European bond holders, had to sanction any abnormal
expenditure, and some of its members did not feel that they
should be pushed to an expensive reconquest at the instigation of Britain: the two members of the Tribunal who felt
this most strongly were Frence and Russia. Nevertheless the
expenditure was sanctioned. But, after protest from France
and Russia that the decision to advance this money must be
unanimous, the sanction was withdrawn. Britain had to pay
for the war after all.

It was, of course, the perfect opportunity for Kitchener.
This was not an occasion when dash, flexibility of mind and
boldness to the point of recklessness would turn the scale.
It was to be a slow grinding campaign over hundreds of miles
of barren country, a campaign in which a fierce but
ill-organized enemy must be worn down then fought to a
standstill. It was not, however, by any standards anything
but a very difficult and dangerous campaign.

There were two main reasons why the idea of reconquering
the Sudan now attracted the British government. One
was that the Conservatives had been returned to power
in 1895 and felt very strongly that if their defeated opponents, the Liberals, had opposed the reconquest of the
Sudan it should and must be done now. The second
was that five years before, in 1891, there had been a
successful precedent when Colonel Holland-Smith, then
the Governor of Suakin, had decided to recapture Tokar.
After a series of spirited engagements and one major
battle his force of 2000 had entirely defeated the best
that Osman Digna could put against them. The significance of this little campaign was not merely that Osman
Digna had been driven from the area by the loss of his
main supply centre but that the newly reorganized Egyptian army had remained steady against the worst that
the Dervishes could mount against it. By calm disciplined

behaviour the Egyptians were able to kill the Dervishes before they could indulge in hand-to-hand fighting. There was some luck in this engagement and the value of the new Egyptian army was probably over-emphasized, but the effect on morale at all levels was enormous.

Kitchener's army was tiny by modern standards. It amounted to 18,000 men, and was divided into fourteen infantry battalions. Of these, eight were composed of Egyptian fellaheen, and six of Sudanese blacks; these latter would add 'fire'. There were four cavalry squadrons and three artillery batteries. There was a small corps of support troops. As it was an army living on credit from the start it must have been one of the most economically equipped forces ever to take the field. It was a parsimonious quartermaster's dream. Uniforms were not 'worn out' until they were threadbare, and not always then. Nothing was ever considered unserviceable until it had almost ceased to exist. At the outset the army looked as if it had survived an arduous campaign without re-equipment; by the time it had been in the field a month or two it was scarcely smarter in appearance than its adversaries. But its appearance bore no resemblance to its fighting efficiency. It was properly paid, properly equipped, and properly led.

There were, on average, 750 men in each battalion; and in each of the battalion's six companies there were four British officers. It made a useful fighting force but, as might perhaps be expected, Egyptian pride was hurt by having so much of the army officered by British. The Khedive was most sensitive on this point, and made even more so by the fact that he was considered such a bad security risk that he was only informed about movements after they had actually begun. However, he was well thought of by the army if not by the Higher Command.

The campaign of 1896 was a triumph of logistical planning over fierce adversaries fighting in the depths of almost impossible country. In this, the railway was to prove all important, but there were many other factors involved as well. Inevitably there were camels and steamers. Before the expedition even set foot in the Sudan it would be 800 miles from its main base. Long before the vanguard had reached Wadi Halfa the Dervishes knew from their spies what was portending. Similar news came to them from the Eastern Sudan where reinforcements had been put in. The advance up the Nile was led by Major H.A. Macdonald, a tough enterprising soldier who had risen from the ranks. He advanced forty miles and took Akasha without opposition. This was then fortified while the rest of the expedition closed up. It was March 1896. The Dervishes were known to be very strong at Firket, a mere ten miles away, but apart from a few skirmishes no real fighting took place before June. By that time Kitchener had brought up a formidable force which included ten infantry battalions, with supporting artillery and cavalry. On 7 June this army overwhelmed Firket, and two days later had taken Suarda, twenty-five miles farther on. As the line of communications lengthened supply became an increasing problem. Up to the First Cataract (at Aswan) supply had been handled very competently by Thomas Cook's river steamers; after that it had to go overland. There had been a railway between Wadi Halfa and Firket but little of it remained. Winston Churchill, who was accompanying the expedition, observed one grim relic, a railway line which had been torn up to make a gallows; at the foot of it was a heap of bleached bones.

By now the line of communications from Cairo was active along its entire length. So far events had progressed much better than anyone's most optimistic expectations. After Firket the situation began to change. The autumn of 1896 brought floods and, almost inevitably, with them cholera. There were over 2000 men at Suarda and a further 7000 at Firket. This was no mean supply problem in itself. It was obvious that further successful progress depended on the railway.

The next step forward would obviously be a difficult one. Although the railway builders were pressing on at all possible speed they did not reach Koshesh (six miles beyond Firket) till 4 August. The next step was eighty-six miles by land, and

127 miles by river. This was Kerma, where the Dervishes were known to be ready and waiting. Over the years the Dervishes had learned the military lesson that it is better to fight your opponent where his lines of communication are stretched to near breaking-point, even if the battlefield is on your own doorstep. It was considered desirable therefore, if not essential, for a flotilla of gunboats to assist the Egyptian army. The total number eventually made available was ten, although only three were new and three were not gunboats at all but hastily converted Nile steamers. But the new gunboats, which were shipped out in sections, were well worth having. They were 140 feet long, compared with the 90 feet of the others; they were well protected by steel plates and they had an impressive array of armaments: one 12-pounder, two 6-pounders, and four Maxims. Their equipment was modern in every way, and included such refinements as ammunition hoists and searchlights; but one of their greatest assets was that they drew only thirty-nine inches of water. These were so good and so efficient that it was rumoured at one time that they must be German. In fact they were north-country British.

Similarly, it was assumed that the creator of the railways was French. He was in fact French-Canadian, and a product of Kingston, Canada, but he had joined the British army and specialized in railways. His name was Lieutenant E.P.C. Girouard, of the Royal Engineers. Building a railways is always a complex matter, and on this occasion more so than usual. Components came from a variety of different places, the terrain was extremely difficult, the weather was exhaustingly hot, and the labour force had to be trained.

H.L. Pritchard, who published a book entitled *The Sudan Campaign* in 1899 under the pseudonym of 'An Officer', described the feelings of the soldiers taking part in the expedition. It was clear to the army long before the expedition was officially sanctioned that something would have to be done to settle the Dervishes. The latter had employed various irritating methods of frontier raiding which needed to be stopped. They used to come across the desert with a supply of water-skins and having dropped them half-way would descend on a village, murder every man, woman, and child, and then retreat. The Wadi Halfa garrison would then set off in pursuit, but before they had been overtaken the Dervishes would have watered their horses at the water cache, and set off again. The pursuers, having no such staging point, would be forced to turn back. On one occasion the Dervishes had even raided a game of polo, and got away before they could be suitably chastised.

Pritchard had a good idea of the logistical problems involved in subduing the Dervishes.

'How was the force to be supplied on the march to the battle and, more especially, after it. Behind them would be one hundred miles of continuous cataract, preventing the supplies being brought by river; to bring them by camel over one hundred miles of bad road through the burning desert, where not an ounce of food could be got, would mean a most stupendous number of camels for even a small force. A baggage camel will carry 300lbs twenty miles a day. He eats 10 lbs of food a day. He occupies ten days in going one hundred miles and back, so he only brings up 200 lbs for the force. He must have rest every now and again and he will die on the least provocation. To take a month's supply one hundred miles for ten thousand men, about fifteen thousand camels are required, and then when a further advance of two hundred miles is made to Dongola and the Merowi, what is to be done then?'

The answer was clear: river transport and a railway. 'It looks a simple plan but it needed a man who knew the country and the enemy to make it, and a mistake in the scheme would be heavily paid for. Any one who has seen the inhospitable, barren, grilling Batn el Haggar, will understand what a mistake in the supply of a force would mean. It stopped the Romans, Greeks, and Persians. Simple the plan looks, but it was not so simple to execute.'

He mentioned some of the problems:

'A railway battalion was formed by enlisting under the conscription act several hundred of the fellaheen, who had no more idea how to lay a railway than to fly. To superintend them several so-called native platelayers were sent up from Lower Egypt. Naturally they proved with few exceptions to be all the useless scoundrels discharged from the Lower Egypt railways; the same with the engine-drivers, they were nearly all native stokers, with the most limited knowledge of how to drive or look after an engine, and with the most reckless disregard of consequences. When one puts an ignorant but reckless native engine-driver on a patched-up condemned locomotive with no brakes, to drive a train of worn-out trucks along a track laid by men who have never seen a rail and don't understand a straight line, or the necessity for exactitude; and when this track climbs up and down and in and out among switchback gradients and sharp corners then you get all the elements required to produce the most exciting and exhilarating railway travelling.'

At Gemai cholera took a steady toll. Alford, a young subaltern, wrote:

'In times like these the ties that bind officers and men together are drawn closer; and in time of peace the British soldier is inclined to think that his officers are put over him solely for the purpose of giving him his pay and "telling him off". This is a survival of olden days, when the officers looked on their duties and responsibilities from much the same point of view. That class of officer, however, is happily extinct; and the officer of today realizes it is his duty to interest himself in his men's welfare to the best of his ability; and the soldier is beginning to realize his best friend is his officer.'

The next stage of the advance began on 23 August:

'It was like going on leave when we marched out of Koshesh, after the long hot period of waiting and preparing. The weather was still very hot, but we did not feel the heat so much now we knew we should soon be in touch with the Dervishes and turning them out of Dongola.'

The force was as follows:

Half a battalion of the North Staffordshire Regiment
One Maxim battery Connaught Rangers
Six squadrons Egyptian cavalry, under Lieutenant-

Colonel Burn-Murdoch.

Camel Corps under Major Tudway

Three mule and one horse battery

1st Brigade under Major Lewis; 9th and 10th Sudanese and 3rd and 4th Egyptian

2nd Brigade under Major Macdonald; 11th, 12th and 13th Sudanese

3rd Brigade under Major Maxwell; 2nd, 7th, and 8th Egyptian

4th Brigade under Major David; 1st, 15th, and half 5th Egyptian

Four gunboats under Commander Colville, R.N., with Lieutenants Beatty and Robertson, R.N., and Captain Oldfield, R.M.A., commanding boats

The total strength was about 12,000.

The 6th Battalion had been left at Koshesh, and half the 5th was to stay at Fereig.

The 5th, 6th, 7th and 8th Battalions were commanded and entirely officered by Egyptian officers. All the others were commanded by English officers, with two other English officers to each Egyptian, and three to each Sudanese battalion.

There were also three unarmed steamers.

Kerma, their destination, was on the east bank of the Nile, six miles beyond the top of the cataract. By 14 September the cavalry were reconnoitring the area. In Pritchard's words:

'During their reconnaissance they encountered a few Dervish cavalry, which gave rise to an incident more suitable to ancient warfare. The Emir commanding the Dervish scouts, seeing one of our squadrons approaching, galloped out brandishing his spear and sword, and making his horse prance the while he shouted insults at the Egyptians. An Egyptian trooper promptly took up the challenge and charged him, but the Dervish dodged the lance point and missed the Egyptian with his sword. Captain Whitler then put an end to this tournament business by riding out and shooting the Emir.'

The boats made good progress with the exception of one which stuck on the very last rock of the cataract. This was

(*Above left*) Rudolf Slatin in formal dress
(*Below left*) Charles Neufeld in captivity
(*Above*) The Sirdar: Maj.-Gen. Sir H. H. Kitchener

(*Above*) The execution of the Batahin. This tribe had refused to send any more soldiers to the Khalifa's army

(*Below*) The Khalifa's flag. The inscription reads: 'In the name of the most compassionate and merciful/Thou Living, Thou Existing and Most Glorious source of generosity/There is no God but God. Mohammed is the messenger of God/Mohammed El Mahdi is the Khalifa of the messenger of God'

The Sirdar's flotilla

(*Above*) Gunboats being hauled through a cataract

(*Below*) A Nile gunboat in action

Snapshots taken after the battle of the Atbara—(*above*) Mahmud in bloodstained *jibbah* is questioned by Col. Wingate; (*below*) Guards officers at ease in the desert

(*Above*) Camerons and Seaforths bury their dead after the battle of the Atbara

(*Below*) Looters 'souvenir-hunting' on the battlefield of Omdurman

(*Above*) The Mahdi's shell-damaged tomb after the battle

(*Below*) Prisoners passing the Khalifa's prayer-house in Omdurman

After the campaign: Lt. the Hon. R. Molyneux talking to Lt. Winston Churchill

sheer bad luck for although the water was high enough for the boats to negotiate the cataracts – even if it occasionally meant some assistance by rope haulage from the land – there was always the chance of a strong eddy lowering the level temporarily. 'All night long,' Pritchard wrote, 'the gunboats were snorting and puffing, trying to get the unfortunate one off, but without success.'

By 9.30 a.m. on 19 September the force reached Kerma and to their surprise found the fort evacuated. On examining the good position and thick embrasured walls, they were relieved to find it empty, for to have taken it by force would have been costly. However, when they came to examine the new Dervish position on the opposite bank they realized that the next move would be even more difficult.

'The navigable channel of the river at this point is not very wide, and to get through the gunboats would have to pass close by the Dervish position. The Dervishes were occupying some excellently placed low trenches connecting six earth gun emplacements. Behind in the desert could be seen about three thousand Dervish horse and foot waiting out of range of the gunboats to fall on any force that attempted to cross the river. It looked a very stiff nut to crack. The gunboats were having a pretty warm time. They are provided with steel plates which protect the great part of the boat from rifle fire; but people walking about from one part of the boat to the other are exposed, and, of course, the boats are not proof against shell-fire. One shell passed right through the magazine of a gunboat but did not explode, and did not touch any ammunition.'

After half an hour Commander Colville was hit in the wrist. While he was having a quick dressing put on the Egyptian helmsman decided it would be a good idea to alter course and retreat downstream again. The Dervishes were so elated at seeing the gunboat in retreat that they jumped up on to their parapets; however they soon took cover when the Maxims were turned in their direction. As soon as he took in the situation Colville brought the boat round again.

However, for the moment, Kitchener's army was in

177

deadlock. If he tried to cross at this point the casualties would be enormous. There were, of course, plenty willing to try it. Nevertheless Kitchener decided that the best policy was to let the gunboats push on past the Dervish position without taking it. By this means they could reach Dongola, further up the river on the same side. Once there, however vulnerable their position, there was every chance that their presence would be sufficiently disconcerting to the Dervishes to make their main force fall back. Once this happened the expedition could cross the river at Kerma. The appreciation proved correct. Although the Dervish commander, Wad Bishara, did his utmost to make his men hold the Kerma position, he was unable to do much as he had been wounded in the head by shell-fire. It was a lucky shot for the expedition, for Wad Bishara showed more ability at generalship than anyone else it encountered then or later. The rest of the Dervishes, knowing very well what would have happened to enemy property had they themselves penetrated behind the lines, could not wait to see what the gunboat crews might not be up to in Dongola. As a result the expedition crossed unopposed – at Kerma.

The gunboats returned from Dongola and reported it empty of troops, but as they came down river they had seen the Dervish army marching upstream and estimated its numbers at 5000. The expedition tackled the thirty-five miles of the next leg by setting off at 5 p.m. on 21 September, marching till midnight; halting till 4 a.m., marching till 9.30 a.m., halting during the heat of the day, marching again from 4 p.m. till midnight, and so on. Six miles outside Dongola they halted and prepared for a possible attack on their position. It did not come and they were able to listen to the gunboats bombarding Dongola: 'The land force were rather sore at the gunboats having all the fun, and I think an officer expressed the opinion of all when he said "Damn those gunboats, why can't they shut up? They will frighten them all away." '

The attack on Dongola was fixed for the following day. By this time it was fully occupied by the Dervish force from Kerma. By the type of miscalculation which was perhaps occasionally inevitable, but was becoming too familiar in this campaign, Dongola was several miles farther on than had been thought. The expedition was therefore an hour later in reaching it than they had expected.

On a ridge ahead of them the invasion force saw what they estimated as 2000 Dervishes. In front was a body of Dervish cavalry. As the army closed up the Dervishes began a steady fire from their brass cannons. Naturally enough, the mounted elements in Kitchener's force were ordered to work their way around the Dervish flanks while the infantry brigades attacked from the front. Had the Dervishes possessed sufficient machine-guns and artillery their frontal assault, even with cavalry diversions, would have finished off Kitchener's force then and there, but to everyone's astonishment the cavalry advance caused the Dervishes on the ridge to disappear promptly from view. And soon it became obvious that they were not going to stand and fight. The town was found to be empty.

The reason for the Dervish retreat was not clear at the time and is still somewhat of a mystery. It was certainly not for lack of courage. However, after a series of defeats and the constant drain on their manpower from other battles, internal and external, it was probably becoming clear to the Khalifa that resources should not be carelessly squandered. At Dongola they had probably decided to retreat in good order, drawing the expeditionary force further and further into bleak country until it could be annihilated as the unfortunate Hicks's column had been. Certainly, any further advance to which Kitchener might have been tempted would be sown with perils. The portion of the Nile which lay ahead was one of the most difficult stretches, containing the fourth cataract, which impedes navigation for 135 miles. On land, there was the formidable Bayuda desert.

However, events did not go according to Dervish plan. The Egyptian army followed up the retreating Dervishes faster and more skilfully than anticipated. Some of the Dervish rearguard were drawn into a fight they did not want and could not win. Finally the Dervishes lost control of the retreat and let it turn into a rout. As the gunboats were patrolling up and down the Nile at this point the Dervishes struck off into the desert to avoid being harassed by machine-gun fire, but the effect of trying to take a route they did not know across a barren desert was disastrous. Many died of thirst; others, including 700 Sudanese riflemen who, like mercenaries, sold themselves to the highest bidder, returned and cheerfully joined the Egyptian army. The pursuers were able to press right on to Korti and Merowe, which were empty.

Everyone was pleased. The first part of the campaign had gone so well that its hardships, the heat, the floods, the cholera and the administrative failures, tended to be overlooked. Deaths from cholera and other causes were six times as high as deaths in battle, and many officers had to be sent home as being unfit for further service.

The Nile battles were not, however, the only successes. The Suakin situation, for so long a poisoned thorn in the foot of the British lion, was now ready for surgery. This view was also held by Osman Digna, with different reasoning. His feeling was that the foot of the lion should be amputated altogether and in April 1896 had brought up to Suakin a force of 300 cavalry, 70 camel soldiers, and 2500 infantry.

Against this was a force commanded by Lieutenant-Colonel G.E. Lloyd, D.S.O., of the South Staffordshire Regiment, which included a squadron of Egyptian cavalry, two mountain guns and eight companies from different parts of the Egyptian army. It was subsequently joined by 250 men from the 10th Sudanese Battalion. It was highly mobile; each man carried 200 cartridges, six days' forage and rations, a day's reserve of water, and a blanket.

Progress was steady but not uneventful. After nineteen miles the cavalry was attacked by Dervishes and suffered a number of casualties before driving them off. Other parts of the force were more fortunate, and had several less costly engagements against the Dervishes. Here as at Dongola (later in the year although earlier in this narrative) the Dervishes showed no plan of campaign against well-disciplined forces with better fire-power. The British force was surprised that the redoubtable Osman Digna should submit to his soldiers being driven out of the area without more attempts at ambushes or counter-attacks. However, as we will see later, the Dervishes were pinning everything on a culminating victory at the very gates of their capital. Furthermore Osman Digna was not the sort of general to ·fight a battle his opponents wanted him to fight, unless he had a better reason for doing so than they had.

When the campaign had been carried as far as seemed feasible the column returned to Suakin and Osman Digna's forces were able to continue much as before in the hinterland. However, in order to relieve the column now based in the unpleasant station of Suakin 4000 troops from the Indian army were sent as replacements. This brigade, commanded by Colonel Egerton, D.S.O., an officer with an excellent and enterprising record, was then left to rot away in Suakin. The summer temperature varied between 103 °F and 115°F. For seven months the brigade endured scurvy, malaria, abscess of the liver and a variety of other depressing diseases. Even the horses developed new diseases. After seven months, now a wreck of its former efficient, mobile self, it was returned to India. By that time the question of who should pay for its transport to, and uselesss sojourn in, Suakin, had developed into a bitter argument between England and the government of India. In the end India paid approximately £35,000 and England met the remaining total of about £280,000.

From start to finish it had been a sorry enterprise.

9

Doldrums in 1897

'Dongola', as Pritchard put it, 'was not exactly the place one would choose to live in. It is barely above water at high Nile so that we found the whole place saturated with every sort of fly.' He continued:

'When an expedition reaches its goal and the strain of urgency is removed, a reaction sets in. Small indispositions that one does not notice while struggling to reach the goal make themselves felt. One notices that one has run down considerably in health and energy. Six months of hot weather in a tent or hut or without any shelter, with indifferent food, with frequent calls on one for exceptional spurts of hard work, take it out of fellows; so that when the objects of the expedition had been attained, fellows began to speculate on the chance of leave.'

But, needless to say, fellows had to soldier on without it — except for special cases, of which there were few. The Khalifa was very angry at having lost Dongola and even more so at the fact that the tribes of the Bayuda desert had gone over to the invader and were holding all the wells for them. No leave. Instead an inspiring reminder that 'these times of working in monotonous uncomfortable places are far the greatest tests of discipline and soldierly qualities that troops have to undergo'. Meanwhile: 'One notices how beastly the food is, how montonous and dreary the country, how hard it is to amuse oneself; one longs for the sight of fresh green vegetables, fresh butter, to find that one's things are not smothered in sand, to get out of the sight and smell of a camel, to see a real green field; or with the many who are living entirely, or almost, by themselves on the line of communications there is a strong desire to walk into a mess again, and hear several fellows chaffing one another, to go into a theatre where one will forget ammunition, equipment, camels, water-supply, food arrangements, boats, railways, angarebs, natives, drill, baggage, etc. etc.'

However, boring though it all was, the expedition was able to train for the next leap forward by being prepared and practised in every detail. Tedious though these interludes may be when troops come back from active service with a light-hearted and casual attitude to life (or death), these are the times when the hard-learnt lessons of the past few months can be turned to a training session, so that when the unit goes back into the line it moves with a flexible precision of which it is secretly very proud. But, in their camps, which were models of layout, comfort and neatness, clothes were bizarre in the extreme:

'Many had cut holes in the corners of corn sacks to put their arms through, others had cut holes to put their legs through, and either way it made a most serviceable coat. They patched their clothes with anything they could get, and it was not uncommon to see a man wearing trousers of which the right leg was blue, the left khaki, and the seat a bit of corn sack. When a transport requisitioned for clothes they were given the cast-off clothes of the railway battalion. When the railway battalion requisitioned for clothes they were given the cast-off clothes of the transport to patch their garments with, and no man's trousers were condemned unless both the knees and the seat were gone.'

Meanwhile Dongola was under military law with Major-General Hunter as Commandant. When he took over there were no police, there was no justice, and what was one of the most fertile provinces in the area had been allowed to lapse into a thin selection of peasant patches. Within a year he had rebuilt the province and established a flourishing trade. But, as Alford pointed out:

'It is a remarkable fact that all the trade, which has been revived here by the British and Egyptians, is now exclusively in the hands of the Greeks. The troops had scarely time to encamp anywhere in the reconquered country before a crowd of Greeks arrived with their camels and goods, set up their stalls, and established their business. Here are the English and the Egyptians toiling with the sweat of their brows under the desert sun, and bringing hundreds of miles of territory back to civilization and commerce, and here is England looking out all over the world for new markets where she can send her goods whilst this excellent opportunity of developing her trade in Africa is allowed to quietly slip away, and the Greek coolly monopolizes what the British and Egyptians have acquired.'

But there were still 500 miles to go, for the expedition was under half-way to the objective. Even then, if the Dervishes decided, there could be more travelling and, indeed, for some of the expedition there was. Five hundred miles and a few battles should see it through, but no one in his senses could underestimate the skill and effort required to get the expedition to Khartoum; nor could anyone discount the possibility of the Dervishes mounting a counter-offensive in which they could cut the line of communication in half a dozen places and annihilate the starving, cut-off remnants of the expedition at will.

Much depended on the route chosen, and with a railway the choice is necessarily limited. However, there *were* half a dozen possibilities, including a route from Suakin, but the problem in each case was that the route could not reach its destination without conquering a major town on the way, and a major town could not be conquered unless the railway had almost reached it. Eventually, against a weight of advice to the contrary, Kitchener decided to discontine extending the railway which had been used to reconquer Dongola and to build instead an entirely new line from Wadi Halfa (where the other railway had begun) and to take it through Abu Hamed to Berber. At Berber the expedition would still be on the Nile and would be within easy reach of Khartoum. The work began on New Year's Day 1897.

At first the new railway made slow progress. Although the

Dongola railway was not to be extended to approach Khartoum it was vital for holding Dongola, and it had to be extended to link the ports of the Nile which were not impeded by cataracts. That task was not completed until May, during which time the new line had only covered thirty-four miles. But when the Dongola line was complete the experienced builders were switched to the other line, and progress became very rapid indeed.

But to decide to build a railway over 235 miles of unmapped and waterless desert which was known to be in the hands of Dervishes was no mean decision. It was fortunate for all concerned that it turned out to be the right one. Although the rail party could exist without finding water on the route its future would be hazardous in the extreme if they did not. In the event water was found at two places, one seventy-seven miles and the other 126 miles from Wadi Halfa. How lucky the finds were may be gauged from the fact that no water has been found anywhere else along the route since. The names of the two young sapper officers who surveyed the country and advised the boring party to try at the only two possible spots in this arid desert seem to have been unrecorded. Girouard was in England at the time, but one may have been Lieutenant Cator of the Royal Engineers. He died of fever three weeks later.

While the railway was being built Pritchard was often sent on camel patrol. On one of these tedious journeys he related:

'Presently we notice that the Arab is looking keenly at something ahead. "What is that?" he says, pointing ahead. We can see nothing, but a desert Arab can see as well with his eyes as we can with field-glasses; eager to satisfy his curiosity he makes his camel break into a swift trot. He does this without any effort, and it is impossible to see or describe how he does it. If we want to quicken our pace we have to use the whip and drum with our heels, but he glides off instantly and apparently without effort. He almost disappears from view, and when we came up with him again we find him standing in the midst of a number of broken earthenware water-pitchers. The Arab is as astonished as we are. We are well away from the ordinary camel track so he has never seen them before, nor has he heard of them. They are quite a different shape to any Egyptian or Arab pot. They are exactly the same shape as Greek pitchers. Just as this occurs to us the Arab says "Those do not belong to this country, they are very, very ancient, they belonged to the Greeks." '

Optimistically they hope that these broken pitchers betoken the presence of water on that spot; they start digging but there is none to be found. One night, when they have halted and are waiting for the evening meal, they can hear the noise of flowing water. Their servant is using it for washing the plates:

'This is a most heinous offence. Water in the desert is more precious than gold and can only be used for drinking. The plates can be thoroughly cleaned by rubbing them in sand. The same method will, unfortunately, not do for cleaning ourselves, and it is very uncomfortable having to spend three hot days and nights without a wash, and it adds considerably to the fatigue.'

The next day a sandstorm blew up:

'A positive wall of sand, through which one cannot see six feet, comes surging over the desert, and strikes one with a rush, stinging the face and hands. Now for several hours we shall be enveloped in sand. There is no chance of dinner, so we bury our heads under a blanket, and with this protection manage to eat some biscuits without swallowing much sand. Then we lie down to leeward of our saddles, wrap ourselves in blankets and go to sleep. When we awake the storm is practically over; our eyes, noses, and ears are absolutely full of sand, also our hair and clothes; it is caked all over one's skin, it is everywhere . . . .'

The railway was now progressing at the rate of a mile a day, and on one record occasion 5000 yards were laid in twenty-four hours. By July 1897 the railway had reached a point from which further progress would be unsafe without previously capturing Abu Hamed. So far the Dervishes had not threatened the railway but it could hardly be supposed that such a state of affairs could continue much longer:

'It seemed rather a cool cheek making a railway towards a place which was still in the hands of the enemy, while the construction party of three thousand men depended for their water upon a single line of hastily constructed railway. Two or three times they had to go on half and quarter rations of water, drawing on the reserve which was always kept. On one occasion, when half rations of water had twice been issued there was only one tank left for the next issue when the water-train turned up.'

The capture of Abu Hamed was well-organized:

'The Abadba Arabs were ordered to make a reconnaissance to ascertain the strength of the place. This they did in a very ingenious way and sent in a report that could not have been made better even by an officer from the Staff College. They did not ride direct on Abu Hamed but on a small village called Abteen, about seven miles below it. As they approached from the desert they opened out into a long line, and, riding rapidly forward, they drove in front of them every man they came across, and gradually closing in they surrounded the place and enclosed in it all its inhabitants so that no one could get away to give the Dervishes warning. They then got hold of the village sheikh, and, having threatened him with every threat imaginable, they got the most complete and, as it turned out, the most accurate information of the Dervish strength and dispositions. They then watered their camels, and, in order to avoid pursuit they took all the inhabitants, man, woman, and child, out into the desert with them, so that they could not send news to the Dervishes. About six miles out they released them all and rode back to Murat Wells.'

The intelligence report thus compiled stated that there were 450 Dervish riflemen and fifty cavalry in Abu Hamed, but there were also 600 local inhabitants armed with spears and clubs. The supply problem kept their numbers low but, when needed, they could be reinforced from Berber.

Abu Hamed was a tough proposition. To reach it the assault column had to cross approximately 130 miles of trackless desert in a march which often involved climbing up and down steep, rocky hills.

For speed and secrecy the attackers' numbers were kept low. Contemporary accounts give them as 2,500, mainly Sudanese. The column, which was commanded by Major-General Archibald Hunter, a soldier of much dash, courage and experience, averaged fifteen to sixteen miles a day:

'It was the hottest time of the year, so General Hunter did, most of the marching by night. Although this is no doubt the best · thing to do in hot weather it has the drawback of depriving men of their sleep, as no one can sleep well in the hot day. The result was that after two or three days marching every one had the greatest difficulty to keep awake even on the march. The ground was execrable and the column had to go in single file, while the transport tailed out for miles.'

On their route they passed the battlefield of Kirkeban and the point where General Earle had been shot when the battle was virtually over. They also passed Hebbeh where Colonel Stewart had been decoyed to the sheikh's house and murdered. Relics of the shipwrecked boat were strewn around. By dawn on 7 August the column was within a quarter of a mile of Abu Hamed. They were tired, they were footsore, but they were there. But there was no sign of the Dervishes. The column had, of course, been seen, but had the Dervishes once more evacuated? Presumably they had, and Major Kincaid of the Royal Engineers, rode forward to reconnoitre. The town is in a sort of crater, and as Kincaid looked down at some deserted trenches and began to write in his note-book a message beginning 'There is no enemy . . .' the first fusillade suddenly rattled around him. As the General Staff were also pressing on behind him they too came in for some of the benefit of this volley. An artillery bombardment was then ordered, and while this was going on Macdonald drilled the infantry in review order.

It may seem incredible but it was probably the best thing to do. The Dervishes could not see the infantry, let alone hit them, over the lip of the crater, and while the gunners were trying to pound the enemy trenches, half of which they could not see, it was desirable to give the infantry something else to think about.

The stalemate was useless, if not worse, to the column and Hunter therefore ordered the infantry to go in:

'As soon as our troops reached the edge of the crater a roar of musketry broke out from the Dervish trenches, and a hail of bullets was poured at our men but, fortunately, as before, most of it went high. Colonel Macdonald's intention was to rush the place with the bayonet but, without any word of command, first the 11th, and then the other battalions broke into rapid independent firing and no one could advance without getting shot by their own side, so there were our troops on the sky-line with the enemy shooting at them from a trench eighty yards off. In the first few seconds four out of the five mounted officers of the 10th Battalion were brought to the ground, two killed and two with their horses shot; every man of the colour party was either killed or wounded. It was a most unpleasant position. Colonel Macdonald immediately came out in front swearing at the men and knocking up their rifles. The officers did the same, and in a few minutes our firing ceased.'

The Dervishes then left their trenches and moved into the houses. Alford wrote:

'The village of Abu Hamed is a network of houses, crowded together, and separated only by twisting narrow alleys. Most of the fighting was at the point of the bayonet, the Dervishes repeatedly charging in the narrow lanes and streets. When the Dervish horsemen had lost about half their number the remainder fled, being the first of the enemy to do so. They were followed by about 100 infantry, and these were all of the garrison that escaped.'

Among the British officers killed was Major H.M. Sidney, formerly of the Cornwall Light Infantry; he was leading a charge across open ground. At the same time Lieutenant Edward FitzClarence of the Dorsetshire Regiment was shot through the heart when only forty yards from the enemy walls. He was a great-grandson of William IV, and was described as 'the keenest soldier that ever lived'.

Once inside the town the Sudanese soldier proved that he

is 'a splendid chap at house to house fighting, and rapidly worked through the place, though it must be admitted that some of their methods are almost as dangerous to friend as to foe. Before entering a house they fire several volleys into it (and as it is mud most of the bullets come out on the other side), then they rush in, and if a Dervish comes for them they stick their bayonet in and at the same time pull the trigger. Before turning a corner from one street to another they reach their rifle round the corner and pull the trigger on chance, regardless of the fact that there may be some of their own troops coming up the street. Nevertheless they are A1 at clearing an enemy out of a village. In a twinkling they were all over the place, on the roofs, through the windows, and in no time had worked through the place and formed up beyond, firing volleys at the few flying Dervish cavalry, who were the only ones to escape.'

The local inhabitants, who had been armed only with spears and clubs, made practically no resistance and were all taken prisoners and soon released, but the genuine Dervishes with few exceptions refused to surrender and died fighting.

While Hunter's column was marching across the desert, a patrol of the Camel Corps under Major Tudway had been sent to Gakdul; this move was intended to alert the Dervish force at Metemmeh and, if possible, convince them the main attack was coming in that quarter. At the same time the gunboats were pushing up the Nile. This meant negotiating the Fourth Cataract, as the sixty miles of obstructions at that point are known. It was not easy: Butler, who had been on the Nile expedition of 1885, described it as follows:

'No wilder scene can be imagined than this waste called Dar Monassir. For miles together there is no vestige of vegetation; silence is broken only by the noise of the foaming water; the rocks left bare by the subsiding current, and black and polished by sand and sun; whenever it is possible to climb one of the rugged hills on either shore, the eye ranges only a wider area of desolation, burnt and cindery rocks rise up in every direction, from amid wastes of sand.'

The bed of a river or lake, as every fisherman knows, is

much the same as the surrounding countryside.

Prichard described a scene which was repeated all too often:

'In the meantime the gunboats under Commander Keppel R.N were having a hard time of it in the cataracts. The usual plan was followed of attaching ropes on which several hundred men pulled while the gunboat put on all steam, but at the first bad place the leading gunboat capsized and was wrecked. A side current caught it and swung the bows round so that the rope came across the deck. The men on the rope, in the hope of saving her, pulled all the harder, whereas they ought to have let go.

'The result was that she capsized in a twinkling; Lieutenant Beatty, R.N. in command of her, although a good swimmer, was twice sucked under in the eddies, but the second time he saw a loose telegraph pole, and catching hold of that he managed to stay on the surface till he drifted ashore. As the capsized gunboat went dashing down the cataract, some men on the bank said they thought they heard some knocking inside her, so they followed it down until it ran aground, and then ripped open the bottom plates, and out crawled the engineer and stoker alive and well. This mishap did not serve to encourage the other gunboats, but they managed to negotiate the place safely, and went on in the same fashion pulling and steaming through the next hundred miles. One of the reises (native steersmen) had a most dangerous habit of leaving the tiller and falling on his knees to pray just at the critical moments, and Commander Keppel had to instruct him that the right time to pray was before and after the critical moment and not exactly when it occurred.'

Just before the first gunboat reached Abu Hamed General Hunter received a report that the Dervishes were evacuating Berber. It was, of course, only rumour and not to be relied on, but not to be disregarded either. Hunter thereupon boarded the first gunboat and set off up river. Meanwhile on the bank a force of 200 friendly Arabs on fast camels were ready for a swift reconnaissance (and retreat too if needed).

However the gunboat struck a rock in the Fifth Cataract (the Rapid of the Asses):
'The nearest pillow and blankets were stuffed into the hole to keep the water out. Immediately the accident occurred three or four fellows rushed to the place with blankets and pillows, but it was observed that each man brought someone else's bedding not his own.'

Because of this mishap the Arabs found themselves well ahead of the gunboat and soon on the outskirts of Berber. While making a very cautious approach they were told by local natives that the Dervishes had left. Doubtfully and with considerable apprehension they rode in. It was true; there was not a Dervish in the town.

Why the Dervishes had evacuated so important a place without a fight was never made completely clear. The most likely explanation seemed to be that the nearest Dervish General — Mahmud — did not feel he could hold the position with the troops available (about 5000) and it would therefore be better to keep his force intact for the inevitable greater battle to come.

Exciting though the news from Berber was, it provided a major headache for Kitchener. Berber was 135 miles farther up river than Abu Hamed; it was also, on the route which had to be followed, nearly 1200 miles from Cairo, the main source of supplies. When the Nile floods subsided it would be necessary to use camel portages round the cataracts. Should he therefore try to hold Berber, or was it suicidally risky to do so? The prize was great; it was a position of such strategic importance that it would not only put the expedition within striking distance of Omdurman but would also wreck Osman Digna's efforts in the Red Sea area and clear the Suakin–Berber route completely. But the cost of failure would be as high as the prize for success. He decided to hold it.

Luck was on his side. The Khalifa still thought that the best place to destroy the expedition was at the gates of Khartoum. He therefore deferred any proper counter-offensive until the expedition was right on his doorstep. Subsequently he changed his mind, but his inaction over retaking Berber and cutting Kitchener's line of communication gave the latter sufficient time to extend the line first to Abu Hamed and later to Berber. Once the railway had gone this far the supply position became an asset rather than a dangerous liability. For by now the Suakin to Berber route was also open. Berber was officially occupied on 13 September; the railway was following up as fast as possible and by 31 October had reached Abu Hamed.

A train on the railway usually carried 200 tons of supplies at 25 to 30 miles per hour. Derailments were rare, which was astonishing considering the difficulties encountered in construction. In the early stages it had been assumed that one contingency the line would never have to contend with was floods. The Sudan was known — in the north at least — to be waterless. The assumption occasionally proved incorrect and when floods came they either left stretches of the line buried under lakes or washed away the foundations so that the line hung like a trellis in the air. Eventually the line was being laid with clockwork precision, with a survey camp always six miles ahead, an embankment party of 1500 one day ahead, a plate-laying party of 1000, and gangs laying lines, fishplates, bolts and sleepers in the places where they would be needed. There were spiking parties, and ballasting parties, and finishers, while all around would be a screen of watchful defenders in case the Dervishes should decide to intervene.

Locomotives and rolling stock were a problem. Steevens expressed it as follows:

'There is no trouble about labour — the Railway battalions supply that. But if navvy labour is abundant and cheap and efficient, everything else is scarce and cheap and nasty. English firemen and drivers are hard to get and Italian mechanics are largely employed. As for the native mechanics there are branches of work in which they are hopeless. As fillers they are a direct temptation to suicide, for the Arab mind can never be brought to see that a tenth of an inch more or less can possibly matter to anybody. "Malesh", he says, "it doesn't matter; shove it in." And then the engine breaks down.

'As for engines and rolling-stock the Sudan Military Railway must make the best of what it can get. Half a dozen new engines of English breed there were when I got to Halfa — fine, glossy, upstanding, clean-limbed powerful creatures; and it was a joy to watch the marvelling black sentry looking up to one of them in adoration and then warily round lest anybody should seek to steal it. There were others ordered but — miracle of national lunacy — the engineering strike in-tervened and the orders had to go to Baldwins* of Phila-delphia. For the rest the staff had to mend up anything they found about. Old engines from Ismail's abortive railway, old engines from Natal, from the Cape, broken and derelict, had to be patched up with any kind of possible fittings retrieved and adapted from the scrap yard. Odd parts were picked up in the sand and fitted into their places again, if they were useless they were promptly turned into something else and made useful. There are a couple of Ismail's boilers in use now, which were found lying miles away in the desert and rolled in by lever and hand. In the engine-shed you see rusty embryos of engines that are being tinkered together with bits of rubbish collected from everywhere. And still they move.'

After the railway had reached Berber, both sides engaged in harassing activities. Kitchener's force operated from water as well as land. The gunboats had a lively time. Keppel took them up to Metemmeh and bombarded it twice, but the Dervishes were alert and the gunboats were hit several times.

Pritchard recorded:

'This was the first of many reconnaissances by the gun-boats. One gunboat was always on patrol for a week at a time, making life unbearable for the Dervishes, so that the gunboat fellows had plenty of small skirmishes and a trip on one of these patrols was eagerly sought after. An Egyptian brigade was now encamped at the junction of the Atbara with the Nile, and set to work to build a fort, inside which were built huts for stores and men, and everything was done to prepare the place for being the advance base of the

*Who supplied three excellent locomotives.

Khartoum expedition. The gunboats made it their head quarters and started from it on their patrols.'

The raiding was by no means confined to one side. The Dervishes at Metemmeh who had not been supplied with food for some time were now near starvation. Their efforts to repair this situation from the neighbouring villages proved unsatisfactory as the villagers were now reasonably adept with their Remingtons and could distinguish friend from foe.

'One party was observed in the act of raiding on the left bank, by Lieutenant Hood, in the *Nazir*, whilst patrolling south of Ed Damer. Hood immediately landed fourteen men of the 10th Sudanese, three native gunners, and a sergeant of Marine Artillery, who were charged by sixty Dervish horsemen, but the latter were repulsed with the loss of four killed and one wounded.'

The commanders of these gunboats achieved fame in a wider sphere later. Beatty become Admiral of the Fleet, Earl Beatty; and Keppel, Hood, and Colville all became Admirals.

Atbara was going to be a name they would remember, but for the time being their actions with the Dervishes were small though vigorous. One had been a raid on the line four miles behind Berber, another on the village opposite. After the latter raid it was decided to issue the villagers with Remingtons for their self-protection. It was not perhaps the wisest of moves, for the new gunmen fired at everything moving; the first day after the issue General Hunter and his staff were fired at all the way from Berber to Atbara.

Hunter on one occasion tried a raid with a small flying column on Adarama, the headquarters of Osman Digna. However, the wily Arab leader was not at home.

At long last Kassala came into the news again though scarcely in the way that had been envisaged at the start of the expedition. Kassala, which lies at the head of the Atbara river, was very important strategically as it was the centre of an important grain district. (It came in very useful for feeding the starving Jaalin tribe whose men had all been killed in the Baggara raid the previous July.) If the Dervishes had been able to capture it they could have maintained a large force there and acted as a constant threat to Berber. The Italian presence had proved very useful but by the end of 1897 the Italians were hard put to hold it. In fact, the Dervishes had already re-established posts close by. To march to Khartoum with an enemy force still at Kassala would be tantamount to suicide. However, after their reverse at the hands of the Abyssinians at Adowa, the Italians were happy to hand back Kassala to Egypt. This took place on 25 December 1897. It was a blow to French ambitions in the area. For some time past Anglo-French rivalry had been at its keenest, nowhere more so than in Africa. Major Marchand was already on his way from West Africa to stake a French claim at Fashoda; from the east Major Clochette was planning to meet him. Once they joined forces the French would straddle Africa. However, as we shall see later, the French government had other concerns besides imperial rivalries in deepest Africa and, with a view to the developing threat from Germany, was ready to be conciliatory in order to win British friendship.

There was still the problem of the Dervish posts around Kassala. The task was handled with military dash and diplomatic efficiency by Colonel Parsons. His first task was to secure the allegiance of a battalion of Arab Irregulars who were mainly of the Hadendowa tribe. He secured their willing co-operation by allowing them to continue to wear the medals they had won under the Italians and at the same time promising them a first-class fight. No news could have been better received.

The first Dervish post, El Fasher, was quickly disposed of; the second, at Osobri, proved rather different. Alford gives the story as follows:

'Assabala [the Irregular leader] arrived before Osobri at daybreak on the 22nd, took the occupants completely by surprise, and captured 23 camels and 70 head of cattle; but the 60 Dervish riflemen, forming the garrison, sought refuge in the fortress and made a most heroic resistance, worthy of a better cause. For six days they held out against thirst and hunger, waiting for help from their comrades at Gedaref — 120 miles distant — whilst Assabala invested the fortress as well as could be expected with his 180 men.

'Desperate sorties were repeatedly made but were repulsed by fierce Arabs forming the investment. The moon had already set, when, at about 10 o'clock, it being very dark, a body of 50 Dervishes, carrying food and water with them, who had come from Safir, made a most gallant effort to relieve the garrison. Assabala's force being insufficient to complete the investing cordon, the fort was surrounded by a ring of isolated companies, with a considerable interval separating the one from the other. Thus when the Dervishes engaged one of these companies, it was not possible for Assabala to send supports, as by doing so he would have left a broad space open for the escape of the garrison. The men of this particular company exhausted all their ammunition in repelling the enemy, and killed, according to the first accounts that reached us, 20 out of the 50, but these numbers are probably exaggerated. They then fell back on the next company in order to procure ammunition, and the relieving Dervishes, promptly taking advantage of the opportunity, rushed through the gap thus left in the cordon, passed through the gate which was open to them, and joined their comrades in the fort, when the gate was once more quickly closed. It was certainly a most heroic performance on the part of those 50, for, in view of all the circumstances, they were going to almost certain death.

'At this juncture Aroda [the other Irregular leader; he had once been one of Osman Digna's cavalry leaders] arrived from El Fasher with 200 men, and the cordon was made much closer. The Dervishes from Safir had been so hard pressed that they had failed to carry any water with them into the fort for the succour of the suffering garrison; consequently, about an hour later, 20 mounted men, led by an Emir, made a desperate rush from the fort towards the walls outside. The besiegers were ready for them, and the Dervishes were shot down to a man, the Emir himself falling into the water which he had succeeded in reaching. After this there was a desultory exchange of rifle fire between the besiegers and the besieged, until a few hours before dawn when a small body of Baggara horsemen suddenly appeared. They attacked a party of our men who were guarding the Safir road; and the besieged, on hearing the rifles, began to open a very heavy fire in the direction of the wells which are on the other side of the fort. This was intended as a feint, and it proved wholly successful. Our men closed in round the wells to keep the Dervishes off the water but the Dervishes suddenly issued from the other side of the fort, where the road was now left open to them, and fled in the direction of Safir, their retreat being covered by the Baggara horsemen.

'Most of the wretched garrison that escaped the bullet or spear met with a worse fate. In their hasty flight they had left behind them their luggage, provisions, and water. Between them and the nearest wells was a twelve hours march over the parched desert. They had suffered dreadfully during the siege from thirst and hunger, and were, at the time of the escape, well nigh physically exhausted.

'The siege demonstrated that the Dervish was still capable of great bravery in the face of the enemy; not mere reckless bravery during the heat of battle, but bravery that unflinchingly faces hunger and privation, and that most awful of agonies, thirst.'

10

Closing in

At the beginning of 1898 the position of the two armies was much more closely balanced than the Khalifa appeared to realize. The railway was now at Abu Dis, roughly thirty miles south of Abu Hamed. Thus one detachment of Kitchener's force was at Merowe, the other at Berber 130 miles away; the line of communication for both was extremely vulnerable. Nevertheless, they were an excellent springboard for a further attack.

Numbers, however, were greatly in favour of the Dervishes who had 40,000 warriors at Omdurman and nearly 20,000 at Metemmeh, their advance post. The latter force was commanded by Mahmud and contained Osman Digna. If used intelligently, their large numbers could destroy each outpost in turn.

In January a rumour spread that Mahmud was going to come down the Nile and attack Berber. It was not at first felt probable because Mahmud was thought to be short of every essential except men. However, to be on the safe side, Kitchener telegraphed to Cairo for British troops. The first battalions of the Royal Warwickshires, Lincolnshires and Cameron Highlanders were then ordered to the front while the 1st Seaforths and the Northumberland Fusiliers were brought over from Malta and Gibraltar respectively. This force was put under the command of Major-General W.F. Gatacre, who had seen service in Burma and India.

The likelihood that Mahmud would descend on Berber with tens of thousands of Dervishes caused Kitchener to concentrate a substantial force there. He took all but a token holding force from Merowe. The record march of the campaign — in which there were many notable achievements — was then made by the 4th Egyptian Battalion commanded by Major Sparkes. It marched from Suakin to Berber in thirteen days, an average of twenty-one miles a day.

There now began a game of bluff and counter-bluff. The Khalifa was aware the railway represented a real threat to his future but had never personally seen a railway. It was explained to him that 'it was like a steamer except that it went on wheels on the land, and could not go in the water and every time it came it brought a pile of supplies as high as a mountain'. Dervish strategy remained unaltered in the main, in that the great Armageddon would take place within sight of the Mahdi's tomb, when all the army of the infidels would be destroyed, but this did not mean that the British and Egyptians would be unharassed in the meantime.

The harassment had begun in January when Osman Digna had raided the village of Gamer with 200 men. However his force had been overtaken by an Egyptian force from El Damer and lost all its loot. Other raids took place in January with very moderate success. None of them was large enough to be serious. If at this time the Dervishes had mounted a series of really vicious attacks they would have goaded the British force into taking action, and the only action they could have taken was to press on to Metemmeh and thus extend an already well-stretched line of communication.

In late February Mahmud came out of Metemmeh and crossed the Nile. It was an unwise move. If he had stayed in Metemmeh he could have inflicted punishing blows on Kitchener's force, and then, if need be, could have fallen back on Omdurman. It was said that the Khalifa had given Mahmud orders that he was either to destroy Kitchener's army and the railway or return to Omdurman and await the great battle. Mahmud decided on the former course but even his Nile crossing gave him a taste of things to come for Keppel took up his gunboats and sunk several of the nuggers Mahmud was using to ferry his troops across. However, the Dervishes did not then move north from Shendi (on the opposite bank) with any great speed, and it looked as if, after a few probing raids, Mahmud might have changed his mind. Alternatively he might be up to something fairly subtle and, in case he was, it was decided to move the British brigade to Berber.

The order to march reached Gatacre at 1 p.m. just as the Brigade was returning from a long and arduous route march. However, they did not have to begin immediately. That night they travelled up the line and next dawn set off on a seventy-four mile march; it took them four and a half days, an average of sixteen and a half miles a day. They had a day's rest at Berber and then went a further fourteen miles towards the Atbara. This gives them six and a half days for eighty-eight miles (Pritchard's version).

Alford and Sword give sharper timings. According to them the indent order came just as the Brigade came in from manoeuvres and they were at once entrained to the railhead. From their starting point at Abu Dis to Shereik on 25 February they went by rail. They then set off two hours after arrival, i.e. at 10 p.m., marched all night, and covered a further twenty-two miles the next day. Then they rested for a few hours at Wadi Amur and pushed on to Berber and to Kunur, ten miles north of the Atbara, arriving on 4 March. This gave a total march of 134 miles in six and a half days, of which ninety-eight miles were covered in four days (counting the 16½-mile route march which immediately preceded the move).

The significance of this march was not the distance or the time taken but the conditions under which it was made. The Brigade being fit and well-trained, the march was accomplished with morale high. What was extraordinary was the fact that the issue boots were so badly constructed and of such poor quality that the stitches burst and soles fell off; many of the men finished the march barefoot. On that ground in that climate the journey must have been a saga of endurance. Army boots improved very considerably after the Sudan campaign and in the Second World War the British 'ammunition' boot, as it was called, stood up to wear in jungle or desert better than any other footgear in the world. (It is not, of course, a beautiful or shapely object, although meticulous attention can produce a mirror like finish to the toe-cap.*)

It seemed at first that the Brigade had force-marched to Kunur for no good reason, but soon the gunboats reported Dervish movements along the Nile; clearly action would take place before long. On 17 March Kitchener inspected his 10,000-strong army at Kunur. It was an efficient, balanced force: the British Brigade plus a battery of Egyptian artillery, an Egyptian Infantry Division which included two artillery batteries, eight squadrons of Egyptian cavalry, three batteries of Artillery, and a Transport Corps which was commanded by Lieutenant-Colonel Kitchener, the Commander-in-Chief's brother. Knowing that there were 19,000 Dervishes further up the Nile, Kitchener tried to lure them on to attack Atbara fort. He aimed to do this by leaving the fort apparently lightly defended by one Egyptian brigade. As soon as the Dervishes had committed themselves he planned to bring up the rest of the army and take the Dervishes on the flanks and in the rear.

However, Mahmud was not prepared to be so obliging. The gunboats, with the irrepressible Beatty ever to the fore, had had daily skirmishes with the Dervishes but reported no large movement. It was surmised, and rightly, that the Dervishes had struck eastward across the desert. Their object was to ford the Atbara river at Hudi, outflank Kitchener's force, attack Berber, and destroy the railway at Gineinetti. Fort-

---

*Steevens said 'a certain stir' followed the publication of his criticisms in England, penetrating as far as the House of Commons, and even the War Office. The official reply was that 'the boots were very good boots only that the work done by the brigade over bad ground had tried them too severely'.

It was, as Steevens said, not much of an argument that the boots were good boots but no good for the purpose intended. He himself walked the distance in riveted boots without mishap. He thought little of it. As he put it, 'Of course, you and I could easily walk twenty-five miles a day for as long as anybody liked to name. But would you like to try it with kit and rifle and a hundred rounds of ammunition?'

unately for Kitchener his intelligence service, run by Wingate assisted by Slatin, was so good that there was no chance of his being surpised in this way. Instead, on 20 March, he took his army up to Hudi, a five-hour march. On arrival, looking a brave sight as they marched in with the Union Jack at the head and with cavalry and horse artillery screens on the flanks, they constructed a strong zareba. That done they settled for the night.

The same day Mahmud reached the Atbara at a point near Nakheila, about twenty-five miles further up river than Hudi but where there was also a ford. There on the eastern side of the river he built a formidable zareba and waited for Kitchener to attack. He was now well-entrenched at a point from which — if matters went well for him — he could threaten the whole of the Eastern Sudan. Meanwhile an encouraging report reached Kitchener that Osman Digna's brother, Ali Digna, had attacked Adarama, held for Egypt by friendly Hadendowas, but had been repulsed. On the 21st Kitchener moved his army up to Hudi and sent out patrols to find out Mahmud's intentions.

As far as Kitchener could tell, the situation was satisfactory. If Mahmud came straight down the Atbara he would be met squarely. If he tried to march round to Berber he faced a twenty-five-mile march through waterless desert, and was all the while liable to a flank attack. If he reached Berber by some swift and lucky move there was a battalion there to keep him occupied till the main force returned. However, war is an unpredictable business, and Kitchener could by no means count out the unforeseen circumstance. But both sides were clearly puzzled as to what the next move should be. Both therefore sent out patrols in very difficult, bushy country, and many were the surprise encounters. Pritchard wrote:

'On one occasion the cavalry had completed their morning reconnaissance, all patrols had come in and reported the country quite clear of the enemy for fifteen miles in every direction. Accordingly they began watering and feeding the horses; the English officers were squatting on the ground together having some lunch, when suddenly their attention was attracted by grunts from the Marquis of Tullibardine, whose mouth was so full of bread he could not speak, and could only grunt and point with his fork. Looking in the direction he was pointing they saw a group of Dervish horsemen dashing down on them. The English officers were in a group by themselves, the remainder of the cavalry on the river one hundred yards off. Every officer sprang for his horse. Captain Baring who was nearest to the Dervishes, was so closely pressed that while he was in the act of mounting, and before he had quite thrown his leg over the saddle, he was obliged to shoot the leading Dervish to prevent being cut down. As it was, most of the officers would certainly have been cut down if it had not been that one troop of cavalry was on guard and mounted, and they dashed up to the rescue, and assisted the officers to put the Dervishes to flight.'

Eight years before, in Zululand, Prince Louis Napoleon, son of the exiled French Emperor Napoleon III, had been killed in almost similar circumstances. He was serving in the British army: his patrol had halted near some tall grass in which Zulus were concealed. In the same war the second battalion of the Royal Warwickshire Regiment had fought with great gallantry at Isandhlwana and been wiped out to a man. When re-formed later it became the South Wales Borderers. The first battalion was now with the British Brigade under Gatacre.

While no action took place both Kitchener's army and the Dervishes became daily more uncomfortable. The British Brigade had set off under the impression that they would be in action at once and back in camp the next day; consequently they had taken very little baggage. The Egyptians with the same orders but a vast amount more campaigning experience had taken just enough to make life tolerable under any circumstances. The Dervishes, with a much larger force, were having considerable problems over feeding. Their logistical arrangements were sketchy at the best of times and they were at their worst when the army had to stay in one place. They were reduced to a ration of two dom nuts a day. Dom nuts have a hard kernel which can be ground into a paste; they scarcely make a meal fit for heroes. However, Mahmud had decided that his previous strategy was impracticable and so would sit back and let Kitchener make the next move.

On 22 March there was a notable brush between the cavalry of the two forces at Abadar. After an initial reverse the Egyptian cavalry squadrons charged the Dervishes, drove them back and pursued them for four miles. The situation still remained static, for these brushes between reconnaissance patrols affected nothing but morale. What was not static was the railway, which was creeping up at the rate of one and a half miles a day and would soon reach Abadieh; at that point the new gunboats could be assembled and put on the Nile. However, with 19,000 Dervishes entrenched just beyond the point where the Atbara joined the Nile, progress of any sort was liable to reach a sudden stop.

Kitchener decided to take the initiative. On 25 March he decided to cut Mahmud's supply route. Three miles south of Shendi the Dervish general had left a dump of stores, half way along his line of retreat. Kitchener decided to eliminate this. With complete stealth and secrecy the 15th battalion of the Egyptian army embarked on three gunboats, commanded by Keppel, Beatty and Hood respectively and launched a dawn attack on Shendi. Surprise was so complete that resistance was ill-organized. One hundred and sixty Baggara were killed, the forts were destroyed, stores were captured and the town was burnt.

Next Kitchener ordered a full reconnaissance of the Dervish encampment. This was conducted in such force that the Dervishes clearly believed it was the prelude to a full-scale attack. As a result they stayed in their trenches, holding their fire for close-quarter work. But, to their surprise and disappointment, it did not come. Instead, General Hunter made a long thorough appraisal of Dervish strength from a ridge 600 yards away, and then retired. The Dervishes watched them but took no action. Clearly they expected a full-scale attack to follow and would not be drawn out of their trenches. The party retired without molestation, in spite of attempts to draw the Dervish fire.

Despite the destruction of Shendi and the successful reconnaissance of the Dervish zareba the situation was not entirely to Kitchener's liking. Mahmud was undoubtedly cornered but unless he could be brought out of his trenches any battle was likely to be costly and very bloody. Mahmud was unlikely to retreat to Omdurman, sensible though that procedure would have been, for the Khalifa was liable to feel his subordinate commander had behaved foolishly, if not cravenly, and might well make an example of him. He could perhaps reopen a supply line but his main hope was that Kitchener, who had already reconnoitred his position, would come in and attack him. By now his camp was looking almost impregnable. Lack of food had caused some drop in morale but summary executions were effectively controlling the waverers. Osman Digna would have had him retire beyond Adarama where he would still be sitting on Kitchener's flank, but Mahmud would have none of it.

On 4 April Kitchener decided to tempt Mahmud. He moved the entire army five miles nearer — to Abadar — then sent another reconnaissance party under Hunter, right up to the zareba. This time it was engaged but, after a brisk encounter, managed to retreat in good order. In spite of the death penalty which was inflicted on those caught, deserters were now coming in daily from the Dervish camp. Hunter reported that the Dervish position was in an oval by the river, and was honeycombed with trenches. Like Abu Hamed it was in a crater.

On 6 April Kitchener, who was so uncertain that he had wired to Cromer for advice as to whether he should assault, moved his army to the village of Umbadia, about seven and a half miles from Mahmud's zareba. There they too made a zareba. Each man was given 127 rounds of ammunition, and on the night of 7 April they moved up in battalion-square formation, a total of some 14,000 men. It included a rocket party commanded by Lieutenant Beatty.

April 8 was Good Friday. At 0345 the army halted one mile and a half from the Dervish position. At 0430 they were deployed into attack formation and at 0600 hours were on the ridge overlooking the Dervish camp. As they looked down they realized that their arrival was known, for the Dervish leaders were already making their dispositions. At 0545 twelve guns opened fire, assisted by Beatty's rocket battery. For an hour and a half they pounded the Dervish position. The Dervishes stayed in their trenches and took no action. This was the unexpected, almost uncanny, quality of the Dervishes. Almost any other army in the world would have reacted for good or ill. The Dervishes sat tight waiting.

The main attack went in at 0810. The exhortations were few and brief. The Seaforths were told 'The news of victory must be in London tonight.' They listened in silence; they had made up their own minds long ago.

The best account of the battle came from Alford and Sword:

'Headed by their officers, the Camerons rush through the gaps. Captain Findlay was the first of the British Brigade to cross the zareba, but ere he had gone many yards he was mortally wounded, being shot in the chest and stomach, besides being wounded by a spear. "Go on, my company, and give it them" he called out and a quarter of an hour afterwards he was dead. The Seaforths rush into the zareba, following closely on the heels of the Camerons, then the Lincolns and Warwicks got through, and the whole of the British Brigade presses on in line, or rather in the best attempt at a line that the circumstances permit. The scene inside the zareba is indescribable. One sees trench after trench filled with Dervishes, all firing point-blank as fast as they can load, whilst the British and native troops dash forward clearing the trenches with bullet and bayonet. It is not a question of merely driving the enemy out of the zareba, but rather of despatching every single Dervish separately. The enemy remain at their posts, firing steadily, and officers and men were falling right and left.

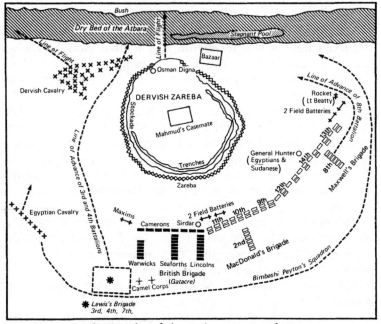

The battle of the Atbara, 8 April 1898

'Major Urquhart (Camerons) was one of the first to fall, shot through the sporran top by a Dervish who lay hidden amongst his dead comrades in one of the trenches. He managed to call out "Never mind me, lads, go on", and then fell dead. Soon afterwards Major Napier of the same regiment was dangerously wounded in the thigh by a large conical bullet from an elephant rifle. The Camerons had sixty men *hors de combat* after being in action less than that number of minutes. The Seaforths also fared badly; one of the first of that regiment to cross the zareba was young Gore – who had only joined the service a few months – and he was gallantly pushing on across the trenches when he fell, shot through the heart. The leading company of the Seaforths had eleven men killed and wounded and four men with bullets through their helmets. General Gatacre had a narrow escape; whilst pulling away the zareba, a Dervish sprang at him with a huge spear, the General called to his

208

orderly (Private Cross of the Camerons) "Give it to him my lad" and Cross rushed forward and bayoneted the Dervish just in time. Poor Cross, who showed great gallantry throughout the fight, died a few weeks afterwards at Darmali.

'Meanwhile, on the right, the Egyptians and Sudanese, led by Major-General Hunter waving sword and helmet, had entered the zareba slightly in advance of the British Brigade, and had with the greatest bravery and tenacity fought their way over the terrible trenches.

'Some of the fiercest fighting took place at a stockade, about thirty yards from the trenches. It was here that Piper Stewart of the Camerons met his death. He had got on some rising ground and, nothing daunted by the bullets whizzing round him was vigorously playing "The March of the Cameron Men" to cheer on his comrades when he was struck by no fewer than five bullets — four in the body and one in the head.

'At last the troops succeeded in hewing their way right across the zareba, and it was a case of *sauve qui peut* with the enemy, who now fled helter-skelter through the palm-belt into the broad, dry bed of the Atbara. Many of the Dervishes disdained to run, and walked calmly away with that dignified air which is one of their chief characteristics.

'The scene in the zareba after the battle was horrifying. The trenches were filled with the slain Dervishes in every position that the agony of death could assume. Many were mangled into mere fragments of humanity far beyond recognition. The artillery fire had played a fearful part in the battle and the coolness and pluck with which the enemy contained themselves during the bombardment proved that the Dervish was truly brave, not merely when fired with enthusiasm in a fanatical rush but when face to face with death, without hope of escaping or hope of killing his foe. Many unfortunate blacks were found chained by both hands and legs, in the trenches, with a gun in their hands and their faces to the foes — some with forked sticks behind their backs.'

Mahmud was captured, with 2000 other prisoners, but

Osman Digna had got away to Adarama with a substantial contingent of Dervishes.

The battle of the Atbara had been won, but the final round between Kitchener and the Khalifa was still be fought. At this moment there suddenly blazed up a row between the army and the war correspondents.

Kitchener, like many another commander, regarded the war correspondents not so much as a necessary evil as a dangerous liability. As far as he could see there was no reason why the general public should not wait for news till the campaign was over. The view has been widely, but not exclusively, held till recently. Even today there may be a few who share Kitchener's views but the vast majority appreciate the advantages of full co-operation with press and publicity, which they willingly give. In the Crimea, nearly forty years before, W.H. Russell of *The Times* had devastatingly exposed the shortcomings of the British supply system, and caused the British public to galvanize the War Office into immediate remedial action. That was excellent, but before long there were bitter complaints about the freedom permitted to correspondents; detailed accounts of the British military dispositions were published in British newspapers and read with interest in Moscow. Similar incidents had happened in the Franco-Prussian War. Infuriating though this was, everyone knew that the burrowings of war correspondents can work for one's own side, and that some of their sources of information are a very useful supplement to military intelligence. Nevertheless in August 1897 Kitchener had issued an order that correspondents were not to go beyond the railhead 'because of the difficulties of transport and feeding'. The correspondents, not believing a word of the excuse, complied, with grace, but when a similar order was issued in January 1898 there was a burst of indignation. The resentment was not entirely justified. Admittedly the Khalifa did not read the London papers but there were plenty of others hostile to Britain who did, and they spared no time and effort in letting the Khalifa have any information they thought might be useful to him. There were a number of

French missionaries wandering about in the Sudan and some of these formed a useful source of transmission.

Meanwhile military preparations went on steadily. Atbara became a fort and a supply depot; Abadieh became an arsenal. The three new gunboats proved to be a disappointment. Although better armed, and drawing a foot less water, they could only carry sixty-five men instead of the 250 managed by the others, and their shallow draught made them almost useless for towing purposes. As one of the principal functions of a Nile gunboat was to tow river craft, the inadequacy of the new acquisitions was a serious matter.

In July a second brigade was sent up the Nile; and the two brigades then constituted the British Division under Major-General Gatacre known, because of his untiring energy, as 'General Backacher'. Brigadier-General Wauchope was given command of 1st Brigade, and Brigadier-General the Hon. A.G. Lyttelton, the second. The new brigade was made up of the 1st Battalion Grenadier Guards, 1st Northumberland Fusiliers, 2nd Lancashire Fusiliers, and 2nd Rifle Brigade. (At this time four was the operative figure in the British army; units marched in columns of four, formed 'fours', had four battalions to a brigade, and so on.) In addition to the new brigade, the 21st Lancers, the Maxim battery detachment of the Royal Irish Fusiliers, 32nd and 37th Field Batteries, Royal Artillery, and suppporting units from Royal Engineers, Army Service Corps, and Royal Army Medical Corps were sent up. There was, as might have been expected, a certain amount of comment, not all of it good-natured, that regiments should be sent up at the last minute to get a medal out of a campaign that was all over bar the shouting. However, as events turned out, the critics ate their words for the medals were to be truly won.

In spite of the recent row the ranks of the war correspondents were now reinforced by some notable figures. They included Colonel Frank Rhodes, brother of Cecil Rhodes, for *The Times*, and the Hon. Herbert Howard, who was killed by one of the very last shots fired at Omdurman, after he had ridden unscathed with the charge of the 21st Lancers; he represented the *New York Herald*. (Many of the newspapers represented are now extinct, like *The Globe*, the *Daily Chronicle*, the *Morning Post* and the *Daily News*). However when the army moved quietly up to Wad Hamed at the end of August the correspondents were prohibited from cabling the information home. Elements of the army were a few miles farther on than Wad Hamed, at Wad Habeshi, and from a nearby hill the dome of the Mahdi's tomb could be seen; it was thirty-four miles away. Appropriately, Major Staveley Gordon, General Gordon's nephew, was the first to spot it.

However, the remaining distance contained its tactical problems. Between Wad Hamed and Omdurman lay the Sixth Cataract, with a nine-mile-long gorge flanked by sheer granite walls 300 feet high. The entrance was defended by strong forts which came right down to the water's edge; the land on each side was full of rocks and boulders. It would have made a formidable obstacle if the Khalifa had decided to defend it, but, wisely, he did not. Although Kitchener's army would have had to pay a heavy price for forcing a way through, the Khalifa would have had to pay a heavier one in the defence, for nearly all his army would have had to be committed in ineffective units on terrain which could not be made entirely impenetrable.

One curious incident at this time was an attempt to destroy the gunboats in a 'frogman' enterprise. The protaganist was a Tunisian prisoner, said to be an expert on explosives. His mission was to tow a box of explosives into mid-stream at Kemeri where an advancing gunboat would certainly hit it — a fixed mine, in fact. Unfortunately for him the mine exploded on the way and killed him; it also damaged one of the Khalifa's boats.

The total strength of Kitchener's force was now 25,000, with ten gunboats in support. On Thursday 25 August, they started to move up; after an eight-hour march they reached Wad Bishara, eleven miles away. It was hard going, particularly for the newly arrived troops, for it was blisteringly hot and the way led through heavy sand. That night, and all the others, they slept in their clothes, with only a blanket each.

The nights were as cold as the days were hot. The next day they went a further nine miles to Um Teref. Their presence was now well enough known to the Dervishes, but they were still not attacked. On the Sunday night the rain poured down with tropical intensity and when the march was resumed at 4 a.m. on the Monday morning the soldiers wanted nothing more than to deal with the Dervishes who had put them to all this trouble. Moving a large army alert for surprise attack over very bad country is a slow business and it was not until Thursday 1 September that they reached Egega, six miles from Omdurman. The previous night they had once more been drenched with all-night rain. Guns were soon in position and Omdurman, Khartoum and Tati Island were shelled. The Dervish army was deployed in full view outside the city, 60,000 strong, and had been in that position for twenty-four hours. Kitchener's army hastily constructed a zareba. It seemed inevitable that the Dervishes would launch an attack during the hours of darkness, when rifle fire would be difficult and close-quarter fighting, at which the Dervishes were supreme, would be paramount. But, for some unaccountable reason, the chance was lost; it was said that the Khalifa expected to be attacked himself, because Kitchener had spread rumours to that effect.

At long last, as it seemed to the troops, the day of battle had arrived. It was Friday 2 September. Kitchener's army was now facing an open plain, with scarcely any cover except for one or two 'Khors' (dried-up watercourses); one of these would play a significant part later. The army was drawn up in a horse-shoe formation with both flanks touching the Nile, where they were covered by gunboats.

At 0530 the gunboats and howitzers opened up. Almost at once came the welcome news that the Dervishes were advancing, and at 0600 their flags came into view at 3000 yards. On their right was the Khalifa's brother Yacoub, with his black banner; on the left were the blue and white banners carried by the Khalifa's son, El Din. At 0630 the Gunners brought down their sights on to the advancing horde but although the shells burst right in the middle of their lines

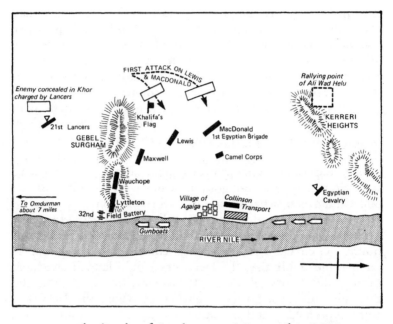

The battle of Omdurman, 2 September 1898

the Dervishes did not check or waver. On they came, to 1500 yards, 1000, 800, and at that point their riflemen were beginning to take a toll of the men inside the zareba. Rhodes of *The Times* was shot in the shoulder and had to be evacuated, protesting loudly, and Williams of the *Daily Chronicle* was also wounded. With the attack being pressed home from all sides, the great slaughter was taking place by the front of the zareba, but the flanks were also hotly engaged. On the right a force of 10,000 Dervishes pushed the line back but on coming under concentrated fire from the gunboats had to withdraw out of range. At 0800 the Khalifa withdrew the entire army for reorganization and re-grouping. The battle was by no means over but the preliminaries were reasonably satisfactory for both sides. If the Dervishes could cover those few final yards — and they had the courage and desperation to do so — the superior fire power of Kitchener's army would be nullified; if the army could hold them at a safe distance, time would bring victory. But Kitchener knew that that was what the Khalifa would expect, so instead he ordered a surprise counter-attack.

The manoeuvre was very difficult. The ground, though clear of major obstacles, was very rough, and progress in formation was slow. As the British came forward the Khalifa's troops and those of his sons mounted an all-out assault on the advancing line. Alford and Sword described it in the passage with which this book begins.

The line was held, but at a cost. The full force of the attack fell on to the 1st Egyptian Brigade, commanded by Lieutenant-Colonel H.A. MacDonald. It contained the 2nd Egyptian battalion and the 9th, 10th and 11th Sudanese. As soon as Kitchener learnt what was happening he brought up Lyttelton's and Maxwell's brigades to the right, to catch the Dervishes in cross-fire, while sending Wauchope's men as reinforcements. But by the time these moves took effect the steadiness of MacDonald's brigade, mainly Sudanese, had won the day.

At 0900 it seemed as if the tide had turned. Kitchener therefore ordered the cavalry into action to cut off retreating Dervishes from Omdurman and force them away into the desert. The Egyptian horse took the right; the 21st Lancers the left. As the latter trotted forward they came to a Khor in which they estimated some 200 Dervishes might be concealed. The regiment wheeled into line and the charge was sounded. As they came to the Khor 2000 Dervishes suddenly appeared in front of them; they themselves were 320 in all. The Dervishes got in one volley before the Lancers were among them. Among the 21st's many casualties was Lieutenant R.S. Grenfell, attached from the 12th Lancers; he was Sir Francis Grenfell's nephew.

There were other attached officers with the 21st that memorable day. One was Winston Churchill from the 4th Hussars, another was Major Pincher of the R.A.M.C. Pincher was not, of course, a combatant officer, but there to deal with casualties. He nearly became one himself, for he was one of the very few to be unhorsed — by the usual ham-stringing but not instantly killed. He owed his life to Sergeant-Major Brennan, who rode to him, fought off Dervishes, and took him out of danger on his own horse. Captain the Marquis of Tullibardine of the Blues (Royal Horse Guards) saved a trooper with great gallantry. Lieutenant Wormald (7th Hussars) came to single combat with an Emir who was wearing crusader chain mail. His sword bent up at the first slash but before the Dervish could take advantage Wormald caught him a blow across the head with the bent sword. Courage was by no means restricted to the officers. Trooper Byrne was wounded by a Dervish sword and then by a bullet, but continued to fight to the end, Sergeant Freeman had his nose cut off and a spear planted in his chest but remained mounted throughout, and Trooper Ayton rescued a fellow soldier in near-impossible conditions. Of the 320 men involved 21 were killed, and 46 wounded. 119 horses were killed. It was the first time the 21st had been in action, for they were a young regiment. Although an error, and a costly one, the charge had accomplished its purpose and the Dervishes were headed off from Omdurman. At 1130 hours the battle was virtually over, although casualties were still being caused by supposedly dead Dervishes as the army advanced over the battlefield. By 1200 victory was complete and at 1430 the occupation of the city of Omdurman began.

Winston Churchill wrote of the 21st's charge as follows:

'The intentions of our Colonel had no doubt been to move round the flank of the body of Dervishes he had now located, and who, concealed in a fold of the ground behind their rifle-men, were invisible to us, and then to attack them from a more advantageous quarter; but once the fire was opened and losses began to grow, he must have judged it inexpedient to prolong his procession across the open plain. The trumpet sounded "Right wheel into line", and all the sixteen troops swung round towards the blue-black riflemen. Almost immediately the regiment broke into a gallop, and the 21st Lancers were committed to their first charge in war!

'I propose to describe exactly what happened to me: what I saw and what I felt. I recalled it to my mind so frequently after the event that the impression is as clear and vivid as it was a quarter of a century ago. The troop I commanded was, when we wheeled into line, the second from the right of the regiment. I was riding a handy, sure-footed, grey Arab polo pony. Before we wheeled and began to gallop, the officers had been marching with drawn swords. On account of my shoulder I had always decided that if I were involved in hand-to-hand fighting, I must use a pistol and not a sword. I had purchased in London a Mauser automatic pistol, then the newest and the latest design. I had practised carefully with this during our march and journey up the river. This then was the weapon with which I determined to fight. I had first of all to return my sword into its scabbard, which is not the easiest thing to do at a gallop. I had then to draw my pistol from its wooden holster and bring it to full cock. This dual operation took an appreciable time, and until it was finished, apart from a few glances to my left to see what effect the fire was producing, I did not look up at the general scene.

'Then I saw immediately before me, and now only half the length of a polo ground away, the row of crouching blue figures firing frantically, wreathed in white smoke. On my right and left my neighbouring troop leaders made a good line. Immediately behind was a long dancing row of lances crouched for the charge. We were going at a fast but steady gallop. There was too much trampling and rifle fire to hear any bullets. After this glance to the right and left and at my troop, I looked again towards the enemy. The scene appeared to be suddenly transformed. The blue-black men were still firing but behind them there now came into view a depression like a shallow sunken road. This was crowded and crammed with men rising up from the ground where they had hidden. Bright flags appeared as if by magic, and I saw arriving from nowhere Emirs on horseback among and around the mass of the enemy. The Dervishes appeared to be ten or twelve deep at the thickest, a great grey mass gleaming with steel, filling the dry watercourse. In the same twinkling of an eye I saw also that our right overlapped their left, that my troop would just strike the edge of their array, and that the troop on my right would charge into air. My subaltern comrade on the right, Wormald of the 7th Hussars, could see the situation too; and we both increased our speed to the very fastest gallop and curved inwards like the horns of the moon. One really had not time to be frightened or to think of anything else but these particularly necessary actions which I have described. They completely occupied mind and senses.

'The collision was now very near. I saw immediately before me, not ten yards away, the two blue men who lay in my path. They were perhaps a couple of yards apart. I rode at the interval between them. They both fired. I passed through the smoke conscious that I was unhurt. The trooper immediately behind me was killed at this place and at this moment whether by these shots or not I do not know. I checked my pony as the ground began to fall away beneath his feet. The clever animal dropped like a cat four or five feet down on to the sandy bed of the watercourse, and in this sandy bed I found myself surrounded by what seemed to be dozens of men. They were not thickly-packed enough at this point for me to experience any actual collision with them. Whereas Grenfell's troop next but one on my left was brought to a complete standstill and suffered very heavy losses, we seemed to push our way through as one has sometimes seen mounted policemen break up a crowd. In less time than it takes to relate, my pony had scrambled up the other side of the ditch. I looked round.

'Once again I was on the hard, crisp desert, my horse at a trot. I had the impression of scattered Dervishes running to and fro in all directions. Straight before me a man threw himself on the ground. The reader must remember that I had been trained as a cavalry soldier to believe that if ever cavalry broke into a mass of infantry, the latter would be at their mercy. My first idea therefore was that the man was terrified. But simultaneously I saw the gleam of his curved sword as he drew it back for a ham-stringing cut. I had room and time enough to turn my pony out of his reach, and leaning over on the offside I fired two shots into him at about three yards. As I straightened myself in the saddle, I saw before me another figure with uplifted sword. I raised my pistol and fired. So close were we that the pistol itself actually struck him. Man and sword disappeared below and behind me. On my left, ten yards away, was an Arab horseman in a bright-coloured tunic and steel helmet, with chain-mail hangings. I fired at him. He turned aside. I pulled my horse into a walk and looked around again.

'In one respect a cavalry charge is very like ordinary life. So long as you are all right, firmly in your saddle, your horse in hand, and well armed, lots of enemies will give you a wide berth. But as soon as you have lost a stirrup, have a rein cut, have dropped your weapon, are wounded, or your horse is wounded, then is the moment when from all quarters enemies rush upon you. Such was the fate of not a few of my comrades in the troops immediately on my left. Brought to an actual standstill in the enemy's mass, clutched at from every side, stabbed at and hacked at by spear and sword, they were dragged from their horses and cut to pieces by the infuriated foe. But this I did not at the time see or understand. My impressions continued to be sanguine. I thought we were masters of the situation, riding the enemy down. I pulled my horse up and looked about me. There was a mass of Dervishes about forty or fifty yards away on my left. They were huddling and clumping themselves together, rallying for mutual protection. They seemed wild with excitement, dancing about on their feet, shaking their spears up and down. The whole scene seemed to flicker. I have an impression, but it is too fleeting to define, of brown-clad Lancers mixed up here and there with this surging mob. The scattered individuals in my immediate neighbourhood made no attempt to molest me. Where was my troop? Where were the other troops of the squadron? Within a hundred yards of me I could not see a single officer or man. I looked back at the Dervish mass. I saw two or three riflemen crouching and aiming their rifles at me from the fringe of it. Then for the first time that morning I experienced a sudden sensation of fear. I felt myself absolutely alone. I thought these riflemen would hit me and the rest devour me like wolves. What a fool I was to loiter like this in the midst of the enemy! I crouched over the saddle, spurred my horse into a gallop and drew clear of the *mêlée*. Two or three hundred yards away I found my troops already faced about and partly formed up.

'The other three troops of the squadron were re-forming close by. Suddenly in the midst of the troop up sprung a Dervish. How he got there I do not know. He must have leaped out of some scrub or hole. All the troopers turned upon him thrusting with their lances: but he darted to and fro causing for the moment a frantic commotion. Wounded several times, he staggered towards me raising his spear. I shot him at less than a yard. He fell on the sand, and lay there dead. How easy to kill a man! But I did not worry about it. I found that I had fired the whole magazine of my Mauser pistol, so I put in a new clip of ten cartridges before thinking of anything else.

'I was still prepossessed with the idea that we had inflicted great slaughter on the enemy and had scarcely suffered at all ourselves. Three or four men were missing from my troop. Six men and nine or ten horses were bleeding from spear-thrusts or sword cuts. We all expected to be ordered immediately to charge back again. The men were ready, though they all looked serious. Several asked to be allowed to throw away their lances and draw their swords. I asked my second sergeant if he had enjoyed himself. His answer was "Well, I don't exactly say I enjoyed it, Sir; but I think I'll get more used to it next time." At this the whole troop laughed.

'But now from the direction of the enemy there came a succession of grisly apparitions; horses spouting blood, struggling on three legs, men staggering on foot, men bleeding from terrible wounds, fish-hook spears stuck right through, arms and faces cut to pieces, bowels protruding, men gasping, crying, collapsing, expiring. Our first task was to succour these; and meanwhile the blood of our leaders cooled. They remembered for the first time that we had carbines. Everything was still in great confusion. But trumpets were sounded and orders shouted, and we all moved off at a trot towards the flank of the enemy. Arrived at a position from which we could enfilade and rake the watercourse, two squadrons were dismounted and in a few minutes with their fire at three hundred yards compelled the Dervishes to retreat. We therefore remained in possession of the field. Within twenty minutes of the time when we had first wheeled into line and begun our charge, we were halted and breakfasting in the very watercourse that had so very nearly proved our undoing. There one could see the futility of the much vaunted *Arme Blanche*. The Dervishes had carried off their wounded, and the corpses of thirty or forty enemy were all that could be counted on the ground. Among these lay the bodies of over twenty Lancers, so hacked and mutilated as to be most unrecognizable. In all out of 310 officers and men the regiment had lost in the space of about two or three minutes five officers and sixty-five men killed and wounded, and 120 horses — nearly a quarter of its strength.

'Such were my fortunes in this celebrated episode. It is very rarely that cavalry and infantry, while still both unshaken, are intermingled as the result of an actual collision. Either the infantry keep their heads and shoot the cavalry down, or they break into confusion and are cut down or speared as they run. But the two or three thousand Dervishes who faced the 21st Lancers in the watercourse at Omdurman were not in the least shaken by the stress of battle or afraid of cavalry. Their fire was not good enough to stop the charge, but they had no doubt faced horsemen many a time in the wars with Abyssinia. They were familiar with the ordeal of the charge. It was the kind of fighting they thoroughly understood. Moreover, the fight was with equal weapons, for the British too fought with sword and lance as in the days of old.

. . . .

'A white gunboat seeing our first advance had hurried up the river in the hopes of being of assistance. From the crow's nest, its commander, Beatty, watched the whole event with breathless interest. Many years passed before I met this officer or knew that he had witnessed our gallop. When we met, I was First Lord of the Admiralty and he the youngest Admiral in the Royal Navy. "What did it look like?" I asked him. "What was your prevailing impression?" "It looked," said Admiral Beatty, "like plum duff: brown currants scattered about in a great deal of suet." With this striking, if somewhat homely, description my account of this adventure may fittingly close.'

Occupying a captured city invariably has its moments of tension. As the army moves through narrow streets, fully alert but completely exposed, there is always the thought that a fanatic will send the bullet with your name on it. There was, however, little opposition. The prime objective was the Khalifa's house, which was found to be barricaded. There was clearly no point in keeping the weapons at their disposal idle, so the gunboats were ordered to fire a few rounds to break the walls. It was not an easy target and one shell nearly killed Kitchener; another finished off Howard. Only a few Baggara, fighting to the death, remained inside; the Khalifa had gone.

Kitchener went personally to the prison where Neufeld and other prisoners were released. The scene was not particularly dramatic: all concerned were too emotionally drained to feel very much at the time. Neufeld had been a prisoner for thirteen years.

It had been a hard day. 9700 dead Dervishes were counted and there were over 10,000 wounded. And when a Dervish was too wounded to fight on he was wounded indeed.

But wars do not finish neatly and tidily, and even when peace is ensured there are often portents of further trouble looming. Within five days of the battle, while the congratulatory telegrams were still pouring in, astounding news was received: Fashoda, on the Blue Nile, was occupied by the French. As this was on Egyptian territory, even though at the time there could be no Egyptian force there, this was a serious diplomatic matter. The news came in a curious way. It was brought by a Dervish steamer which had sailed up river on a patrolling mission and had been fired on. The captain was able to describe the flag he had seen flying at Fashoda.

On realizing its identity, Kitchener promptly sent all the war correspondents back to Cairo. He then went up with three battalions to see for himself. The ensuing proceedings were courteous in the extreme. Major Marchand, in command of the 128-strong force, was politely requested to haul down his flag. Equally politely he explained that he could not do so without orders from the French government. Kitchener thereupon landed and hoisted the British and Egyptian flags alongside. Then he cabled the Foreign Office and left them to sort it out.

There were, of course, other incidents, less meaningful, elsewhere. Colonel Parsons, from Kassala, retook Gedaref, but nearly lost it again in a desperate counter-attack.

The Khalifa was not tracked down till two months later. Then he was caught at Um Dabrekat, about 250 miles south of Omdurman. It was a triumph for Wingate, not only for his intelligence service but also for his skill as a military commander, for the final surprise was made after a forced night march. The Khalifa fought to the death but Osman Digna once more got away; he was eventually captured in the Red Sea by a small force of Sudanese policemen on 19 January 1900. He was then sixty-four. He lived till 1926, and although officially in captivity appeared more like a minor princeling than a dangerous captive guerrilla. He made a pilgrimage to Mecca when he was eighty-eight.

By the time Osman Digna was captured the Anglo-French crisis at Fashoda had been resolved. On 11 December 1898 the French flag was hauled down and Marchand departed by way of Abyssinia. It was a portent not of British triumph but of saner Anglo-French relations after hundreds of years of bitter fighting and acrimony.

Kitchener went on to win fresh laurels in South Africa during the Boer War and in Britain during the First World War before being drowned in 1916 when the troopship which was taking him to Russia struck a German mine in the North Sea. In the Sudan he was succeeded by Wingate. Wingate's task was not easy but there is no doubt that he would not have wished to change it. He remained in the post of Governor-General for seventeen years, and they were by no means uneventful. Almost immediately he had a small army mutiny on his hands; throughout his governorship there was a series of troubles usually engineered by would-be Mahdis. His great achievement was building the Sudan into a sound and well-run country, a task in which he was ably assisted by his Inspector-General Rudolf Slatin. Slatin was knighted and made an honorary Major-General in the British army. He resigned his post in 1914, not wishing to fight for or against Britain. He lived till 1932. Wingate outlasted him by twenty-one years.

The subsequent history of the Sudan does not concern us here but it would be a rash man who would say that Mahdism is extinct or the Sudan will see no more upheavals. The Dervish Empire, or the Mahdiyah as it is often known, was undoubtedly a tyranny, but that was the work of the Khalifa, not the Mahdi. Whether the Mahdi could or would have been anything but a tyrant had he lived, it is impossible to say, but it seems from those who knew him that he was of a different quality from his supporters and successors. Many of the criticisms of the Sudan in the period of Dervish supremacy would have been valid in many other primitive countries, and the unfavourable comments made on the sanitary conditions in many Sudanese cities were somewhat self-righteous in view of the conditions which had existed in Europe in the Middle Ages. There were, however, three features of the Dervish story which need to be remembered because they must be almost unique. One is the astonishing quality of courage shown by the Dervishes, which has been illustrated frequently in this book; the second is the fortitude of the men who fought them, whether British, Egyptian or Sudanese; and the third is the British achievement in rebuilding the country afterwards. On the second point it will not be overlooked that the story of this period — with some exceptions — was one of courage in defeat, which is the hardest moment of all. Of the last part Theodore Roosevelt, who was by no means pro-British, said:

'During a decade and a half, while Mahdism controlled the

country there flourished a tyranny which for cruelty, bloodthirstiness, unintelligence and wanton destructiveness, surpassed anything which a civilized people can even imagine. The keystones of the Mahdist party were religious intolerance and slavery, with murder and the most abominable cruelty as the way of obtaining each. During these fifteen years at least two-thirds of the population — probably seven or eight millions of people — died by violence or by starvation. Then the English came in, put an end to the independence and self-government which had wrought the hideous evil, restored order, kept the peace and gave to each individual a liberty which during the evil days of their own self-government not one human being possessed, save only the blood-stained tyrant who at the moment was ruler.'

The tyranny, the bloodshed, the cruelty, were not, of course, unique to the Sudan. Almost every country in the world has had a period of bloodshed and anarchy. What is unusual, if not necessarily unique, is the sharp contrast between good and evil, the good with which Mahdism began and the evil into which it was distorted, the good of courage and self-sacrifice, the evil for which they were perverted, and, lastly, the almost unbelievably severe setting in which all this action took place. Well might one say

Ex Africa semper aliquid novi.

Appendix: The Dervish Army

The Dervish army was composed of four elements:
1. Horsemen – all Baggara Arabs.
2. Camel men – all Danagla and Jaalin tribesmen.
3. Jehadia. These were riflemen, mainly Sudanese blacks, but their numbers included some Arabs, and some Baggaras in command. The 'Jehad' was the Sacred War and these troops had been specially embodied to fight in it.
4. Swords and spearmen. These were organized in *Rubs* or battalions. They were armed with swords, spears and some rifles, and were commanded by Emirs (Arab chiefs). Some *Rubs* were composed of Baggaras, others of Jaalin, others of Danaglas.

The numbers given by Slatin were:

Cavalry	6,600
Jehadia	34,350
Swords and spearmen	64,000

The Dervishes had 40,000 rifles or smooth bores. As some of these weapons had been shortened or otherwise altered to suit the user their reliability had suffered, but there were at least 22,000 Remingtons in good condition. The heavy guns consisted of six large-calibre Krupps, eight machine-guns, and sixty-one brass muzzle-loaders. Ammunition for all guns was short and there was nothing to spare for practice; furthermore, as some of it had been manufactured locally it was of inferior quality. Ammunition was accounted for with scrupulous care and the Dervishes were warned to hold their fire till the last possible moment in order to to be sure of finding targets.

Rations were measured out in *ardebs*, a capacity measure equal to 5.6 bushels. The monthly ration was measured out to a fraction, and was as follows:

Arabs — 3/24ths per month

Jehadia — 4/24ths per month

Baggara — 6/24ths per month.

Every Baggara therefore received twice as much corn as an Arab.

The Jehadia was organized in the simple style of many primitive armies. Twenty men (roughly equivalent to a platoon in the British army) would be led by a *maggudam*. A hundred men (roughly a company) would be led by a *Ras miya*. Groups of 'hundreds' would be commanded by Emirs in proportion to their status. There was no system of training or manoeuvres, although they were required to parade at regular intervals. But innate tactical skill and fighting ability made the Dervishes first-class troops.

Index

Readers will note that place-names are spelt differently by writers whose works are quoted. Thus we have Merowi and Merowe, Ferkeh, Ferket and Firket, and many others. There was, of course, no standard spelling, and names sometimes changed completely. It might be apposite to quote General Gordon on the subject: 'The language everywhere causes confusion. There is the *town* El Obeyed and the *sheikh* El Obeyed; there is the Haloman of Cairo and the Haloman of Khartoum. I became irritable and said I would write to *The Times* about it.' By following the campaigns on the map on page 8, the reader should have no such difficulty.